The
White Wine
Companion
A CONNOISSEUR'S GUIDE
Godfrey Spence

The
White Wine
Companion
A CONNOISSEUR'S GUIDE
Godfrey Spence

FIREFLY BOOKS

Dedication
To Catherine, Rosalind, and Isobel

A FIREFLY BOOK

First published in Canada in 1998
by Firefly Books Ltd.
3680 Victoria Park Avenue
Willowdale, Ontario
M2H 3KI

Published in the United States in 1998
by Firefly Books (U.S.) Inc.
P.O. Box 1338, Ellicott Station
Buffalo, New York 14205

Cataloguing in Publication Data
Spence, Godfrey D.
The white wine companion

Includes index.
ISBN 1-55209-258-5

1. Wine and wine making. I. Title
TP548.S63 1998 641.2'222 C98-930459-0

This book was designed and produced by
Quintet Publishing Limited
6 Blundell Street
London N7 9BH

Creative Director: Richard Dewing
Art Director: Silke Braun
Project Editor: Clare Hubbard
Designer: Ian Hunt
Editor: Andrew Armitage
Photographers: Adrian Swift and Philip Wilkins
Illustrator: Louise Boulton

Typeset in Great Britain by
Central Southern Typesetters, Eastbourne
Manufactured in Singapore by
Pica Colour Separation Overseas Private Limited
Printed in China by
Leefung-Asco Printers Limited

TABLE OF CONTENTS

Introduction
6

PART ONE
THE *story of* WHITE WINE
7

PART TWO
THE WHITE WINE *directory*
48

Introduction

White wine has been the lubricant of a million lunches, and the introduction for most wine drinkers to the pleasures of the fermented juice of the grape. Made throughout the world, it is at once refreshing and relaxing, thirst-quenching and inebriating. Wine sharpens appetites. Food is digested more readily, and conversation flows more freely with a glass or two of chilled white wine. Despite this, or perhaps because of it, we rarely give white wines the attention they deserve. Diners will stop and ponder the claret, wax lyrical about the red Burgundy, yet drink the white wines almost without comment, as they might hear background music, noticed more by its absence, present but all too often ignored.

To do this is to miss a fascinating range of flavors. White grapes are often more aromatic than their red counterparts, and the wine-making can fine-tune the flavors to a greater degree. True, few white wines keep as well as red. Fewer still develop complexity with age, adding extra facets of flavor as the wine slowly evolves in the bottle. Still, such white wines do exist. This book has been written to encourage you to try a broader range of white wines, to experience the flavors offered and get more out of your drinking experiences, and to do so with confidence, knowing that the premium price paid will be justified.

Wine is a friend,
wine is a joy,
like sunshine,
wine is the birthright of all.

André Simon

A WINE PRIMER

PART ONE

THE
story of
WHITE WINE

A SHORT HISTORY

Wine has always been part of human culture, but was around before that culture began. When man first made the transition to humanity, wine had probably already been discovered. Discovered it almost certainly was, for, though one knows when wine was first made, ancient man surely found it rather than inventing it. Grapes growing wild would have been a welcome part of the diet in many parts of the world. Those gathering the grapes would be gathering all the necessary raw materials for wine.

Grapes contain sugar, acid, and flavor that can become wine. Moreover, the agent that converts the sugar into alcohol is the yeast that flourishes on the stalks and in the waxy bloom on the skins. The first wine would probably have resulted from the juice of wild grapes spontaneously fermenting in the bottom of whatever receptacle the early hunter-gatherers had. Such wine, however, would not have been wine for very long. The natural yeasts that created it in the first place would soon have given way to bacteria called acetobacter, rapidly turning the wine to vinegar.

But, even though we do not know when wine was first *made*, we can be certain that those early examples were prized more for their effect than the complexity of their bouquet, or elegance to the palate. This strange juice, sweet and innocuous one day, dry but intoxicating the next, must have brought great comfort in those harsh times.

Archeological evidence can date the first serious attempts at winemaking to being some 10,000 years ago. Sizable accumulations of grape pips, suggesting the grapes had been pressed, rather than just eaten, have been found in Turkey, Lebanon, Syria, and Jordan, all dating from Neolithic times, about 8000 BC. These were wines from wild vines, but the earliest evidence of vine cultivation comes from Georgia, dated some 3,000 years later in the Stone Age.

The first mention of grape growing in the Judaeo-Christian world appears in Genesis, Chapter 9. When the ark landed, Noah planted a vineyard, and became intoxicated on the results. Christians thus believe winemaking can be said to date from the great flood. However, the very fact that Noah knew how to grow grapes and make wine shows that wine was a normal part of every-day life in antediluvian times.

As to where wine originated, we can be more sure. South of the Black Sea in Transcaucasia may be the most likely starting point for *Vitis vinifera*, the wine vine.

From there it spread to the eastern edge of the Mediterranean and throughout the Middle East. Muscat and Syrah (Shiraz in Australia) are believed to be the oldest of today's vine varieties, their names still bearing witness to the Middle Eastern origins of organized viticulture.

ANCIENT CIVILIZATIONS AND WINE

The ancient Egyptians cultivated the vine, and through their well-preserved antiquities we have the oldest pictorial references to viti-culture. One tomb painting in Thebes details every stage of the winemaking process, from picking the grapes to transporting the

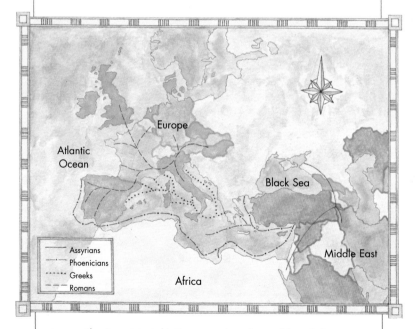

The vine originated in Transcaucasia and spread through the
Middle East and Europe as ancient civilizations moved westward.

finished product down the Nile by boat. So detailed is it that the picture even depicts the pickers making a tally of the crop, the ancient equivalent of the weighbridge that stands at the entrance to so many wineries.

These wines were, it seems, mostly red. Only black grapes, which thrive in warm climates, are depicted in the paintings, and the treading, as still used today for the best (red) ports, is clearly shown. In the hot climate of North Africa the grapes would be super-ripe, yielding high-alcohol wines.

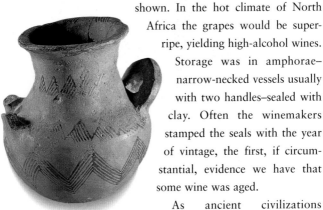

Storage was in amphorae–narrow-necked vessels usually with two handles–sealed with clay. Often the winemakers stamped the seals with the year of vintage, the first, if circumstantial, evidence we have that some wine was aged.

As ancient civilizations changed, the skills of viticulture and vinification moved to the

Late Bronze Age amphora.

north shore of the Mediterranean. Initially Crete and then Mycenae were the culturally dominant nations. Both were wealthy trading nations and recognized the value of wine and traded in it. Homer's *Iliad*, written much later, is liberally peppered with references to wine, showing just how important it was to the civilization.

Mycenae fell to an unknown army, but refugees moved to the Greek mainland taking with them their culture based on vineyards and olive groves. Gradually the Greeks moved into what is now Italy, which they named Enotria, the land of the vine, so prolific were the vines there.

It was because of Italy, through the emergence of the Roman Empire, that most other Western European countries first developed viticulture and winemaking skills. A few regions claim the Phoenicians, an ancient seafaring Syrian people, brought the vine, but the wine history of most regions begins: "The Romans first brought the vine to ..."

Viticulture and vinification illustrated in a fifteenth
century manuscript.

THE NEW WORLD

Grape distribution to the rest of the world started almost as the age
of exploration did. The early explorers were the Spanish and the
Portuguese, both major wine-producing nations, and both Catholic
countries. It would be unthinkable that they would have set sail
without wine and a few cuttings on board to set up a vineyard
when they landed. The first "New World" vineyards were in
Central and South America, originally planted in the early sixteenth
century. Soon viticulture had spread along the west coast of both
North and South America, areas that are still major producers.

The early settlers to the east coast were dismayed to find that
their vines, planted in the early seventeenth century and carefully
tended, died while the forest was full of wild vines. We now know
that these local vines were of different species, tolerant or resistant
to the local diseases and pests, oidium and phylloxera, whereas
Vitis vinifera, the European vine, is not. Later the diseases were to
be imported, accidentally, into Europe, causing devastation
throughout the continent. Fortunately, the cure came from the same
place as the curse. All European vines are now grafted onto
American vine rootstocks to guard against the vine louse,
Phylloxera vasatrix.

The first vines in sub-Saharan Africa were planted in the Dutch
Cape colony during the latter half of the seventeenth century, taken

there along with other fruit to supply the ships on the long sea voyage to the East Indies. Australian and New Zealand viticulture owes its roots to South Africa–the two countries' first vines were from cuttings taken in the Cape.

Most wines are sold predominantly on the local market: an Italian man will typically drink the wine of his local village, as will his Portuguese or French counterparts. If this is true today, imagine how much truer it must have been in the past, before mass transport systems were developed. Small wonder, then, that so few wines are listed in old books and wine lists.

Certain areas made a specialty of export, usually because they had the export facilities, rather than the ideal climate. Bordeaux is a port near a large river estuary, the Gironde, which is navigable. Sherry and port were shipped from Cadiz and Oporto, both on the coast. Wines like these have had a head start in the battle for world markets, and have for a long time developed a reputation other areas hardly dared challenge. Those other countries are now catching up fast, learning from the old masters, but rapidly overtaking them in technology and scientific approach.

Unhindered by millstones of regulation and tradition the New World has been able to look to the market, and supply it. Its strength has been much fruitier wines, more easily understood by the novice and drinkable when released. The Old World has had to take notice of this phenomenon, and is now learning from it. Many vineyards and wineries in the most classic of areas now boast an Australian- or Californian-trained expert.

The earliest South African vineyards were planted in the shadow of Table Mountain.

HOW WINE IS MADE

At the end of the twentieth century making good wine is easier than ever. There is no excuse whatever for anyone to make faulty wine. With all the knowledge, both scientific and empirical, gleaned over the centuries most of the possible mistakes have already been made. In the past a winemaker learned the craft from the previous generation; problems, when they occurred, would be solved by talking to a friend in the village, or at best the next town. Nowadays a typical winemaker is a technocrat. He (or increasingly she) has a degree in the subject and a world of experience available, published in a host of industry journals, and transmitted around the globe both on paper and electronically.

Yet, despite all this, the majority of wine will not excite. Wine can be made to a recipe, but the result is a sameness; the quality will be consistent, but never fine. The chorus, not the soloist. Fine wine requires more than simply good technical expertise: it needs passion. Without exception the winemakers mentioned in this book have a love of the product; winemaking is almost a vocation, not simply a job. Viticulture, or grape growing, is an agricultural activity, and vinification, or winemaking, can be an industrial process; but the best grape growers, and the best winemakers, elevate their respective crafts to an art form.

GRAPE GROWING/VITICULTURE

The ultimate quality of any wine is determined in the vineyard. Without good raw material, perfect grapes, the winemakers cannot make good wine. "Perfect" here means "suitable for the style of wine being produced." For crisp, neutral-flavored whites, barely ripe but healthy grapes are needed, whereas top sweet wines like Sauternes need grapes shriveled by rot and covered in mold.

The best grapes come from top vineyards. The distance between a basic commune-level vineyard in Burgundy and the greatest of the Grands Crus (great growths, or great wines) might be only a few yards, yet the difference in the wines is great.

Climatically the vineyards are identical and the grape variety might be the same, but the difference is in the "*terroir*." Simply

Italian vines trained high on a flat site.

translated as "the soil," *terroir* encompasses the soil's chemical composition, its physical formation, and its aspect–altitude and exposure to the sun can have a dramatic effect on the ripeness of the grapes, or their susceptibility to disease. The grower can control these to a certain extent by training the vine in particular ways or by managing the pruning and spraying programs effectively, but ultimately the factor governing the maximum quality of the grape is inherent in the vineyard.

Traditionally in Europe the most individual wines have come from specific, often very small, vineyards. Blending wines from more than one plot dilutes the character of the wine. Indeed, the whole Appellation Contrôlée hierarchy in France is based on this premise. In the New World, where rules and traditions are less uncompromising, winemakers have the facility to blend grapes from different vineyards, often many miles apart. For the best wines this is done to improve quality, not diminish it. Prime, complementary parcels of wine from a range of *terroirs* will be assembled to make a blend better than any one of the individual parts.

In the Mosel, vines have to be trained on individual posts.

Such wines are, however, still the exception. For most of the best wines the fruit comes from a single vineyard—some recognized as above average for decades or even centuries. It is often difficult to define exactly what it is that makes a particular piece of land better than its neighbors. Hillsides have been known to produce better wines since Virgil was writing on the subject (*Bacchus Amat Colles*). The additional exposure to the sun will help ripen grapes in cooler areas, whereas in hotter climates, the additional altitude will keep the grapes a little cooler.

The structure of the soil will help. Vines prefer well-drained soil, so stones, slate, and chalk are preferred, and clay is positively avoided. Poor soils reduce the yield, while encouraging the roots to search deeper for nutrients. This limits the volume produced but, since quality and quantity are inversely proportional, all else being equal, fewer grapes means better wine. For this reason, too, the vineyard owner will limit the yield through severe pruning, and even thinning the crop, removing a proportion of the bunches

Even in the most mechanized vineyards, pruning usually has to be done by hand.

halfway through the season, encouraging the vine to concentrate its efforts on the remaining crop.

All the natural advantages of even the best site mean nothing if the vineyard is badly managed. Only if care is taken at all stages of the vineyard calendar does the grower stand a chance of producing perfect grapes. Even then, viticulture is a gamble. As with all agriculture, the viticulturist can suffer from the vagaries of the weather. One night of frost in spring, a bad summer hailstorm, or rain at vintage time can destroy a year's crop.

White grapes will ripen with less sunshine than black grapes, and natural acidity is vital to the structure of the wine. For these reasons the best white wines are made in cooler areas. Countries like Germany and New Zealand make best use of their cooler climates to produce racy, fresh wines. In warmer countries, cool areas will be sought, for example Yarra Valley in Australia, or Somontano in Spain. Hotter areas will certainly allow grapes to ripen, but the resulting wines will lack the finesse needed.

HARVESTING

White wine is, perhaps, the simplest of all wines to make, and yet can be very difficult to make well. It is simply the fermented juice of the grape. The maker of red wine has to concern himself with the extraction of color from the skins, but for his white-wine counterpart the emphasis is on preserving the often delicate flavors of the grape. Gentle handling and cool temperatures are *de rigueur* if the wine is not to become flabby and uninteresting.

The moment of picking is paramount. Grapes must be ripe; how ripe will vary from wine to wine. As grapes ripen on the vine photo-

In the spring the pruned vines start to bud.

synthesis produces sugars that accumulate in the berries. At the same time the natural acids in the berries diminish. It's easy to measure the ripeness of the grapes by measuring the density of the juice within them, a task often carried out in the field with a simple optical device, the refractometer. For dry wines, care must be taken not to allow the grapes to become overripe, otherwise the wines might lack the essential acidity.

Sugar and acid levels are easy to measure and give an objective, scientific definition of maturity. Increasingly, however, quality-conscious winemakers all over the world are returning to what may seem a very unscientific method: tasting the grapes. There is more to fine wine than just alcohol and acid: winemakers are looking for ripeness of flavors too–phenolic ripeness. Research in Australia is leading the way, but to date no computer has been programed to have a palate. Wines like Mosel Riesling Kabinetts, bursting with flavor yet only 7 percent alcohol, are proof that high grape sugar levels are not everything.

Harvesting can be back-breaking manual labor.

Harvesting has always been a backbreaking job. Teams of pickers comb the vineyards, snipping with pruning shears, or hooking the bunches with curved blades like miniature sabers, gathering the fruit in buckets and baskets, emptying these in turn into the hods that transport the grapes to the crusher. Such picking is slow, and increasingly expensive. Each year it is more and more difficult to find enough workers willing to suffer such pains and discomfort, all for the sake of a minimum wage and bed in a dormitory, even if the evening meal is hearty, and the wine flows freely.

Terrain is not a problem–even the steepest slopes are manageable–but the greatest advantage of hand harvesting is selection. Not every bunch of grapes is perfect: some will be underripe, others affected by rot, or mildew. Trained pickers know to discard these, favoring only the perfect bunches. Alternatively, for certain types of sweet wine (*see* Sweet Wine Production on page 23), only rotten berries will be selected. Pickers might go through the vineyard five or six times, each time looking at each bunch, but picking only those affected by noble rot.

Where the topography permits, machines are now used. Mechanical grape harvesters straddle the rows of vines while motorized beaters shake the branches so vigorously that the berries are torn from the vine. While it is quick, efficient, and a godsend if the weather threatens to turn bad, mechanical harvesting is economical only for large vineyards or where a group of owners can share the enormous cost of the machine. No selection is possible, but where the climate is warm and dry, and vineyard husbandry up to scratch, very high-quality wines can result.

Where terrain allows, machines are increasingly taking over.

After the harvest nothing can be done to improve the intrinsic quality of the grapes: the potential is there in the berries. All a winemaker can do is to preserve that quality, enhancing it by making up for any deficiencies of structure perhaps, but not improving the flavor.

Once harvested, the grapes need to be processed. As we have seen, wine is a natural product, but for reliable, stable wine the fermentation process must be monitored and controlled. At each stage decisions have to be made, and many options are available. The skill in vinification is choosing which route to take–take a wrong turn and some of that potential quality will be lost. The mark of the greatest winemakers is their understanding of the processes and the effect they will have on the raw material, which may well differ from the previous vintage.

A winemaker has only one chance with each batch of grapes, and each vineyard will produce grapes only once a year. For many, a lifetime's experience might be only a few dozen vintages; memory and knowledge are vital, but, for the most individual wines, so is vision.

VINIFICATION

No skins are needed, so when the grapes arrive at the winery they will be crushed, gently breaking the skins without damaging the pips, which, as anyone who has ever bitten one knows, contain bitter oils. Occasionally the winemaker will leave the skins in contact with the juice, called "must," for added flavor pickup, but normally pressing follows very rapidly.

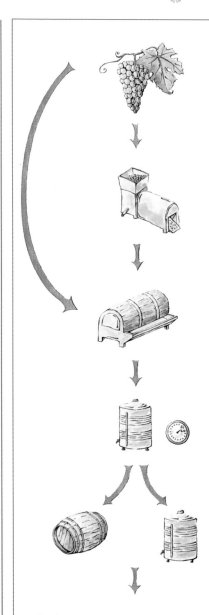

GRAPES
Received from the vineyard.

CRUSHER
Most grapes are crushed before they are pressed.

PRESS
Gentle pressing gives the finest must (juice).

Some grapes are pressed without being crushed first.

SETTLING TANK
The must is held at a low temperature for a period of time to allow the solid matter from the grapes to settle. For cheaper wines this can be done by filtration or centrifuging.

FERMENTATION
This can take place in inert containers or in wooden barrels. The latter will add a vanilla spice character if the oak is new.

After fermentation the wines are matured, either in barrel or tank, until the winemaker decides they are ready for bottling. Most wines will be fined and filtered to ensure stability before bottling.

The first must from the press is the most delicate, with the finest flavors. Much of this drains out before pressure is applied; this is the free-run juice. As pressing progresses more bitter flavors can be

Grapes being loaded into the press directly from the vineyard.

extracted from the skins, so the finest wines are made from the first pressings and the free-run. Green-yellow in color, as opaque as pea soup, this sweet grapy liquid will need to be cleared if a healthy wine is to result. Cold settling, overnight in refrigerated vats, is gentle, the preferred method for the noninterventionist enologist. For cheaper wines, made in bulk so speed is vital, centrifuging is common.

Once clear, the must can be fermented. Enzymes in the yeast convert the sugar in the must into alcohol, and thus the juice becomes wine. Natural yeasts, the indigenous microflora of the vineyards and winery, give fine wine some of its individuality, although commercially cultivated yeast strains offer greater reliability. There are two fundamental ways in which the options for fermentation can affect the taste of the wine: the temperature and the vessel used.

Cool temperatures are required to preserve the flavor of the grapes. Fermentation is naturally exothermic, so the vats are cooled with running water to maintain a temperature of between 50 and 64°F. A higher temperature will speed up the biochemical reactions so the fermentation will be quicker, increasing the winery's productivity. But aromatic components in the must will be lost through evaporation.

Too cold a temperature can also be a problem. Very cold conditions, a frequent natural hazard in northern European wineries, can result in stuck fermentations. It is not unknown for a Burgundian winery to need heating in the fall.

The majority of wines are fermented in inert vats. Large vats of old wood, stainless steel, or lined concrete can be seen in wineries throughout the world. The difference between these types of vat is more to do with ease of use than wine quality. A new winery would probably choose stainless steel as a matter of course, but an existing concrete or wooden vat can be just as serviceable, if more difficult to maintain. Ideal for aromatic varieties like Riesling or Muscat, these vessels do not contribute any additional flavors to the wine. If an enologist using these wants the complexity that comes with oak, it must be added later through maturation.

To get the full effect of oak many winemakers are turning to barrel fermentation. The traditional way of making wine in Burgundy, the practice of fermenting musts in small new barrels, almost died out because of the extra work involved in dealing with a large number of small fermenters. Fashion in the last 20 years or so has, however, turned full circle so that what was once rare and specialist has become flavor of the month. Suddenly "Barrel-fermented" or "Barrique-fermented" are appearing on labels from all four corners of the world. The important point here is the newness of the wood. Barrels have only a finite amount of the oaky flavors, particularly the vanillin, within them. Fermenting in barrel extracts these faster than static maturation so a barrel can be effectively used for barrel fermentation only a few times before it becomes a small and inconvenient inert vessel.

Fermentation produces alcohol and CO_2, seen here bubbling in the vat.

Many different oaks are used in winemaking. The most popular are French– from the forests of either Allier or Nevers–and American. American forests are warmer than the central French ones, so French oaks have a finer grain. Furthermore, the American oak is usually sawn, whereas French oak is split. The net result is that American oak gives more obvious vanilla and smoky oak flavors to any wine fermented or stored in it. French oak is considerably more expensive than American, another factor for the winemaker to bear in mind.

A word about chips. Oak has long been used to add structure to wine, and enrich the nose and palate. Ideally you should never notice the wood. If the wine is mature, and the fruit properly ripe, it will be integrated into the flavor, and will not stand out as it so often does when the wine is young. However, many wine drinkers associated oak flavors with high quality, creating a demand for oak flavors in an ever-increasing range of wines. Inevitably, this search has led to cheaper alternatives. Barrels are expensive to buy and costly to use, so why not add oak chips, or powdered oak in a sort of overgrown teabag? These methods have their place, and are frequently used for mass-market wines, but never for the finest, where real barrels are still the norm.

All wines spend some time maturing before being bottled. Whether this is a matter of a few weeks in inert tanks, or an

White wines are sometimes matured in old oak.

extended period in a barrel, eventually the wines will be blended and bottled. Blending is a normal practice for all wines. Even a single vineyard may produce a range of qualities, and different barrels will behave differently. The final act of the maker of fine wines then is to select only the best parcels, those that will marry together well, and blend them to make the finished wine. After filtration and stabilization, all that remains is bottling.

Certain basic components of a wine's structure can, quite legitimately, be adjusted by the winemaker to make up for any inconsistencies or deficiency in the must. These adjustments are best done before fermentation. Strict limits are set by the various governing bodies around the world, and the aim is not to adulterate but to improve the product. Acidity can be adjusted up or down, depending on the climate; alcohol can be increased by adding sugar *before* fermentation (this is always fermented out so the system cannot legally be used to sweeten wine).

One natural adjustment which has to wait until the primary, alcoholic fermentation is malolactic fermentation. Some overacidic wines contain a high proportion of malic acid, the acid that gives apples their tart flavor. A natural bacterium, called lactobacillus, can be encouraged to break this acid down into lactic, or milk, acid, much softer on the palate. This is encouraged with almost all red wines, but only selectively with whites–many winemakers want to preserve the freshness in the flavor.

Malolactic fermentation does have another important feature, though. Other chemical components are produced as by-products which have an effect on the taste. The buttery character so often attributed to Chardonnay is often a result of malolactic fermentation rather than the grape itself. Malolactic fermentation is, therefore, more than simply an adjustment to the structure: it can be a positive change in the wine's flavor.

SWEET WINE PRODUCTION

To make a medium-sweet or fully sweet wine special techniques are required. The typical sugar content of ripe grapes is sufficient to give about 12 percent alcohol. Under normal circumstances yeast can easily ferment to this level, so the resultant wine will be dry.

If the winemaker wants to make a sweeter style several options are available. Yeast generally dies when the alcohol level reaches about 15 percent. Some sweet wines are made by stopping the fermentation by artificially raising the alcohol level. This is achieved by adding spirit, a technique used in port and the French *vins doux naturels*. For the cheapest sweet wines it is possible to sweeten a dry base wine with concentrated grape must. The results are usually dire.

A variation of this is used in many medium-dry and medium-sweet wines. A small amount of unfermented (and unconcentrated) must is reserved and blended back into the wine just before bottling. In Germany, where the unfermented must is called *Süssreserve*, there are very strict controls upon its use. For example, if a Riesling Spätlese wine is to have *Süssreserve* added then the *Süssreserve* too must be Riesling Spätlese must. Fully sweet wines cannot be made this way because the unfermented must is not sweet enough.

The best sweet wines are made from grapes in which the sugar content has been concentrated in some way. The resultant higher sugar level is difficult to ferment–the yeast simply cannot manage it–so considerable amounts of residual sugar remain in the wine. The most usual way to concentrate the sugar is through noble rot. This is the beneficial form of the vineyard fungal disease caused by botrytis (*Botrytis cinerea*). When botrytis hits a red-wine

vineyard or affects underripe berries, it is a disaster, but when it affects certain grape varieties, when fully ripe, and in the correct conditions of temperature and humidity, the wines are absolute nectar.

Most of the world's great sweet wines are made from grapes affected by noble rot.

Botrytis requires certain very specific weather patterns. Misty mornings encourage the growth of the mold, which softens the skin of the grape and lives on the water, sugars, and acids within it. If the sun comes out later in the morning, the softened skins allow evaporation of the moisture, concentrating the sugars. Unfortunately, botrytis is unreliable. It may or may not happen, when it does it affects grapes irregularly so a vineyard will have to be harvested a number of times, with only the most rotten berries being picked each time. Worse still, rain will rapidly turn the rot to gray rot, and waste the crop. For some, though, the risks are worth taking. The finest

The concentration in Icewine results from picking the grapes when frozen.

Sauternes, Hungarian Tokaji, Aszú wines and the great Beerenauslesen and Trockenbeerenauslesen of Germany and Austria are all botrytis-affected wines.

If botrytis wines are unreliable, spare a thought for those trying to make Icewine. Here the frost concentrates the sugars. Healthy grapes are needed. Left on the vine, they are harvested only when the temperature drops to about 17°F, for a continuous period of at least eight hours. The frost freezes the water, leaving super-concentrated juice to be pressed.

In parts of Italy, and for the legendary Vin de Constance from South Africa, concentration is achieved by drying the grapes. Italian Passito wines, including the Tuscan specialty Vin Santo, are made this way. The grapes

Drying the grapes before pressing in order to concentrate the sugars.

are harvested in the fall and laid out or hung up on racks, generally in a dry barn, to be pressed in the middle of winter when some of the water content has evaporated.

Whichever method has been used, the yield for good sweet wine will always be much lower than that for dry wine from the same vineyard. In Sauternes the Appellation is for sweet wines only, so, unless a producer is prepared to get a minimum price for basic Bordeaux Blanc, he or she has no choice. But a German grower could make 25 bottles of Kabinett wine for each bottle of Trockenbeerenauslese. True, the sweet wine is more expensive, but not that much more. These great sweet wines are made more for love than money and, although prices are rising, they still represent astounding value.

Do not be afraid to experiment with sweet wines. These are not just wines for desserts, but are confident partners for many dishes. The French prefer sweet apéritifs, and Sauternes is the ideal accompaniment to foie gras. Sweet wines with creamy cheeses or with nuts are other combinations worth trying.

Complementary partners—a sweet wine with creamy cheese.

GRAPE VARIETIES

All but a handful of fairly localized and obscure wines are made
from grapes of the *Vitis vinifera* species. There are other vine
species, and some of these have a role to play in modern
viticulture, supplying rootstocks and material for
developing new varieties, but *vinifera*, the "wine vine," is

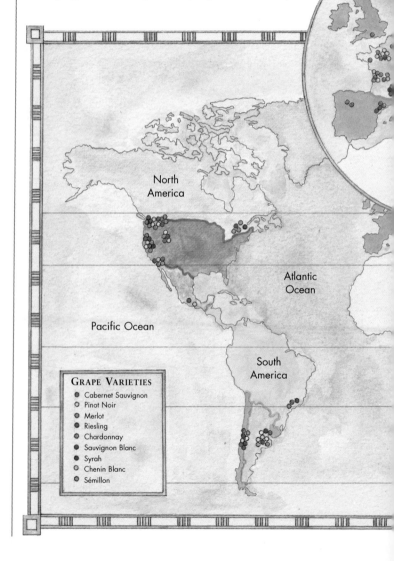

North
America

Atlantic
Ocean

Pacific Ocean

South
America

GRAPE VARIETIES
- Cabernet Sauvignon
- Pinot Noir
- Merlot
- Riesling
- Chardonnay
- Sauvignon Blanc
- Syrah
- Chenin Blanc
- Sémillon

dominant. Within *V. vinifera* there are thousands of recognizable
varieties, or, to use the horticulturally correct term, cultivars.
Many of these have developed in Darwinian fashion,
to suit local conditions and tastes, and are
destined to remain anonymous to the wider
wine-drinking world. Certain varieties are,
however, recognized as superior, often to

Europe

Asia

50N

30N

Africa

Equator

Indian
Ocean

30S

Australia

50S

the extent that winemakers throughout the world have adopted them from their original home in Western Europe. These "noble" grapes have characteristics that winemakers and wine drinkers find appealing, and which are distinctive to the particular grape, wherever it is grown.

For white wine, the noblest half-dozen of the noble grapes are:

CHARDONNAY

The world's most popular grape. Wherever it is grown, whatever the price, if "Chardonnay" is on the label, it will sell. Chardonnay is forgiving, both in the vineyard and the winery. It is an easy grape to grow and process, and it sells–the perfect combination.

Chardonnay is unfussy about climate. Plant it in thin acidic soils, too poor to maintain any other crop, in the cold, gray, wet climate of northeast France and the result is Champagne or Chablis. Barely ripe fruit gives steely, lean flavors, almost austere in youth but developing marvelously with some age. Alternatively it will grow well in the hottest irrigated vineyards in Australia, where big rich buttery wines full of the flavors of tropical fruit and often approaching 15 percent alcohol result.

Relatively neutral in its unadorned state, it is a blank canvas on which the winemaker can work his artistry. Options include oak fermentation or not, oak maturation or not, use of malolactic fermentation, and so on, each giving its own facet to the final wine.

Chardonnay grapes.

RIESLING

Riesling is the best white grape in the world. No other white grape can give the range of flavors that Riesling can, dry to sweet, light and floral through fruity to oily and waxy, depending on its provenance and age. It also ages in a remarkable way. Of all the white grapes, only Riesling will age literally for decades.

Riesling is choosy as to where she puts down her roots. The best sites only will do, with good exposure to the sun, but paradoxically cool regions are better than warm. Ideally, Riesling needs a combination of just enough sun spread over a long season: plenty of time during a long, dry fall makes for the best wines. If the weather is right, the fungus botrytis will occur in its benevolent, noble form, permitting the very later-harvest Beerenauslese and Trockenbeerenauslese styles. Warmer areas can, and do, grow Riesling, but rapid ripening results in diluted flavors.

In contrast to Chardonnay, Riesling is most attractive in a pure form. Chardonnay has been described as a "tart," not unattractive but plain enough that one would not notice it but for the vivid makeup and alluring clothes of added oakiness. By contrast, Riesling is a countess–sophisticated rather than popularist. To appreciate Riesling takes time, but it is time well spent.

SÉMILLON

Like the Chardonnay grape, Sémillon can make a range of wines from the frankly unexciting to the very finest. Similarly unaromatic, it can make low-acid, high-alcohol wines with a great affinity for barrel fermentation and maturation. One feature that distinguishes it in its dry-wine form is a strange waxy flavor, along with a lemony character.

Few grapes produce such peaks and troughs of quality. Most of the world's Sémillon is bland but in a few areas it can achieve exceptional magnificence. The Hunter Valley in New South Wales is one, Bordeaux another. In Bordeaux it can be, and usually is, blended with Sauvignon Blanc, for the aromatic character and the marked acidity of the latter, in both sweet and dry whites.

The one factor that puts Sémillon firmly into the Noble Grape category is its propensity to rot nobly if the weather permits.

Southeast of the city of Bordeaux, in the commune of Sauternes, and at Château d'Yquem in particular, arguably the world's best sweet wines result.

CHENIN BLANC

Another variety capable of a host of styles. In South Africa this is the workhorse, producing gallons and gallons of neutral, off-dry to dry cheap quaffing wine. In the Loire valley this venerable variety produces some of the most long-lived sweet whites in the Appellations of Quarts de Chaume, Bonnezeaux, and, in good vintages, Coteaux du Layon, and some fantastically full-flavored drier whites such as Savennières.

Mass-produced Chenin smells of next to nothing, yet the fine ones have a hugely aromatic nose, floral in youth developing into lanolin and wax with age–making it easy to confuse with Riesling at times.

Chenin Blanc.

SAUVIGNON BLANC

The twin Appellations, Pouilly Fumé and Sancerre, standing either side of the Loire river in Northern France would, 10 or 12 years ago, have been seen as the archetypal Sauvignon wines, pale, with a pungently aromatic grassy nose, often described as "cats' pee." However, that was before the start of the New Zealand Sauvignon Blanc revolution. Realizing the suitability of the grape variety to their cool climate conditions, New Zealand's winemakers have adopted Sauvignon Blanc, developing a style uniquely their own, so much so that now New Zealand is considered "benchmark" Sauvignon.

Whether Sauvignon Blanc is related to Cabernet Sauvignon is open to debate, but their geographical origins are certainly similar, Sauvignon's natural home being Bordeaux as well as the central vineyards of the Loire Valley.

Widely grown throughout the world, most Sauvignon relies on its own aromatic flavors, gooseberry, elderflower, grass, asparagus, and green bell peppers being frequent descriptors, rather than additional flavors from wood. Some producers, however, do use wood, either subtly, as in the case of Cloudy Bay in New Zealand, or more overtly so that the oak flavors dominate when the wine is still young. This is a shame, since few Sauvignon wines ever get the chance to age, most consumers preferring the vibrance of the grape in youth.

GEWÜRZTRAMINER

If there is one grape the wine-trade trainee prays for in a blind tasting examination, it is Gewürztraminer. The perfumed, floral, spicy, litchi-like nose is quite unlike that of any other wine, making a good Gewürztraminer a banker.

Originally a natural mutation of the Traminier, a native of the village of Termeno (Tramin) in the Italian Tyrol, the best examples now all come from Alsace in northeast France. Look for Grand Cru wines if you can afford them to get the most headily scented versions, often lowish in acidity, which makes them seem less dry, with alarming levels of alcohol, usually well covered by the intensity of the flavor.

OTHERS

Many examples of very individual wines are made from grape varieties that are, or have until recently been, very localized. The great white wines of the Northern Rhône, Condrieu, and Château Grillet are made from the Viognier, a strange variety which at best gives notes of honey, peaches, and ginger all rolled into one. Difficult to grow, Viognier was very much confined to the steep slopes between Côte Rotie and St Joseph until very recently. Now intrigued growers all over the world are experimenting with it, with some very interesting results.

Furmint and Harslevelú make the great Hungarian dessert wine, Tokay. Furmint is susceptible to botrytis, and gives full, high-alcohol, high-acid wines. Harslevelú adds smoothness and character, softening the blend. Neither on its own would classify as noble anywhere else, but together they make one of the few truly legendary wines.

Austria's most famous grape is the Grüner Veltliner. Restricted to Austria, Grüner Veltliner produces all styles from dry to sweet, with a musky aroma reminiscent of Pinot Gris and Gewürztraminer, but different from either. It deserves a wider audience, but will never be as internationally famous as Chardonnay.

Italian white wines are typically fresh, crisp, dry but fairly neutral, in contrast to the full-flavored reds. One area that has taken this mold, and added a certain twist of Italian style and an extra layer of sophistication, is Gavi where the Cortese variety is king. Here neutrality is replaced by subtlety. The flavors are there, but they are difficult to find, almost ethereal, but worth searching out.

Think of Spain and you think of Rioja. Few non-Spanish would think of high-priced, crisp, white wines being made in Spain. All the more surprising, then, to find that one of the most highly regarded wines on the home market is made from the unheard-of Albariño. This Galician variety is also found across the border in northern Portugal, under the name Alvarinho, where it produces better-than-average Vinhos Verdes. The Spanish wines from Rias Baixas are highly prized in the restaurants of Madrid.

VINTAGES

Wine lovers around the world are concerned about the qualities of the various vintages. Was the wine made in a good year or not? To talk about good and bad vintages is a shorthand way of talking about the annual weather pattern in the region from which the wine came. A good vintage is from a year when rain fell when it was

Grapes need ample sunshine to ripen properly.

wanted, and the sun shone when needed, when hail and frost were kept at bay, and the grower was able to tend to the vines when they needed tending, unhindered by the weather.

It is impossible to give a complete vintage list for the whole world. Even within different countries the weather in one area can be very different from another. For instance, 1992 and 1993 were very poor in Bordeaux–rain at harvest diluted the quality appallingly. In Burgundy, on the other hand, they were stunning. In general the cooler the area the more variation in annual weather conditions, and therefore vintages.

The ideal vintage starts with a cold winter. This allows the vine to rest, and limits the development of the vineyard pests and diseases. Not too cold, though. A really severe frost can damage the vine, but in winter it has to be very severe. In winter the vines will be pruned ready for the year ahead.

Frost is more of a problem in the spring. As the vine starts to bud the embryonic shoots are very prone to frost damage. One night of frost in spring can destroy a year's production before it has even started to grow.

Once they start the shoots grow rapidly in the spring. They will need to be tied up to facilitate access, and need sunshine and a little rain to promote growth. By early summer the vineflowers will form. Vines are self-pollinating. Gentle breezes, warm sunshine, and dry weather are needed. Rain now will prevent pollination so no grapes will form.

The growing grapes need sun to develop and ripen. Occasional rain helps photosynthesis, or in some very dry areas irrigation may be needed to avoid stressing the vine.

In the fall the grapes are ripe and ready to pick. In many European vineyards the fall brings rain and there is always a balance to be struck. Should the grower pick today when the weather is fine? Or leave the grapes on the vine for a few more days to catch a few more hours of precious sun, but risk the weather turning wet? Rain now will dilute the fruit, and can encourage rot as the thirsty berries swell and burst.

Once the grapes are harvested the vine's leaves will fall, the vine will become dormant, and the cycle will start over again.

BUYING WINE

White wines in particular tend to be sold young. For most wines this is not a problem, because they are meant to be drunk young, but if you want a mature white Burgundy it is difficult to buy one. For this reason it is worth building up a wine collection.

Make sure you have somewhere suitable to store the wines. Ideally this should be a cellar, but for smaller collections, in modern homes without cellars, one of the special electric wine-storage cabinets now available is ideal. If you can keep wines only in the kitchen or living room, do not keep them too long. Wine deteriorates if not correctly stored and you will find you have wasted your money.

The number of outlets selling wine seems to increase every year. It is no longer the preserve of traditional merchants and liquor stores, and almost every grocer now has a range of wines, with the quality getting better all the time.

The corner grocer store or the all-night delicatessen is all very well for the emergencies in life–we all have times when we need a bottle at short notice–but they are not usually the place to build up your collection of fine wine. The range is probably limited, the storage questionable, and the prices reflect the convenient opening

Specialist stores are the best place to find
the finest wines.

hours. To buy fine wines, visit the vineyard or search out the specialist. Each merchant has its own specialty, and a few minutes' browsing will tell you whether it specializes in New or Old World wines, whether the policy is one of individual service, or if it is a cheaper self-service establishment. Every type of outlet has its place, and the typical wine consumer will buy from a range of outlets depending on the wine he or she is looking for, but bear in mind the specialty when buying.

Having sorted out the storage (*see* Storage and Service of White Wine on page 37) and selected the retail outlet, the next step is to start building your collection. There is very little money to be made in white wine investments. Apart from top-flight Sauternes, few white wines ever appear at auction. Your first priority should be, therefore, to buy wines that you intend to drink. Be true to yourself, and buy wines that you and your friends or household like. If your taste is for aromatic varieties like Riesling or Sauvignon Blanc, buy those. It doesn't matter if the pundits tell you that a particular Chardonnay is the greatest white wine ever–if you don't like oaky dry whites leave it on the shelf. That said, lay in a small stock of the wines you occasionally drink. Few people drink dessert wines frequently, but it is as well to have a few bottles tucked away for when the mood strikes you.

Do not restrict yourself to the very finest wines. Unless money really is no object, buy wines at a range of prices. That way, when the unexpected weekend guests arrive, you don't have to broach that old bottle you were keeping for that special occasion, just to wash down the salad at lunchtime. Most merchants will offer a discount on 12 bottles or more so buy the case whenever you can. Buy mixed cases too. If you buy, say, eight bottles of everyday drinking wine, and four finer bottles to lay down, your collection will build rapidly.

Once the collection is built up, maintain it. Continue buying wine to replace what you drink, but also keep an eye on what you have left. Wine, especially white wine, will not keep forever. Occasionally the odd bottle that has been forgotten about for decades turns out to be marvelous, but more wine has disappointed by being kept too long than by drinking too young.

STORAGE AND SERVICE

Commentators often describe wine as "a living thing" because it will develop, changing over time sometimes for the better, sometimes not. "Living" is an exaggeration. Wine should have no living organisms present. It is a very complex mixture of chemical components, and these certainly can change with time, but they are not alive. However, like living things, wine does need to be cared for correctly. Light, heat, and vibration will all accelerate the aging process and can quickly lead to spoilage.

The vast majority of wines are ready to drink when released for sale; there is no advantage in keeping these wines. Quite the opposite, the wines will gradually fade, however well they are looked after. Increasingly, in a world ever more hurried, producers are making even the finest wines with youthful drinking in mind. The patient connoisseur knows, however, that the best wines, both red and white, will repay keeping by developing more flavors, gaining complexity, finesse, and elegance with increasing maturity, albeit not indefinitely.

Fewer white than red wines repay keeping, because they lack tannin, but the choicest white Burgundies or single-estate Rieslings become exquisite after 10 or 15 years in the bottle.

Ideally the cellar should be cool. The perfect temperature is 55°F, but slight variation on either side is acceptable, between 50 and 59°F. Consistency is important: better at 59°F all the time than have wide fluctuations of temperature. An underground cellar or basement dedicated to

Wines should be stored on their sides to keep the corks damp.

wine storage is ideal, but the pressures of modern living mean that such luxuries are rare these days.

If a traditional cellar is used, it should not be too damp. High humidity will cause deterioration of cartons and labels, and can encourage cork weevils, which burrow through corks, ultimately destroying the wine. On the other hand, if the atmosphere in the cellar is too dry, the tops of the corks will dry out, which can cause problems for long-term maturation.

Bottles should not be exposed to strong light. The ultraviolet component in particular will age a wine prematurely. The clear glass so often used for white wines exacerbates the problem. The cellar, or other storage area, should therefore be dark. If you must keep wines in a living area, store them in boxes, or cover each bottle with one of the cardboard packing tubes so often used by wine retailers.

To keep the corks moist, bottles should be kept lying on their sides. Cork shrinks as it dries out, reducing the effectiveness of the seal and allowing in air, which will lead to oxidation. Keeping labels uppermost makes identification easier.

The storage area should be free from any vibration. This can disturb the wine, again leading to premature aging. For the same reason, avoid moving the bottles too much while the wine matures. Wine lovers and collectors enjoy seeing their possessions as much as the philatelist does, but resist the temptation. Allow the cobwebs to form, ignore the dust, and leave the wine in peace.

WINE SERVICE

White wine should always be served chilled, but not too cold. We appreciate much of the flavor of wine by smell. If it's too cold, the vital aromatics are trapped in the glass, and even the most aromatic of wines will smell neutral. Normally half an hour in the body of the refrigerator is sufficient.

If unexpected guests arrive and you need to chill a bottle rapidly, use an ice bucket, or a large bowl filled with cold water and ice, which is far quicker than ice alone. Ten minutes will suffice. Light-bodied white wines are perfect at cellar temperature, between 50 and 59°F. Sweet whites can be served a little colder.

The screwpull and waiter's friend corkscrews, and the butler's friend.

OPENING WINE

A capsule protects the cork. Remove the top by cutting around the lip of the bottle. Use a sharp knife, or one of the special capsule removers now available. Corkscrews often have knives attached, but all too often these are not sharp.

Capsules were made of lead until quite recently, when health fears led to their being replaced with tin, plastic, or wax. Treat tin capsules with the greatest of respect–removing them all too often leaves a razor-sharp edge, inconveniently close to where your hand will be.

Do not panic if mold is found on the top of the cork: just clean the neck of the bottle with a clean cloth. Be particularly careful to clean the tops of old bottles if lead capsules have been used. Any wine seepage will react with the capsule to form poisonous lead salts.

Producers are moving away from cork as a seal for many cheaper wines, but bark of *Quercus suber*, the cork oak, remains the closure of choice for the best bottles. This natural medium is not without its faults: leaks and taints are all too common. Furthermore, many people, particularly those with hand or wrist injuries or ailments, find removing a cork very difficult, or even painful. Despite this, and the relative difficulty of removal, consumers still demand proper corks, much to the chagrin of the producer, and the relief of the Portuguese cork manufacturers.

Draw the cork. There are many types of corkscrew available; buy the best you can, but avoid gimmicks. A good corkscrew will draw the cork as gently and cleanly as possible, with little effort and without ruining the cork. Look for a long, open helix, with a sharp point placed on the circumference of the helix itself. Avoid solid or gimlet types of corkscrew. They do not work well with new corks, and will completely destroy an old, crumbly one. A well-designed waiter's friend, with a long helix, or the screwpull are always safe bets.

Pour a sample into a glass for approval. Not too much, a tasting sample only. Swirl the wine around the glass and sniff it, gently at first. This is the last, but vital, part of the quality-control process. Most wines are healthy, but a significant number are faulty, either through contaminated corks or inadequate storage. If you are having a large dinner, with more than one bottle of each wine, remember that faults happen randomly, so taste every bottle, not just the first. A sign of a good restaurant sommelier is whether or not these subsequent tastings are offered. (*See* Tasting White Wines on page 42).

To get the most from your glass it should be two-thirds full.

Never fill the glasses more than two-thirds full. This inhibits the full appreciation of all the characteristics of the wine as one cannot swirl it round the glass, or put one's nose in the glass to collect the maximum aroma. For white wines, there is another reason: temperature. Wine stays cooler in the bottle than the glass,

White wines can vary in color from almost water-white to a deep gold.

where it will warm up remarkably quickly. Far better to top the glass up frequently than have the wine get too warm. White wines are often served in smaller glasses than red for this very reason– they need topping up more frequently.

As to what glasses to use, often the simplest design is the best. Cut crystal may look good, but plain glasses allow the wine to shine through. Fine glass, tapering at the rim until it almost disappears, is far more pleasant to use than thick glasses with a molded rim. Wineglasses should never slant outward, except perhaps just at the rim. A tulip-shaped bowl is ideal, allowing the wine to be swirled without spillage, and sniffed without the aromas dissipating.

The Austrian glassmaker Riedel has developed a range of glasses for white wines which are well worth investigating. His top range is pricey, but for everyday use the Vinum range is not too expensive, provided you are very careful when washing them.

SEDIMENTS AND DECANTING

Few white wines ever need decanting. A light sediment may form after many years of storage, which should be removed for appearance's sake. Simply pour the wine carefully from its bottle into a decanter, watch the sediment all the time and stop as it reaches the neck. Fortunately, the pale-colored bottles used for white wine are an advantage here. They make it easier to see the sediment.

One type of sediment causes consumers enormous, but unnecessary, anguish: tartrate crystals. These appear in old German wines in particular, but can occasionally be found in Sauternes and other sweet wines, looking like sugar crystals, or even ground-up glass. They are

It can be useful to decant white wine if it has deposited tartrate crystals.

harmless natural salts which have formed in the bottle during the maturation, and should be welcomed since they show that the winemaker has not overtreated his product. Tartrates taste bitter, so pour with care when reaching the end of the bottle, or decant first.

TASTING WHITE WINES

The purpose of wine tasting, as distinct from drinking, is to assess quality and maturity of the wine and to assess whether it is to your taste. You, the consumer tasting each wine, are the final stage of the quality-control sequence, checking to ensure the wine is in good condition. This is why the sommelier offers the host a sample, not to see if the diner likes the wine, but to check its condition.

When tasting, only a small sample is necessary. Overfilling will distract from your ability to taste, because it becomes more difficult to swirl the wine around the glass. For this reason it is better not to use too small a glass. Different-shaped glasses emphasize different constituents of flavor, so when comparing a number of wines use the same glasses.

The first stage of tasting involves looking at the wine. Look for clarity. The wine should be bright and clear. If it's dull or cloudy, alarm bells might start ringing: this wine may be faulty. Even within clear, healthy wines there are degrees of clarity. Although it is difficult to rationalize it scientifically, very fine wines often seem to have a certain polish, an extra level of brilliance that a simpler wine, even with a similar provenance, does not have. Do not worry unduly if there is a sediment if the wine has had some bottle age–this is natural.

The color might vary from almost water white to deep gold. The depth can be affected by the climate–cool-climate wines are generally paler than warm-climate wines–and by aging, since white wines deepen in color with age. Sweet wines made from nobly rotted grapes are often golden rather than lemon yellow, a result of the concentration process. The range of hues and the brilliance can add to your enjoyment, but beware if the color does not match your expectation. A dry or off-dry German wine of QbA or Kabinett quality or a young wine from the Loire should be pale–if not there may be something amiss, so proceed with caution.

The sense of smell is perhaps the most important part of tasting. Smell and taste are very closely linked (think how little you can taste when you have a cold). Swirl the wine in the glass to release the aromas and sniff gently but deeply. The wine should smell appealing. Any hint of mustiness and it might be corked–reject the bottle. A dull, flat smell comes from slight oxidation, a result of bad handling or insufficient sulfur dioxide in the wine. In an extreme case, your glass might smell of vinegar–again, call for another bottle. Faults can happen, even with the best wine, if the cork is faulty, or storage less than perfect. Unfortunately faults are often random: it could be one rogue bottle or the whole batch, and we can tell only when the corks are drawn.

Assuming all is fine, consider the character and its intensity. Some grapes produce aromatic wines with distinctive characters (*see* Grape Varieties on page 26), while in other wines the wine-making process might come to the fore, particularly if new oak has been used. Young wine will still smell of fruit but, as they age, the best wines develop more complex flavors. Try to assess the maturity this way.

The palate confirms the flavors found on the nose and reveals the wine's structure–the sweetness, the acidity, and the weight.

White wines are made in all styles from bone-dry to fully sweet and luscious, but they should not be cloying. Sweetness should be balanced by acidity, an important component of all types of wine. Acidity manifests itself as a mouthwatering sensation.

"Body" and "length" are terms much used in wine tasting. Body is the feel of the wine in the mouth. White wines can be very light, or quite full. Body and intensity of flavor are important to assess when trying to match food and wine. A wine's length–or finish–is the time you can still taste the wine after it has left the palate, either by being swallowed or, in the case of the professional wine taster, being spat out. Obviously it depends upon the situation you are in as to whether you swallow the wine or spit it out. Generally, the longer the length, the better the wine.

Different parts of the mouth detect different components, so it is important to take a reasonable mouthful and swirl it around the mouth; "chew" it so that it contacts all parts of the mouth, tongue, gums, the roof of the mouth. Additionally, taking in air through pursed lips will help to release extra flavors, but it does make an unsociable noise.

Evaluating wine in this way adds to your knowledge and enjoyment, allowing you to get every ounce of flavor and pleasure out of each glass. But our memories are fallible, so many enthusiasts choose to write tasting notes for each wine as they taste it, building them up over the years into a valuable encyclopedia of wines tasted. A cellar book can be used to list wines "in stock" and to note your impressions of them, providing a personal record of which wines were tasted, when, and with whom. It helps in monitoring the progress of a wine, and is essential for protecting your investment and enabling you to know when to drink which wines.

Wine Tasting

Tasting involves the senses in combination: sight, smell, and taste, and even touch, because some elements, like bubbles, are felt rather than tasted. The more experience you gain, the more pleasure you will get from the wine.

Assess color and appearance.

Swirl the glass to release the wine's aromas.

Professional tastings are always in neutral conditions: good daylight, clean white surfaces, and no distracting odors; before lunch when the palate is freshest and the mind most alert. This is not appropriate for social drinking. Ambience of the decor cannot be so clinical, and can hardly avoid the aromas of food or cologne, but a few small considerations will help. Simple expedients like a white tablecloth, or napkin, and a sensibly shaped glass, not too full, will vastly improve the pleasure you and your guests can get from the wine.

Nose the wine.

Taste the wine.

WINE AND FOOD

Throughout this book you will find recommended food-and-wine pairings. Over the years a whole raft of "rules" has been created about which wines match which dishes; what is acceptable and what is not. Such rules can, however, be either too simplistic or too complicated. The dictum that red wine shall be served with red meat, white wine with white meat and fish, while a useful rule of thumb, ignores both the cooking and the sauces that may be used. On the other hand there are whole books about the subject, some of which set out exactly what wine to drink on any given occasion. The only rule that must be followed is: do not be too dogmatic. If you like drinking young vintage port with your steak, or fino sherry with the dessert, why not?

It is, however, worth bearing in mind a few tips. It is not the color of the wine and the food that matters, but the flavor, and in particular the intensity of that flavor. A delicately flavored dish will be overwhelmed by a big, gutsy Southern Rhône red like Châteauneuf-du-Pape; a fine Chablis might make a better choice. A top Mosel Riesling, fine and elegant with steely acidity and an exquisite bouquet, will be annihilated by a big Provençal casserole, rich in flavorsome herbs. In either case something will be lost.

Most wine is produced to accompany food, and so wine styles have evolved to complement the cuisine of a region. With classic areas this is often a good starting point for finding a good wine-and-food combination.

Some wine-and-food combinations are definitely more success-ful than others. To reach the perfect match you need to analyze the basic elements of taste in both the food and the wine. Try to achieve balance with these, so that neither overpowers the other.

First think of the weight. Rich heavy foods, like game and red-meat casseroles, need a full-bodied wine. Powerful red wines are often the favored choice, although a rich, full-bodied white wine is better than many lighter reds.

Lighter food, like plain white meat or fish, suits more delicate wine. Choose a light-bodied example such as Muscadet, Mosel Riesling, or simple Chablis.

Then consider the other taste elements. Sweetness, acidity, and tannin, along with the fruit characters, help determine to which type of food it is suited.

Dry wines can seem tart and excessively acidic if served with sweeter foods. Balance the sweetness by choosing a wine with a similar or greater degree of sweetness, the sweeter the food the sweeter the wine. Late-harvest and botrytis-affected wines are the ideal choice for desserts.

Such sweet wines with a good level of acidity can also be a superb partner to rich, oily food. Sauternes and foie gras is a classic combination.

Wines with crisp acidity match tart foods, but no wine can stand up to vinaigrette dressing; better to leave the salad undressed, or use just a little oil.

If one particular flavor element stands out, as often happens in a sauce, this should be considered when selecting the wine to accompany it. The spicy flavors in Gewürztraminer call out for spicy dishes, so it is ideal with Asian food. Smoked meats and cheeses will stand up to oaked wines–the stronger the flavor, the greater the oak can be. Rich creamy sauces, whether sweet or savory, need to be accompanied by wines with enough weight and acidity to balance them.

Sauternes and foie gras is a classic pairing.

*B*eing asked to put together a list of top white wines of the world is, for a wine enthusiast, like giving a child the freedom of a toy store. White wines are produced all over the world, in a vast range of styles. Countless wines are made by growers and winemakers around the globe, each one differing slightly from its peers. Every vintage presents another set of challenges for the grower, and developments and changing fashions mean that the winemaker is constantly altering the way the grapes are turned into wine.

Any selection of vineyards or wineries is necessarily arbitrary. No two people have the same list of favorite songs, and no two film critics would give the same list of top films. Wine is, perhaps, a little more objective, there are certain qualities that one can look for. But deciding on whom to leave out is difficult. There are many hundreds of wines worthy of inclusion, but which have had to be omitted, such is the constraint of space. To those who are not included, I can only apologise.

Each entry gives an overview of the winery's history and an outline of the grape growing and winemaking techniques used. The information contained in the fact boxes is as up to date as possible, as supplied by the producers. Production volumes vary from vintage to vintage, depending on the weather. One bottle of wine was tasted for each producer and a tasting note appears alongside each entry. Bear in mind that wines change with time, and vintages and techniques vary, although generally the winemaker will try to keep a consistent style wherever possible. The rating given is for the wine tasted. Many wine companies make a range of wines of varying quality–others in the range would get a different score. The companies are strictly in alphabetical order; if a company's name is preceded by the word "Château" or "Domaine" etc. you will find it under "C" or "D." This has been done for ease of use and also allows for quick comparison between companies.

RATING

★ Relatively inexpensive wine which has proved itself to be consistent and reliable, better than many others at a similar price.

★★ Finer wine with greater character and definition.

★★★ Wines showing true character and individuality.

★★★★ "Special Occasion" wines to be brought out when dining with wine-enthusiast friends.

★★★★★ One of the finest wines you can buy. Expect to pay highly for the privilege.

PART TWO

The
WHITE WINE
directory

ADRIANO RAMOS PINTO

Av de Ramos Pinto 380, 4401 Vila Nova de Gaia, Portugal
Tel: (351) 2 370 7000
*Visitors: Welcome at the Ramos Pinto Port wine lodge in
Vila Nova da Gaia*

Adriano and António Ramos Pinto founded Adriano Ramos Pinto Vinhos in 1880, aiming squarely for the Brazilian market. The company soon built up a reputation both for their wines and the well-planned marketing and promotion. Famous artists of the time were often engaged to produce eye-catching posters, often with hedonistic and mythological themes. They have always been an important port-wine exporter, so it comes as a surprise to many that Adriano Ramos Pinto also produces significant volumes of light wine.

Champagne Louis Roederer now has a controlling interest in the firm but it is still run by João Nicolau de Almeida, a direct descendant of the founder. He is a nephew of Jorge Ramos Pinto Rosas, one of the great names in Douro light-wine production. It was when working for Ferreira that Jorge created the great Barca Velha, the finest Portuguese light wine that

FACT BOX

WINEMAKER: João Nicolau de Almeida
SIZE OF VINEYARD: information not available
PRODUCTION: information not available
GRAPE VARIETY: Sauvignon Blanc
RECOMMENDED VINTAGES: drink youngest available

originates from Quinta da Leda in the wonderfully named village of Meão near the Spanish frontier.

With this background it is not surprising, then, that João takes so much interest in his dry, light wines. His two red Douro DOC wines, Duas Quintas and Duas Quintas Reserva, have been some of the most reliably good light wine from the Douro for some time. The new white wine, Quinta dos Bons Ares, makes a worthy stablemate.

Quinta dos Bons Ares is in the Cima Corgo, the best part of the port region. However, at about 2,000 feet above sea level the ambient temperature is too cool for good port production so the grapes go to make Douro light wine. Duas Quintas, as the name implies, is a blend of wines from here and from Ervamoira, further up the river. This is helpful for the red wines because the heat and ripeness of one site is balanced with the freshness of the other. The wine featured here, however, is purely from Bons Ares.

João has been experimenting with different white grapes here

> ## TASTING NOTES
>
> ### QUINTA DOS BONS ARES 1996
>
> Pale color with quite noticeable legs. Full, quite aromatic nose, but not classic, benchmark Sauvignon. The warmer climate and riper grapes have given this a full, mineral, slightly earthy character, as well as some tropical fruit hints. Dry with moderate acidity, lower than cooler regions might have. Mid-weight with a pronounced flavor. The alcohol is high but it is a tribute to the winemaking that this is hardly noticeable, and is totally in balance.
> Rating ★★★
>
> #### SUGGESTED FOOD PAIRING
> Great with broiled fish and broiled or roasted chicken.

for some years. The most unlikely, and on the face of it, illogical trial has been Sauvignon Blanc. Sauvignon is a cool-climate grape. It produces excellent wines in the Loire and New Zealand, but generally less good in warmer areas. Ramos Pinto took a big risk planting it here. But it has been a gamble that has paid off. Bons Ares Sauvignon, labeled as a Regional wine from Tras os Montes since the grape is not permitted for Douro DOC, is a great success.

A fine-flavored, well-balanced wine, it will be available only in small quantities but is well worth seeking out.

AGRICOLA CASTELLANA
SOC. CO-OP, LA SECA

Ctra. de Rodilana s/n, 47491 La Seca, Valladolid, Spain
Tel: (34) 983 81 63 20 Fax: (34) 983 81 65 62
Visitors: By appointment only

*S*panish wine has come through a renaissance in the last few years. With the exception of a few very high-quality areas, like Jerez and Rioja, all too often Spanish wine was dull and old-fashioned in a very negative way. Yields were low, which should have been positive, but the harvest was often delayed as growers tried to increase the potential alcohol in the grapes, in the hope of a premium price. Winemaking was basic, with little temperature control and rudimentary cellar hygiene. The result was a range of deep-colored, big, fat, over-alcoholic wines in which oxidation was considered normal. Nowhere was this more so than in the wines from the cooperatives.

Azumbre from Agrícola Castellana, the cooperative in La Seca, Valladolid, could not be more different. This wine reeks of modern

FACT BOX

WINEMAKER: D. Angel Calleja Martin

SIZE OF VINEYARDS: 4,500 acres controlled by co-op members. About 25 acres of Sauvignon, and 1,500 acres of Verdejo

PRODUCTION: approx. 600 cases

GRAPE VARIETIES: Sauvignon Blanc, Verdejo, but Viura, Palomino, Tempranillo also grown

RECOMMENDED VINTAGE: 1996

winemaking. Carefully chosen varieties, grown in an appropriate manner, harvested at the right time and processed to get the best out of them, have resulted in a wine any winery in the world would be proud of.

The Agrícola Castellana was founded in 1935 by a small number of local growers. Nowadays 400 growers, controlling 2,000 acres of vineyards, are members. A range of grapes is grown by the members: Sauvignon Blanc is a relative newcomer, joining Verdejo, Viura, and Palomino, the sherry grape. Until fairly recently the region was in what looked like terminal decline. The main styles of wine from here were made in the sherry style: fortified wines from the high-yielding Palomino grape, coarse imitations of Andalucian finos and amontillados. Rapid expansion of the area under the native Verdejo, and the introduction of Sauvignon, have been the saviors of this area.

Some taste combinations seem to have been made in heaven. Lamb and rosemary or tomatoes and basil are universally recognized. Sauvignon Blanc and Verdejo is a newer and less well-known combination. Verdejo is a low-yielding, high-quality grape giving full-bodied wines. Like many warm-climate grapes it lacks aromatic flavors. Sauvignon Blanc, on the other hand, is highly aromatic, but can lack weight and seem rather thin and unsatisfying. The solution is to blend the two.

> ## TASTING NOTES
>
> ### SAUVIGNON BLANC VERDEJO 1996
>
> Pale-lemon yellow in color, much paler than the wines of this area once were. Pungent grassy Sauvignon Blanc character at first but on more careful study the wine reveals a degree of earthy spiciness and some nuttiness too. Really quite complex for a wine of this type. Dry with balanced acidity and full broad palate, the advantage of using the Verdejo.
> Rating ★
>
> #### SUGGESTED FOOD PAIRING
> The aromatic qualities of this wine with its soft palate make it good on its own, or with lighter-flavored pasta dishes.

The grapes are harvested by hand and treated separately. After destalking a few hours of cold maceration increases flavor pickup before pressing and fermentation at 59–62°F–cool by Spanish standards. Blending follows fermentation. The proportion of Sauvignon in the blend has been increasing each vintage as more plantings become available.

AGRICOLA FLLI TEDESCHI SRL

Via G. Verdi, Pedemonte di Valpolicella 37020, Verona, Italy
Tel: (39) 45 7701487 Fax: (39) 45 7704239
Visitors: Monday–Friday 8:30AM–12:30PM and 2:00PM–6:30PM,
by appointment only

*T*edeschi is now run by the fourth and fifth generations of the same family. The firm was started in 1884 by Nicola Tedeschi, succeeded by Lorenzo and then his son Riccardo. Riccardo was responsible for adding some of the finest vineyards to the company portfolio, in particular Monte Olmi and Monte Fontana. As a result and because of his business acumen, Tedeschi started to become better known outside its native Verona.

The next generation was Renzo, who is still in charge of the winery, and Silvino, the viticulturist. The pair continued the expansion of the markets and it was under their joint tenure that the wines became widely available in the export market.

FACT BOX

WINEMAKERS: Renzo, Riccardo, and Sabrina Tedeschi

SIZE OF VINEYARD: Tedeschi own 12 acres, but the grapes for this wine are bought in

PRODUCTION: 34,000 cases total for the company

GRAPE VARIETIES: Chardonnay, Garganega

RECOMMENDED VINTAGE: 1995

LOCAL RESTAURANT: Tratt. La Rosa at Sant' Ambrogio di Valpolicella

The Tedeschi vineyards in Verona, Italy.

International recognition of the brand was greatly improved by a number of successes in foreign wine competitions. Tedeschi are particularly proud of the awards they gained at the London-based *Wine Magazine* International Wine Challenge.

The present generation is made up of Antoinetta, who manages the administrative side of the business, together with Riccardo and Sabrina who, along with Renzo, handle the technical aspects of both vineyards and winery.

Within Italian wine law there is a clear and generally understood hierarchy of grades, and well over 200 individual DOC (equivalent of the French AC) names, yet many choose to go outside the disciplines of DOC and DOCG to produce wines that can carry only the designation of Table Wine, Vino da Tavola–in European parlance the lowest level to which a wine can aspire.

One such is Tedeschi's Capitel San Rocco Bianco. The grapes for this wine are all grown in the Valpolicella area, a region in the Veneto which gives its name to a whole range of wines from the simple and quaffable to very fine, complex wines needing years to mature. All Valpolicella, however, is red. Tedeschi have decided to make a high-quality white wine from a mixture of Italian and foreign grapes in the region.

Unlike many of these "fantasy" wines, Capitel San Rocco Bianco is made very much in the traditional Italian model. No overt oak covering up big fat fruit flavors here. Italian whites are renowned for delicacy and subtlety, which is exactly what this wine has in abundance.

TASTING NOTES

CAPITEL SAN ROCCO BIANCO 1995

Pale straw lemon color with a delicate, refined nose. Some crisp appley characters and a slight hint of herbal tea as well. Very dry with crisp acidity, which is fully balanced by the remarkably full palate, much broader, fatter, and riper than the nose leads one to expect. Again there's a herbal character with a butteriness as well and good length.

Rating ★★★

SUGGESTED FOOD PAIRING
Although full-bodied this is not a full-flavored wine so light-flavored foods are needed. Salads and simple fish dishes are called for.

AGRO DE BAZÁN SA

Tremoedo, 46, Vilanova de Arousa, Ponteverdra, Spain
Tel: (34) 986 56 13 44 & 55 55 62 Fax: (34) 986 55 57 99
Visitors: Weekdays, by appointment only

*F*or centuries pilgrims have walked across the north of Spain on their way to Santiago de Compostela. Over the centuries many thousands must have followed this route, no doubt stopping in places like Navarra, Rioja, and El Bierzo on the way, staying the night and sampling the wine. When they finally reached the end of their journeys the pilgrims would have found, and will still find, the local wine in Santiago to be a fresh, light, and very crisp white, now made under the Denominación de Origen (DO) of Riax Baixas.

Granbazán is a fairly new operation set up by Agro de Bazán SA, a firm specializing in other foodstuffs, including canned sardines and pâtés. Manuel Otero Caneira, a member of the Bazán board, was responsible for searching out a suitable site and bringing it into the Bazán empire. The palatial estate he founded in the

FACT BOX

WINEMAKER: Isabel Salgado de Andrea

SIZE OF VINEYARD: 32 acres supplies 50% of requirements

PRODUCTION: 30,000 cases

GRAPE VARIETY: Albariño

RECOMMENDED VINTAGES: 1995, 1994 (drink youngest available of the un-oaked versions, but this wine will stand a few years' cellaring)

O Salnés valley in northwestern Spain was the result of many years of searching.

The climate here is, by Spanish standards, wet. Santiago is reputed to be the wettest city in Europe, quite remarkable when one considers that the rest of Spain is so dry for much of the year. The lush landscape and cooler climate are ideal for white-wine production, so much so that the wines from this region are among the most prized in Spain.

Here in Galicia, in contrast to the Vinho Verde area on the other side of the Spanish/Portuguese frontier, the vines are low-trained to ripen the grapes fully. The typical alcohol level here is 12 percent by volume, three percentage points higher than the average south of the border, where 9 percent is considered a good vintage. The winemaking here is different too. Rather than aiming for the light, appley but otherwise neutral style, more emphasis is put on extracting flavors from the grapes. A period of low-temperature skin contact is allowed after crushing, to pick up additional aromatics from the skins.

Three levels of wine are made. "Verde" is made from press wine only, "Ambar" from free-run juice, both without oak. "Limousin"–tasted here–is free-run must fermented and matured in French oak casks, including a period on the yeast deposits from the fermentation, and then further matured in bottle prior to release. The result is a much more complex wine than is normal from this part of the world.

TASTING NOTES

GRANBAZÁN LIMOUSIN ALBARIÑO 1995

Pale golden color with a fresh, youthful nose of cinnamon and allspice from the oak with floral and fruit hints. Rose petals and gooseberry, apricot and white peaches are all present here. Dry with marked, cleansing acid balance, medium weight only, as one would expect from the region, with a long, elegant finish. One of few Albariños that could benefit from a few years (but not decades) of bottle aging.
Rating ★★★★

SUGGESTED FOOD PAIRING
White fish, especially oily fish like sardines and mackerel. The acidity of this wine will cut through the oil, which could well prove too much for many other wines.

ANDRÉ & MIREILLE TISSOT

39600 Montigny-les-Arsures, Jura, France
Tel: (33) 3 84 66 08 27 Fax: (33) 3 84 66 25 08
Visitors: Cellar-door sales only

*J*ura wine is unique. This area on the eastern side of France, south of Alsace, on the Swiss border, produces wines quite unlike any others in France. About 150 years ago the area was an important producer, but after phylloxera only a fraction of the vines were replanted. However, the splendid isolation of the areas means that those wines that do still exist are very traditional. Difficulty of communication with the rest of the wine-growing world has resulted in a range of strange wines. Vin Jaune is, like fino, flor-affected. Vin de Paille is made from dried grapes, as happens in some parts of Italy. Add to this a collection of grapes rarely found elsewhere, and you have a recipe for a fascinating range of wines.

André and Mireille Tissot established their vineyard in 1962, with just over half an acre of vines. The family estate now has some 65 acres of vineyard, and one of the best reputations in the

FACT BOX

WINEMAKER: Stéphane Tissot

SIZE OF VINEYARD: total for estate is 65 acres

PRODUCTION: 125,000 bottles per year

GRAPE VARIETIES: Savagnin, but Chardonnay, Trousseau, Poulsard, Pinot Noir are also grown

RECOMMENDED VINTAGES: 1989, 1985, 1983, 1982, 1979

area. It's a strongly family affair, and Mireille and Bénédicte Tissot look after the cellars and the administration, while André is in charge of viticulture, and Stéphane looks after the winemaking.

Two-thirds of the family's sales are to private individuals, many regulars who return to the cellar year in and year out to collect their supplies.

The grape for Vin Jaune is the Savagnin, a local variety said to be related to the Traminer of northern Italy–a forerunner of the Gewürztraminer. This low-yielding variety is well suited to the region, being very resistant to cold, but it does not flourish in the heat.

It is ironic that the region that gave the world Louis Pasteur–who gave his name to a means of killing unwanted microorganisms–should produce a wine that relies on a veil of yeast to give it its style. The grapes are harvested late, late enough to give a natural alcohol of some 14.5 percent, and are pressed. After the alcoholic fermentation the young wine is transferred to casks where it is left "on ullage"–that is to say the casks are never totally filled, an air-gap being left in the top. This is unique in the light-wine world. The only other area that traditionally uses the system is Jerez in Spain, where fino sherry matures beneath a veil of flor.

This yeast veil covers the wine and protects it from oxidation, while changing the characters of the wine. It feeds on acids, alcohols, and glycerin and produces acetaldehyde–ethanal– and chemicals giving a nutty character. The wines spend six years maturing under this yeast before sale.

TASTING NOTES

ARBOIS VIN JAUNE 1990

Deep golden color with a pronounced nose of yeast, fresh French bread and dried apples, spices and walnuts as well. Similar to fino sherry but with more fruit behind the flor character. Dry with marked acidity, again a big difference between this and fino. Full, weighty palate with quite high alcohol and good length. An unusual wine, well worth seeking out.

Rating ★★★★

SUGGESTED FOOD PAIRING

It can seem difficult to place a wine like this. Shellfish is a good start, as is sausage. Think in terms of Spanish tapas, but with French ingredients. It is also sublime with game.

BABICH WINE LIMITED

Babich Road, Henderson, Auckland, New Zealand
Tel: (64) 9 833 7859 Fax: (64) 9 833 9929
Visitors: Monday–Friday 9:00AM–5:00PM;
Saturday 9:00AM–6:00PM; Sunday 11:00AM–5:00PM

*J*osip Petrov Babich was born in Dalmatia in 1896. He emigrated to New Zealand when he was 14 to join his brothers working in the gum fields at Kaikino in the north of the country. He planted his first, very small, vineyard in 1912. Four years later he sold his first wine, and was promptly arrested for selling less than two gallons and for selling out of hours, in contravention of the licensing laws.

Although he was acquitted, the lawyer involved in the case recommended that Babich move the operation closer to the main market, Auckland. This he did and set up a vineyard at Henderson in 1919, where the winery is still situated.

FACT BOX

WINEMAKER: Joe Babich until 1997, Neill Culley from 1997

SIZE OF VINEYARDS: 183 acres spread over Henderson Valley and Hawke's Bay supplies 50% of total needs

PRODUCTION: 80,000 cases total

GRAPE VARIETIES: Chardonnay, Sauvignon Blanc, Chenin Blanc, Riesling, Gewürztraminer, Semillon, Pinot Gris, Cabernet Sauvignon, Merlot, Cabernet Franc, Syrah, Pinotage, Pinot Noir (mostly used unblended as varietals)

RECOMMENDED VINTAGES: 1997, 1996, 1994, 1991, 1989

Josip's son Peter, now chairman, joined the business in 1948. Joseph Babich, now managing director, joined 10 years later. At that point the production was small and concentrated on fortified wines for a purely local market. It was not until the 1960s that the company began to expand into the light-wine production for which they are now famous. Between 1960 and 1970 Babich expanded their light-wine vineyards and in 1977 re-equipped their winery so that it became a totally light-wine establishment. That year too saw the first purchase of grapes from the Gisborne area. The highlight of Josip's career came in 1980 when for the first time Babich wines were exported to Europe, the home of wine production.

Joe and Peter Babich.

Josip died at the age of 87 in 1983 but his sons now run the company, and Joe continued to make the wines until the 1997 vintage when Neill Culley took over as both winemaker and export manager.

The two Irongate wines, a Chardonnay and a Cabernet Sauvignon–Merlot blend, are the flagship wines of the company. Fruit comes from the company's own vineyards in Hawke's Bay where the river deposits give a rich, well-drained soil. For the Chardonnay the must is barrel-fermented in a mixture of mostly French with some American oak. Malolactic fermentation is encouraged both to reduce the acidity and to add a buttery, creamy texture to the finished wine.

TASTING NOTES

IRONGATE CHARDONNAY HAWKE'S BAY 1995

Pale yellow developing some gold hints. Intense nutty and oaky nose with cream and butter, rich and almost oily. Dry with balanced acidity and rich, opulent texture, creamy and rich again on the palate. Full bodied and with a long length. Big, powerful up-front wine.
Rating ★★

SUGGESTED FOOD PAIRING
Excellent with poached salmon in a creamy sauce.

BADIA A COLTIBUONO

53013 Gaiole in Chianti (SI), Toscana, Italy
Tel: (39) 577 749498 Fax: (39) 577 749235
Visitors: Farmgate store and restaurant only

*T*he Badia a Coltibuono estate dates back over a millennium, making it one of the oldest wine estates still in existence. As well as a wine producer, Badia a Coltibuono is an abbey, a historical monument seen by hundreds of visitors every year, and, most important, it is a family home, that of the Stucchi Prinetti family, who have run the estate for the last century and a half. Roberto and his father Piero manage the vineyards and winemaking. Roberto's sister, Emanuela, is in charge of the marketing and public relations.

Badia a Coltibuono is in the heart of the Chianti Classico region of Tuscany. Here, between Florence and Siena, the landscape is the background to hundreds of Renaissance paintings, the rolling hills all

FACT BOX

WINEMAKER: Roberto Stucchi Prinetti
SIZE OF VINEYARDS: 125 acres, in an estate of 2,000 (2½ acres of Chardonnay in vineyard called Sella del Boscone)
PRODUCTION: 1,000 cases of this wine
GRAPE VARIETIES: Chardonnay, but classic Chianti grapes also grown
RECOMMENDED VINTAGE: 1995
RESTAURANT: They have a restaurant on site

Coat of arms over the main entrance to the cellars.

covered with olive trees or vines, occasionally interspersed with a field of dazzling yellow sunflowers, perhaps bounded by a row of cypress trees. At the peak of each major hill is yet another fortified town, the ramparts bearing witness to warfare that long ago turned to friendly rivalry. The abbey house of Badia a Coltibuono sits at the summit of a lesser hill near Gaiole, the yellow sandstone walls visible above the conifers on the hillsides.

The house is not open to the public as such, although courses in Italian cuisine are run here, led by Lorenza de'Medici, wife of the current owner, Piero Stucchi Prinetti. Guests who are invited are as likely to be greeted by a Moreno sheepdog as one of the family; these huge, golden-furred dogs have become almost as much a symbol of the estate as the coat of arms above the gate.

The vines are some way from the house, lower down the hillside where the climate is a little warmer. All of the normal Chianti grapes are grown, because, until recently, the only wine made here was Chianti Classico, and first-rate Chianti at that. So Sangioveto (the high-quality local clone of Sangiovese) Cannaiolo, Malvasia, and Trebbiano were all grown. In the 1970s the prices fetched for even top Chiantis did not reflect their true worth so a number of producers started to make what were

SELLA
DEL
BOSCONE

Chardonnay
1994

COLTIBUONO

called locally "fantasy" wines, better known internationally as "Supertuscans." These are usually of outstandingly high quality, and of course Badia a Coltibuono's is no exception.

About 2½ acres of Chardonnay provides the fruit for Sella del Boscone. Fermentation follows a very brief skin contact and is in new French oak barriques, after which an extended lees maturation in the same barrels is carried out. Bottles are not released until the wine has had a full year of bottle aging, too.

The wines are matured in the cellars of the house, in new,

TASTING NOTES

SELLA DEL BOSCONE CHARDONNAY 1995

Pale golden in color with an almost luminous brilliance. Ripe tropical fruit and butterscotch nose with quite pungent oak and a hint of nuttiness on the nose. Dry with finely balanced acidity and fruity intensity. Great elegance and length.
Rating ★★★★

SUGGESTED FOOD PAIRING
Medium flavored pasta dishes and veal, if the sauce is not too overpowering.

---

small barriques and old oak botti, the traditional large barrels used throughout Italy. These are so large, and the entrance to the cellar so small, that they had to be made, and when necessary have to be repaired, in situ.

The Badia a Coltibuono palace is still the family home.

BLACKWOOD CANYON VINTNERS

53258 N. Sunset PR NE, Benton City, WA 99320, USA
Tel: (1) 509 588 6249 Fax: (1) 509 588 5195
Visitors: Daily, 10:00AM–6:00PM

*M*ike (M. Taylor) Moore of Blackwood Canyon Vintners is renowned for his passion–a passion for viticulture rather than winemaking. The result is a range of wines unique in the North West states of the U.S., very different from other Washington and Oregon wines, and totally different from Californian wines, being far more French in character.

Mike Moore started out as a range conservationist in Idaho. A love of food, wine, and agriculture led to his leaving the rigors of government bureaucracy and, via a course at the University of California, into winemaking. Whilst there he turned his attention northwards to what was then an undeveloped region. The vast majority of U.S. wines come from California, the high quality estates farther north are only now achieving the reputation they deserve.

FACT BOX

WINEMAKER: Mike Taylor Moore
SIZE OF VINEYARD: 49 acres
PRODUCTION: 33,000 cases in total
GRAPE VARIETIES: Chardonnay, Sémillon, Chenin, Riesling, Cabernet Sauvignon, Merlot
RECOMMENDED VINTAGES: for Chardonnay 1990, 1989, 1988

The land that was to become Blackwood Canyon vineyard was bought in 1983. The first "vintage," some 100 tons of grapes, was bought in, as the first vines were not planted until 1984. The following year the winery and the entire stock of wine was destroyed by fire. Rising phoenix-like from the ashes, it was rebuilt in readiness for the 1986 harvest.

Moore, like many European wine-makers, believes that the wine's quality comes not from technical trickery but from the vines. He has gone so far as to call his viticulture "Flavor Farming," thereby emphasizing the long-held belief of so many in the "Old World."

The vines here are grown using integrated pest management. This is a halfway house on the road to full organic viticulture. It recognizes that there are occasions when synthetic chemicals are the best option, but that their use should be limited. Only low residual compounds, those that decompose harmlessly, are used and then only when necessary. Considerable effort is put in to creating and maintaining the ideal habitat for predator species which prey on the vineyard pests. Considerable savings in chemicals result.

TASTING NOTES

1988 YAKIMA VALLEY CHARDONNAY

Deep golden color, a sure sign of maturity and concentration. The nose too, is mature—so unusual to find in a Chardonnay from anywhere but Burgundy, these wines are normally released and drunk when young. Complex fruit and spice flavors, smoke and linseed oil combine with butter and tropical fruit. Dry but very ripe palate. Very full flavor and full body with the complexities of the nose coming through. Great wine. Rating ★★★★

SUGGESTED FOOD PAIRING

This wine needs foods which are in themselves naturally full flavored—fish simply broiled, or veal in a light sauce. This wine could almost match red meats too.

Blackwood Canyon make some wonderful late harvest wines from botrytis-affected Riesling and Sémillon, as well as dry reds and whites from a range of varieties. Superficially you might see the Chardonnay as having been made in the standard fashion of barrel fermentation with maturation and battonage (lees stirring) but Blackwood Canyon use no sulfur dioxide in many of their wines, and avoid fining completely. Also, the wines are not released as soon as they are bottled, they are matured for up to two years in wood. The 1988 Chardonnay is the current vintage offered.

BODEGAS ESMERALDA SA

Guatemala 4565, Capital Federal, Buenos Aires 1425,
Argentina
Tel: (54) 1 833 2082 Fax: (54) 1 833 5660
Visitors: Vineyards are not open to the public

*L*ike so many of the most successful north American wineries, Bodegas Esmeralda was founded by an Italian immigrant, in this case Nicola Catena, from the Marche on the east coast of the Italianate peninsula. He arrived towards the end of the nineteenth century, settling in Mendoza. Whether this was because of an influx of Italians, or whether the Italian immigrants were attracted to the vines, it is difficult to say, but even then Mendoza was beginning to get a reputation for its wine production.

Nicola Catena planted his first vineyard in 1902. The wine was made for the local market only at that stage–exports came much later. Nicola was succeeded by his son Domingo, and eventually his grandson, Nicolas. Throughout this time the company had continued to expand, becoming the biggest producer of bottled wine in Argentina. In 1966 the Catena company bought Bodegas Esmeralda, a winery

FACT BOX

WINEMAKER: José Galante
SIZE OF VINEYARD: 385 acres
PRODUCTION: (export) 60,000 cases
GRAPE VARIETIES: include Sauvignon Blanc, Chardonnay, Sirah, Sémillon
RECOMMENDED VINTAGE: 1996

TASTING NOTES

CATENA 1995 CHARDONNAY AGRELO VINEYARD

Vivid pale-gold wine with moderate legs forming on the side of the glass. Pungently oaky at first. Toast and roast almonds are the first impressions, only later followed up by pineapple and pear fruit with some butterscotch character. Still very young, needing a few months or a year to settle down and marry. Dry but ripe on the palate with good, cleansing acidity that sets this wine apart from some other New World Chardonnays. Medium weight and a long finish.

Rating ★★★

SUGGESTED FOOD PAIRING
Broiled chicken or medium-flavored white fish.

devoted to fine, rather than bulk, wines. But the wines were still strictly for the local market. Heavy, oxidized styles persisted, white and red wines that were nearer brown in color and lacking fruit.

The change came in 1976. Nicola Catena visited California and in particular went to see Robert Mondavi. This was a revelation. Wines that retained their fruit, white wines that still had freshness to them, wines that tasted of the varietal from which they were made. Immediately he changed his travel plans to allow time to visit the University of California at Davis. After a return visit by Professor Kunkee a number of initiatives were started at the Catena cellars: must coolers were installed and less oxidative handling was introduced. Nicola's brother, George, even enrolled at UC Davis to take a Master's degree.

Despite this effort, the style of wine the company made hardly changed. The market, or at least the perceived market, was still for the oxidative style of wines they had always made. Only later, in the late seventies and early eighties, was Argentina ready for the new styles.

The Andes protect the vineyards of Argentina.

After another spell in California, this time as visiting professor at the university, Nicola turned his attention to the vineyards searching out the ideal terroirs to ripen grapes well. Sites were selected that had poor rocky soil, and were rich in minerals but not in organic matter, with cool microclimates. New vineyards were planted with low-vigor rootstocks, and high plant densities to improve quality. Three sites were chosen, the Agrelo vineyard in Lujan being the most promising for Chardonnay.

All the grapes for the Catena Chardonnay come from this vineyard. Harvesting is done entirely by hand. Partial crushing takes place, and part of the crop is whole-cluster pressed. The proportions have been arrived at by experience. All the wine is fermented in cask using for the most part natural yeasts, although a small amount of commercial, cultivated yeast is also used, more as an insurance than anything else.

BODEGAS ETCHART DE CUSENIER SAIC

Lima 229, 1073 Buenos Aires, Argentina
Tel: (54) 1 382 6923/3820310 Fax: (54) 1 383 1495
*Visitors: Monday–Saturday 9:00AM–12:00 noon and
3:00PM–6:00PM*

*I*n most vintages Argentina is the largest wine producer outside Europe. Only Italy, France, and Spain produce a greater volume of wine. Despite this, little Argentine wine is seen on the export markets, largely because of a healthy local market. Political problems too have played their part. Domestic instability and international conflicts, particularly in the early 1980s, put a brake on the embryonic exports, a situation that has only recently been overcome.

In the meantime the country's winemakers have not stood still. From supplying a vast bulk of wines to an undemanding market, they have moved to higher quality, with a few firms now making wines of world-beating class. One such is Etchart, whose interpretation of the Torrontes variety has taken the world by storm.

FACT BOX

WINEMAKER: Michel Rolland
(consultant winemaker)
SIZE OF VINEYARD:
630 acres–supplies 90% of requirements
PRODUCTION: 250,000 cases
GRAPE VARIETY: Torrontes
RECOMMENDED VINTAGE:
drink youngest available

Ninety percent of the volume comes from the Cafayate estate, in the foothills of the Andes. Originally established in the middle of the last century, it was bought by the Etcharts in 1938 who, in 1992, went into partnership with the giant French drinks company Pernod Ricard. Best known for their aniseed-flavored pastis, Pernod Ricard have vineyard holdings and winemaking facilities in many countries and were able to give technical advice as well as financial support to the estate.

Old wine presses kept as museum pieces.

The soil at Cafayate is mostly alluvial, irrigated by rivers and underground water coming off the mountains, the climate here being generally quite dry. The altitude, 5,580 feet above sea level, means the estate is cooler than the latitude might suggest and, the low night-time temperatures encourage the development of aromatic compounds in the grapes.

The main grape here is the Torrontes, not widely grown anywhere other than Argentina, where it has become popular, giving the world an alternative to Chardonnay. It is aromatic in character, and its flavors are best preserved in the wine by modern, reductive handling. Stainless-steel presses and vats, cool temperatures, and careful avoidance of aeration of the must are essential if the winemaker wants to keep the grape's charming perfume. Oak maturation here would be anathema, unnecessarily distracting from the grape.

TASTING NOTES

CAFAYATE TORRONTES 1997

Very pale-colored wine, almost water-white. Light, aromatic almost Muscat nose, rose petals and peaches. A deceptive nose that leads one to expect a gentle, light alcohol and probably sweet wine. How wrong! Dry with a firm structure, and noticeably high alcohol supporting the delicate flavors. This is a wine best enjoyed while it is young. If stored in ideal conditions it will keep. It has the structure, in particular the alcohol, to do it, but it will not improve in the bottle. Better to drink it while it is still fresh.

Rating ★★

SUGGESTED FOOD PAIRING

Chicken, light flavored fish dishes and particularly good with Chinese foods where the aromatics complement the sweet and sour flavors.

BODEGAS JULIÁN CHIVITE

C/Ribera s/n, 31592 Cintruenigo, Navarra, Spain
Tel: (34) 48 811000 Fax: (34) 48 811407
Visitors: By appointment only during office hours (note that Chivite are usually closed in July, not August, as is normal in Spain)

Navarra is a large and disparate region to the east of Rioja. Here tradition and modernity meet each other head on. Navarra has, until recently, looked on with envy as its nearest neighbor built a reputation for its wines that Navarra could only dream of. Here high-alcohol rosado wines, mostly drunk in the local bars, sold; buyers wanting higher-quality wines went to Rioja.

The scene is now changing dramatically, with a whole host of high-quality bodegas becoming better known for finer wines. One that has always been at the forefront of high-quality Navarran wines is Chivite, the oldest bodega in the region.

The present Chivite winery was established in 1860, partly a response to the scourge of oidium in Bordeaux, across the border in France. This disease dramatically

FACT BOX

WINEMAKER: Fernando Chivite
SIZE OF VINEYARD: 840 acres
PRODUCTION: information not available
GRAPE VARIETY: Chardonnay
RECOMMENDED VINTAGES: 1996, 1995, 1994, 1992
LOCAL RESTAURANT: Restaurant Maher, Michelin-starred and very close to the Bodega

cut the production in the Gironde, leaving a gap in the market which was easily exploited by Claudio Chivite. In those days "improving" a wine with a little of something from further south was not the anathema it is today, so many of the period's Medoc and Graves might have had Navarra added. The family go back far longer than the winery, however, and have documentary evidence that the first winery was established in 1647, 11 generations ago.

The current head of the family, and the business, is the octogenarian Julián Chivite, son of Claudio. Day-to-day running is in the hands of his three children, who conveniently are each interested in different aspects of the business. Mercedes and Julián Jnr are responsible for PR and export marketing, while the mustachioed Fernando is the enologist.

The estate comprises three separate vineyards totaling 840 acres, but even this is not sufficient so grapes are also bought in from contract growers in the region. This is because of the success of the basic Gran Feudo range, probably the most widely recognized Navarra of the export markets as well as being well respected in Spain.

All the grapes for the top-of-the-range wines come from the company vineyards. These premium wines, the Coleccion 125, were launched to celebrate the 125th anniversary of the founding of the winery. The white is made from premium-quality Chardonnay fruit from the best sites, fermented after a period of unsulfured skin contact in first- and second-fill Allier oak. Full malolactic fermentation is encouraged and the wines remain on the lees for 10 months before bottling. The result is a thoroughly modern style of white wine with a great deal of elegance to it. Reserva and Gran Reserva red wines and a remarkable late-harvest sweet wine are also made in this range.

TASTING NOTES

COLECCION 125 BLANCO 1996

Pale-lemon yellow. Medium-intensity nose of fresh fruit, lime juice, and melons with the spice of new wood. Unlike with many oaky Chardonnays, the oak is not dominant: it adds complexity without overpowering the fruit. Butterscotch flavors as well coming through. Dry with balanced acidity and medium weight. Thoroughly well balanced.

Rating ★★★

SUGGESTED FOOD PAIRING

Chivite recommends this with fish. It also works very well with roast chicken cooked with a fresh herb stuffing.

CA' DEL BOSCO AZÍENDA AGRICOLA

Via Case Sparse 20, 25030 Ebusco (BS), Italy
Tel: (39) 30 776 0600 Fax: (39) 30 7268425
Visitors: By appointment only Monday–Friday 9:00AM–12:00 noon and 3:00PM–6:00PM

*I*n direct contrast to many of the best wine firms, Ca' Del Bosco is emphatically not an old, traditional family firm. Now one of the best known of the Lombardian wine companies, the firm started making wines commercially only in the late 1970s, and they were made by Maurizio Zanella, the motorbike-racing son of a Milan trucking magnate.

Sandwiched as it is between the better-known Piemonte and the Veneto, Lombardia has never had the international recognition that it deserves. This could be a disadvantage for a newcomer to winemaking. Famous names like Barolo and Valpolicella have a track record that consumers know and understand. Lombardia has no such

FACT BOX

WINEMAKER: Maurizio Zanella
SIZE OF VINEYARD: 240 acres
PRODUCTION: 50,000 cases total
GRAPE VARIETIES: Chardonnay, but also Pinot Bianco (Pinot Blanc), Pinot Nero (Pinot Noir), Merlot, Cabernet Sauvignon, Cabernet Franc, Barbera, Nebbiolo, Sauvignon Blanc
RECOMMENDED VINTAGES: 1995, 1991
LOCAL RESTAURANT: Il Volto

The Ca' Del Bosco winery and cellars.

famous names. Maurizio Zanella has turned this to his advantage. He is able to ignore the traditions of the region to make international-style wines which have been highly praised, even though, or perhaps because, they break the rules attached to Italian DOC wines.

The name, Ca' Del Bosco, means the house in the wood, a fitting name for the impressive winery and cellars. The estate was originally the family summer retreat but, using a bank loan under-written by his parents, the then 20-something Maurizio Zanella built cellars big enough to house considerably more volume than he planned to make. This allowed for expansion, but more important, allowed for long-term aging in the cellars. The cellars them-selves are innovative in their

Inside there is ample storage in ideal conditions.

design. Instead of tunneling *under* the hillside the builders took away a section of it, built the cellars, and then replaced the hill, landscaped it, and replanted the trees.

If the region has a reputation for anything it is sparkling wines, so about half of Ca' Del Bosco's production is sparkling, made from Pinot Noir and Chardonnay using bottle fermentation like champagne. Still wine, both red and white utilizing a range of Italian and international grape varieties, makes up the remainder. Ca' Del Bosco's flagship wine is the Chardonnay.

TASTING NOTES

1994
CHARDONNAY

Deep golden color, indicative of the ripeness of the grapes and the degree of oak aging this wine has had. Very full, pronounced nose of vanilla from the oak with some toast and nuts, backed up by massive ripe tropical fruits, peach and apricot flavors with a hint of lemon butter. Dry but very ripe, with a full-bodied, creamy texture and complex flavors. Something of a blockbuster.
Rating ★★★★

SUGGESTED FOOD PAIRING
This is a full-flavored wine that would dominate delicately flavored dishes. Serve it with fuller-flavored dishes like veal or chicken in a rich, creamy sauce.

Inspiration for this wine came when Maurizio Zanella visited Burgundy when he was 16. This was when he first became fascinated by wine, and after visiting the cellars of the famous Domaine de la Romanée Conti he set himself the goal of creating a wine as good as the white Burgundies.

The result is perhaps more in the Californian model than the Burgundian, but the quality is certainly there. First produced in 1983, the wine has collected a multitude of international awards. It is made in what has become the classic method for Chardonnay. Twenty-four hours of skin contact after crushing is followed by pressing and fermentation in small barrels, half of which are new each vintage. Full malolactic fermentation is encouraged and the wine spends eight months in cask before bottling.

C. A. HENSCHKE & CO

PO Box 100, Keyneton, South Australia 5353
Tel: (61) 8 8564 8223 Fax: (61) 8 8564 8294
Visitors: Cellar-door sales only Monday–Friday 9:00AM–4:30PM;
Saturday 9:00AM–12:00 NOON; public holidays 10.00AM–3:00PM

*S*tephen and Prue Henschke have an enviable reputation for their red wines. Hill of Grace and Mount Edlestone are among the best Shiraz wines in the world, the former being made from vines approximately 130 years old, making them the oldest Shiraz vines on the planet. Henschke are perhaps less well known for white wines that are equally interesting.

Johann Christian Henschke founded the company. An immigrant from Silesia (then in Germany, now in Poland), he arrived in 1841 and settled near Bethany. Eventually he bought a plot of land in what was then called North Rhine, now known as Keyneton. It is recorded that he continued living in Bethany while building on his new property, walking from one to the other

FACT BOX

WINEMAKER: Stephen Henschke
SIZE OF VINEYARDS: 247 acres
PRODUCTION: 30,000–40,000 cases
GRAPE VARIETIES: Semillon for this wine; also Shiraz, Chardonnay, Sauvignon Blanc, Riesling, Gewürztraminer, Cabernet Sauvignon, Malbec—mostly used in varietal wines, some blends also made
RECOMMENDED VINTAGES: 1994, 1992, 1990

each day. Along with wheat he planted a few vines, to make wine for personal consumption. He probably made the first wine in the mid-1860s, and the first record of any being sold is dated 1868.

Paul Gotthard Henschke took over from his father, and the third generation, Paul Alfred, took over in the early part of the twentieth century. Until then viticulture had been a sideline but the demand for fortified wine was increasing so viticulture and winemaking became more important. At the same time additional land was bought to ensure financial security.

It was with the next generation, Cyril Henschke, that light-wine making came to the fore. After working at Hardy's he decided to take up the challenge of light-wine production and phased out the fortified. Further research in Germany, South Africa, and California all helped but, despite this and the quality of the wines, he initially found selling the wines very difficult.

The current generation, Stephen, and his viticulturist wife Prue, have no such problems. Such is the reputation of their wines, and the popularity of the styles, that they regularly command the highest prices at auction, and the top wines are available only on the very strictest allocations.

Most of the grapes are sourced from their own land, which gives them total control over the quality. The main Semillon vineyard is in the Eden Valley, a long-term organic vineyard, organic because that was the way it was done, rather than for reasons of fashion. After cold settling, the fermentation is begun in stainless steel at a low temperature and, when it is partway through, the fermenting must is transferred into casks. Hogsheads are used, larger than the traditional barrique, they impart a more subtle oak flavor. About 50 percent new casks are used.

TASTING NOTES

1994 EDEN VALLEY/BAROSSA VALLEY SEMILLON

Mid-lemon yellow with some gold hints. Big, fat, rich, opulent nose. Quite strongly oaky but with floral and fruity hints as well, honeydew melon, peaches, and some spiciness from the oak. Dry with balanced acidity. Again, fat broad texture, almost oily. Mouth-filling, full bodied with quite high alcohol. Drinking well now but it will be interesting to see how it develops, as it certainly will.

Rating ★★★★

SUGGESTED FOOD PAIRING
Full-flavored fish like broiled trout or smoked marlin. Char-broiled chicken.

CARLO PELLEGRINO & CO.
SPA

Via del Fante 37–39, 91025, Marsala, Italy
Tel: (39) 923 951177 Fax: (39) 923 953542
Visitors: Winery open Monday–Friday 8:30AM–
12:30PM and 2:00PM–5:30PM

*P*ellegrino was founded in 1880 by a notary public called Paolo Pellegrino. Like many Sicilian residents, he was a grape grower as well. On his death his son Carlo took over. Carlo was married to a French noblewoman, Josephine Despagne, a member of an influential Sauternais family. With this background they could improve the marketing of the wines.

Pellegrino has always specialized in the fortified wines of Marsala, from the western end of the island of Sicily. They also produce wine from Sicily's sister island, Pantelleria.

The tiny Italian island of Pantelleria lies 87 miles southwest of Sicily, and only 44 miles off the North African coast. Sicilian mythology has

FACT BOX

WINEMAKER: Gaspare Cataeano

SIZE OF VINEYARDS: total over the two islands 990 acres–supplies approx. 60% of needs

PRODUCTION: 500,000 cases total–only a small (unstated) proportion of this is Pantelleria

GRAPE VARIETY: Zibibbo (a.k.a. Muscat of Alexandria)

RECOMMENDED VINTAGES: for Moscato, drink youngest available

LOCAL RESTAURANT: Delfino, in Marsala

it that the goddess Tanit, in an effort to seduce Apollo, disguised herself as a cup bearer and served him the sweet wine of Pantelleria. Finding it even greater than the ambrosia of the gods, Apollo was spellbound.

Viticulture and vinification on the island are fascinating– seemingly all of the most unusual vineyard and winery practices from anywhere in the world are gathered here to make the two unique Panelleria wines. Being on a hilly volcanic island, the vineyards are terraced, hand-built stone walls being used to hold the soil in place. The main grape here is the Zibibbo, the local name for the Muscat of Alexandria. Because of the hot climate the growers train the vines low, in individual bushes, without recourse to wires or trellising. This shades the grapes and helps to retain moisture. The drying winds can be very damaging so, as well as being low-trained, the vines are often planted in craters to afford a little more shelter. The pruning makes each vine look like a large bird's nest.

The two wines are made in very different ways. Moscato di Pantelleria, a Vino liquoroso, is made from grapes pressed soon after harvest, fortified partway through fermentation to retain some residual sweetness as in port and the Vins Doux Naturels of southern France. The Passito wine is made from raisined grapes. After harvest the grapes are spread out on racks to dry in the sun. This concentrates the sugars and the flavors to give a full-bodied, pungently raisin-like wine, ideal with baked puddings or dried fruit.

TASTING NOTES

MOSCATO DI PANTELLERIA 1996

Pale yellow with just a hint of gold. Fine, perfumed floral and peach or apricot nose, young and grapy. Fully sweet with an unctuous, luscious texture. Balanced acidity ensures that it is not in the least cloying and the full weight and noticeable alcohol (15.5%) gives the wine the necessary structure. Good, but not outstanding length.

Rating ★★

SUGGESTED FOOD PAIRING

This is a dessert wine, to be served with the sweetest of sticky foods. Treacle pudding would be ideal. The weight makes this too full and heavy to serve as an apéritif in the way that the French Muscat de Beaume de Venise wines are in their homeland.

CARPINETO SNC. FRAZ. DUDDA

Greve, Chianti, FI, Italy
Tel: (39) 55 8549001 Fax: (39) 55 8549062
Visitors: By appointment only

*C*asa Vinicola Carpineto, based at Dudda in the heart of the Chianti Classico region, Tuscany, was founded in 1967. Here, in one of the most beautiful of all vineyard regions, grapes have been grown for longer than history records. Certainly the Ancient Romans had a settlement which included the Carpineto vineyards.

Although a newcomer by grape-growing and winemaking standards, the company has already built an enviable reputation for the quality of its wines. Most of the portfolio consists of classical Tuscan wines: Chianti Classico, Vino Nobile di Montepulciano, and Vernaccia di San Gimignano are all on the list. From the beginning, though, Carpineto has been prepared to experiment with new techniques and new grape varieties. The range also there-fore, includes spumante wines, unusual in

FACT BOX

WINEMAKER: Giovanni Carlo Sacchet

SIZE OF VINEYARD: 50 acres owned by Carpineto, 173 acres under contract

PRODUCTION: approx. 80,000 cases total

GRAPE VARIETIES: Chardonnay for this wine, but also Sangiovese, Canaiolo, Cabernet Sauvignon, Sauvignon Blanc

RECOMMENDED VINTAGES: for Chardonnay 1995, 1994

TASTING NOTES

FARNITO CHARDONNAY DI TOSCANA VINO DA TAVOLA 1995

Deep gold, vividly clear, polished appearance. Fine elegant nose, complex flavors of spicy cedary oak, vanilla and ginger with soft fruits, peach and melon. Still smells quite youthful. The palate is totally dry, with fine balanced acidity. Medium weight but with a full flavor. The alcohol level is not noticeably high, adding to the overall finesse of the wine. A very stylish example of Chardonnay.

Rating ★★★★

SUGGESTED FOOD PAIRING
Complex enough to be interesting on its own, this is ideal with veal dishes and pastas if the sauce is not too full.

this part of Italy, and a range of "super-Tuscans."

These are wines that, while not entitled to the official quality designations of DOC or DOCG (Denominazione di Origine Controllata and Denominazione di Origine Controllata e Garantita), are often of higher quality. Made outside the disciplines of DOC and DOCG, these wines are often made with international, rather than local, varieties or, in contravention of the rules, might be a pure varietal rather than a blend. Carpineto's range of super-Tuscans, the best sold under the Farnito label, includes a Sangiovese/Cabernet blend, a pure Cabernet Sauvignon, a Sauvignon Blanc and the Chardonnay featured here. All of these are entitled only to that most lowly appellation, vino da tavola.

Carpineto's vineyards cover about 50 acres, but the company has contracts with proprietors of a further 172 acres, and will buy grapes on the open market when needed. The Chardonnay comes from vineyards south of Florence, some 1,000 feet above sea level. The grapes are hand-picked, partly for quality reasons, and partly simple expediency. The hillside vineyards of central Tuscany are difficult terrain for unwieldy machines like grape harvesters. After crushing, a period of low-temperature skin contact is allowed to bring out more grape flavors. Fermentation is in small French oak barrels, one-fifth new each year, followed by four months' oak maturation on the lees, and a further four months in cask away from the lees. The result is a wonderfully complex Chardonnay retaining the crisp acidity that is typical in Italian wines, but with a fruity and spicy palate. A wine that can be kept for a few years yet and will develop further complexity, although it is delicious now.

CHALONE VINEYARD

Highway 146 and Stonewall Canyon Road, PO Box 518,
Soledad CA93960, USA
Tel: (1) 408 678 1717 Fax: (1) 408 678 2742
*Visitors: Monday–Friday by appointment only "unless you have
come to work"; Saturday–Sunday 11:30AM–5:00PM*

*C*halone is the oldest vineyard in Monterey still producing wine, and is unique in having its own AVA or "American Viticultural Area," the rudimentary version of the French Appellation Contrôlée. An estate of 1,000 acres, of which about a fifth is vineyard, the Chalone estate is the only vineyard within the Chalone AVA. A remote mountain retreat, as recently as 20 years ago the estate was not connected to mains power, and the only communication was via a truck radio.

Will Silvear planted the first vines on the Chalone ranch in 1922. An interesting date since the infamous 18th Amendment to the Constitution of the United States of America, or the "Volstead Act," which prohibited the "manufacture, sale, or transportation of intoxicating liquors," was enacted two years before. Somehow

FACT BOX

WINEMAKER: Michael Michaud
SIZE OF VINEYARD: 200 acres
PRODUCTION: (all types) 45,000 cases
GRAPE VARIETIES: Chardonnay, Pinot Noir, Pinot Blanc, Chenin Blanc—sold as varietals
RECOMMENDED VINTAGES: 1996, 1995, 1994

the vines survived and some of the same vines are still used for Chalone Reserve Chardonnay. They sold grapes to other winemakers, including the famous Wente family, until 1960 when the first Chalone label was used, by Philip Togni. His facilities may have been basic–the winery was a converted chicken shed, and the only cooling available was ice brought in from the town of Salinas–but the brand was born.

Perhaps the most important milestone in Chalone's history was the introduction of Dick Graff, a Harvard music graduate who became a winemaker. After studying at UC Davis and in Burgundy, he introduced correct use of malolactic fermentation to the Californians and encouraged the use of French barrels. In 1968 he saved the Chalone vineyard from bankruptcy. His two brothers, John and Peter, have both been winemakers at Chalone at various times.

Until 1994 cultivated yeast, as the "New World" wine colleges teach, was used. Then Chalone experimented with native yeasts for a proportion of their wines. Native yeasts are the natural microflora of the vineyards and winery, the result of a natural selection process over many generations and therefore unique to each winery. The experiment was successful, so, from the 1995 vintage, all Chalone wines are the result of native yeast fermentations. After fermentation, malolactic fermentation is encouraged and the wines mature on their lees–the sediment of dead yeast and grape matter that has settled in the bottom of the barrel. "Battonage"–or lees stirring–is employed to get the full effect and add weight and texture to the finished wine.

The result is a complex, full wine with plenty of fruit in youth but also with the capability to age and develop.

TASTING NOTES

1994 ESTATE BOTTLED CHARDONNAY

Deepish golden color with a ripe, full nose of butter, lemon, and melon fruit overlaid with toasty spicy oak. The fruit dominates. Dry but ripe with wonderfully balanced acids and full, concentrated flavor. Earlier vintages are marked by noticeable tannins, which are now fully under control. Great length and complexity.
Rating ★★★★

SUGGESTED FOOD PAIRING
A full-bodied, full flavored wine like this needs quite a powerful dish. Grilled chicken or trout are ideal.

CHAPEL DOWN WINES LTD

Small Hythe, Tenterden, Kent, TN30 7NG, UK
Tel: (44) 1580 763033 Fax: (44) 1580 765333
Visitors: Welcome at the Tenterden Vineyard Park

*F*ew wine drinkers, even English wine drinkers, realize that there are now over 400 vineyards operating in England and Wales. The climate is marginal, so production volumes vary dramatically from year to year, and many vineyards are very small and can supply only the cellar-gate demand. There simply is not enough volume to sell through the wine trade. Furthermore, owners of even the smallest vineyards often have a range of different grapes, further reducing the availability of each wine.

Chapel Down was established in 1993 to deal with these problems. Sourcing grapes from over 20 different estates, they are able to produce the volumes needed to supply the market, giving assurances to the merchants of consistency in a manner few English growers can. Economies of scale also mean they can afford to invest in equipment.

FACT BOX

WINEMAKER: David Cowderoy

SIZE OF VINEYARD: grapes bought in from over 20 growers

PRODUCTION: 53,000–66,250 cases

GRAPE VARIETIES: Bacchus, Müller-Thurgau, Schönburger, Seyval, Cortega, Reichensteiner

RECOMMENDED VINTAGES: 1997, 1996, 1995

LOCAL RESTAURANT: Vineyard Park has a café and restaurant

Grapes come to the winery in Kent from as far as Oxfordshire and the Isle of Wight. A key role in the whole operation is that of David Cowderoy, the winemaker at Chapel Down. He was born into English wine. His father was one of the pioneers of the modern revival. He still runs the Rock Lodge vineyard and is very active in wine industry administration and education through Plumpton College. David's first experience of viticulture, he says, was when, at the tender age of one, he helped plant a vine of his father's vineyard. Having studied soil management and plant nutrition at London University, he took himself off to Roseworthy to do a postgraduate diploma. Subsequent experience in various New World, French, and central European vineyards makes him one of the best-qualified winemakers in the UK.

TASTING NOTES

EPOCH V 1995

Pale-lemon yellow. An aromatic nose, still very youthful with spice from the partial oak maturation blending with some quite aromatic floral and soft-fruit, peaches and apricot hints. Crisp palate, very refreshing and quite light in alcohol but with a reasonable concentration of flavor and a degree of complexity from the oak. Good lengthy finish.

Rating ★★

SUGGESTED FOOD PAIRING

White meats in a creamy sauce or fine seafood.

Cowderoy's aim is to make a range of reliable, consistent styles of wine which are uniquely English. Convinced that consumers are gradually becoming tired of "the same old Chardonnays and Cabernets" he is sure he will build up a following for the crisp, elegant wines England has to offer.

Epoch V is a blend from a number of vineyards and grapes. This philosophy, which would horrify many continental European winemakers, is, of course, what the great Australian wines rely on. Blending here is to ensure quality, not reduce it. With no concerns here about the wines being typical of their origins, the aim is to take the best from each parcel of vines and use them just as a composer uses the different instruments of an orchestra, each adding its own unique character to the work.

The cellar door sales facility at Chapel Down.

CHÂTEAU CARBONNIEUX

33850 Léognan, France
Tel: (33) 5 57 96 56 20 Fax: (33) 5 57 96 59 16
*Visitors: By appointment only Monday–Friday 8:00AM–12:00
NOON and 2:00PM–5:00PM*

*B*ordeaux is one of the largest of the French Appellation Contrôlée regions, producing a full range of wines, five-sixths of them red. Few parts of Bordeaux treat their dry white wines with the reverence exhibited towards the reds or the finest sweet whites. One area is an exception, the Graves district south of the city of Bordeaux. Here the Appellation is for both red and white, and the classification of properties, which in the Médoc is for reds only, covers both types.

The best part of the Graves is the northern end, just south of the city and extending into the southern suburbs. This is the Pessac-Léognan Appellation, so called because of the two villages of those names within the district. On the top of a small hill just east of Léognan, some six miles south of Bordeaux, is Château Carbonnieux, one of

FACT BOX

WINEMAKER: Bertrand Cherel

SIZE OF VINEYARD: 210 acres, half for white wine

PRODUCTION: 20,000 cases of white, 25,000 of red

GRAPE VARIETIES: Sauvignon Blanc, Sémillon for this wine, the full range of Bordeaux black varieties for the red

RECOMMENDED VINTAGES: 1997, 1996

Château Carbonnieux in the Graves.

the finest dry-white-wine châteaux of Bordeaux. Grapes have been grown on this site for at least the last 500 years and unusually white wine has always been held in high esteem.

The very early history of the estate is still being unearthed, but it is known that Ramon Carbonnieux owned vines in Léognan and these are likely to have included part of what now constitutes the estate. The château building itself is thought to have been built in the fourteenth century, originally a fortified farm with towers at each corner. By the sixteenth century the estate was in the hands of a prominent bourgeoisie family, the Ferrons. After a little over 200 years, finding themselves in desperate financial straits, the family sold the château to the Bénédictine monks who, in their brief tenure, replanted the vineyards and re-established the reputation of the wines which by now had found favor with Thomas Jefferson. This reputation continued after the Revolution in 1789 when the château was confiscated by the revolutionary government and sold to the Bouchereau family.

After owning Château Carbonnieux for 80 years the family sold the property on and it went through a number of changes of ownership, with the inevitable loss of continuity, until the Perrin family took over in the 1960s. Since then considerable effort and money have been expended in returning the estate and its wines to their rightful place.

Château Carbonnieux has very heterogeneous soils. Also, numerous microclimates exist in the vineyards and great care is taken to match microclimate and soil to achieve the greatest ripeness and balance in the wines. The net result is one of the earliest harvests in the region, but also extra work, because, to get the best from the vines, each plot has to be treated separately.

Harvesting here is very selective. Up to five different tries are made through the vineyard to select only the best grapes. All rotten grapes are discarded, and unripe bunches left on the vine. Winemaking here has often been held up as an example for others to follow. Grapes are crushed, and a period of cold skin contact is allowed. After pressing the must is clarified by further cold settling. Fermentation is in new, one-, and two-year-old barrels–one-third of each, to give just the right balance of oak flavors. Long lees maturation follows, with frequent battonage (lees stirring) at first, gradually becoming less frequent as time goes on. This increases the complexity of the wine, adds body and weight to it, and increases its aging potential.

TASTING NOTES

1995 CHÂTEAU CARBONNIEUX

Pale golden yellow color. Fine nose showing some vanilla and spice from the oak with delicate flavors of citrus stone fruit, peaches in particular. A little tropical fruit, probably a function of the warm vintage. Dry with a crisp skeleton of acidity holding the fullish flavor and moderate alcohol together. Great long and elegant finish, but still very youthful overall, needing a few years to marry and develop finer characters of bottle age.

Rating ★★★★★

SUGGESTED FOOD PAIRING

Very fresh white fish, simply and briefly cooked to preserve the natural flavors would be the best choice.

The Chais, or cellar.

CHÂTEAU D'YQUEM

Sauternes, Bordeaux, France
Tel: (33) 557 9807 07 Fax: (33) 557 9807 08
Visitors: Vineyard is not open to the public

*A*sk two film critics to list their all-time top-10 films, and you will have a list of 20 movies. Ask a group of musicians for their top tunes, and each will have a different set. Similarly with wine: no two wine merchants or any pair of wine writers will give you the same "top 10." Yet in everyone's list of the best white wines in the world you will find Château d'Yquem. This historic estate in the small commune of Sauternes is the source of what is without doubt the finest sweet wine in the world.

The Sauternes Appellation, which applies to the communes of Sauternes itself, Barsac (which also has the alternative of using its own name), Fargues, Preignac, and Bommes, is a small enclave, entirely surrounded by the Graves region, about 30

FACT BOX

OWNER: Comte A. de Lur Saluces
SIZE OF VINEYARD: 250 acres
PRODUCTION: varies considerably from about 6,000 cases to nothing depending on the vintage. Typically only a small part of the production will be sold as d'Yquem, and any wine not reaching the mark will be sold through the brokers as basic Sauternes
GRAPE VARIETIES: Sémillon, Sauvignon
RECOMMENDED VINTAGES: all vintages are exquisite

miles southeast of the city of Bordeaux. Here a remarkable, if unreliable, climatic feature makes the production of top-quality sweet wine possible, and makes the wines unlike almost all other Bordeaux. The area is one of gentle hills and sweeping, shallow valleys. Flowing through one, bisecting the region before it enters the Garonne just south of Barsac, is the River Ciron. In the fall, if the weather has stayed fine enough, early-morning mists rise from the Garonne, travel up the Ciron, and blanket the vines in fog. By late morning the mist has lifted and the vineyards are bathed in warm fall sunshine. This is ideal for the development of noble rot. The whole appellation is for sweet wines only, and any other wines made here can be sold only as simple AC Bordeaux.

Château d'Yquem.

Like the Médoc, the best estates were classified in April 1855, listing Premiers Crus and Deuxièmes Crus, but above these, alone at the top of the list was one Premier Cru Supérieur, Château d'Yquem.

The origins of the name are lost in the mists of time, but the history of the property is well documented. During the time that Bordeaux was under the English dominion, from when Henry Plantagenet married Eleanor of Aquitaine in 1152, Yquem was owned by the Kings of England, who were also the Dukes of Aquitaine. It passed to the French crown in 1453 during the reign of Charles VII. Eventually it was passed on to the Sauvage family and in 1785 through the marriage of Françoise-Joséphine de Sauvage to Louis-Amédée de Lur Saluces, to the Lur Saluces. Until 1996 it remained in their hands but then a majority interest in the estate was sold to LVMH, the champagne-to-cognac-to-luggage group. Comte Alexandre de Lur Saluces, who took over the estate in 1968, remains in charge of the day-to-day running of the château, however.

In contrast to most of Bordeaux, the grapes here are, of course, predominantly white. Sémillon and Sauvignon Blanc are grown, the former for its affinity to noble rot, the latter for acidity. Much of the work is still done in old-fashioned, slow ways, but this means greater attention is spent on detail. Plowing is still done by using a horse-drawn plow, pruning and training have to be done by hand. Harvesting is very selective. Numerous pickings are done, each taking only the most rotten berries, leaving others in the hope that they too might become infected before the next picking. The total yield can be as low as around 85 gallons per acre, and in some vintages, on average about once a decade, none of this is considered good enough to sell under the château label.

Pressing still uses the small, old basket presses that have been used for decades–they are still the best because not all the grapes are ready at once. Fermentation is in new oak barrique but, as with all top Sauternes, the concentration of flavor that results from botrytis covers up the vanilla of the oak. The barrels add complexity rather than being the flavor of the wine. Oak maturation follows, the period in barrel depending on the quality of the vintage.

Not all the wine is released at the same time. Château d'Yquem sells through a couple of Bordeaux brokers and makes an offer of a limited number of bottles three or four times per year. These are not all from the latest vintage to be released. A reserve of about eight vintages is used in order to maintain the prestige of the wine, and to ensure supplies of a few moderately mature wines.

TASTING NOTES

CHÂTEAU D'YQUEM 1989

Deep golden amber color with thick legs forming on the sides of the glass, a sign of the concentration to come. Pungent but very youthful nose, even now nearly a decade after the harvest. Strong botrytis hints, honey, and tropical fruit, and even a hint of coconut. Very complex but not yet knitted together properly. Sweet, of course, but along with the huge intensity of a very fine vintage, an elegance that is impossible to convey using the standard vocabulary of a wine taster. Magnificent.

Rating ★★★★★

SUGGESTED FOOD PAIRING
Traditional pairings include foie gras and desserts, but top Sauternes is remarkably versatile. Chefs throughout the world have created all manner of dishes to accompany this wine, from herbed liver terrines and simple bread and butter pudding, to, of all things, chicken and pineapple cooked in and served with Yquem.

CHÂTEAU LAVILLE HAUT-BRION

Domaine Clarence Dillon S.A., B.P. 33602, Pessac, France
Tel: (33) 5 56 00 29 30 Fax: (33) 5 56 98 75 14
Visitors: By appointment only

*F*or well over one hundred and fifty years Château Haut-Brion has been recognized as the finest red wine château of Graves. So high was its reputation in 1855 that it was the only estate in the district to be included in the classification of the wines of the Médoc–not just included, but listed among the top four granted Premier Cru Classé status.

Although Château Haut-Brion produces a small amount of white wine, it is the neighboring Château Laville Haut-Brion which is best known for its whites. Some commentators have described the Château as the "white Haut-Brion." It is fitting, therefore, that in 1983 the estate became part of the Domaine Clarence Dillon S.A., also owners of Châteaux Haut-Brion, La Tour Haut-Brion, and La Mission Haut-Brion.

Vines have been cultivated on the site for centuries, but in the Middle Ages Laville

FACT BOX

WINEMAKERS: Jean-Bernard Delmas and Jean-Philippe Masclef

SIZE OF VINEYARD: 18 acres

PRODUCTION: 1,000 cases

GRAPE VARIETIES: Sémillon, Sauvignon Blanc

RECOMMENDED VINTAGES: 1996, 1995, 1990, 1989

Haut-Brion was often blended with La Tour d'Esquivens. This was then a more important estate in the area, and what is now Laville Haut-Brion was a holding of theirs. After the French revolution in 1789 the feudal system came to an end and the estate took the name of its manager, Monsieur Arnaud de la Ville.

Fifty years later it passed to Pierre David Bouscasses and in 1912 it was taken over by a Bordeaux dealer, Léopald Bibonne who sold the estate in 1931 to Frédéric Woltner who already owned La Mission Haut-Brion, the Grand Cru property on the other side of the railroad track. When the Dillons, owners of Haut-Brion, bought La Mission in 1983, they also took over Laville, forming the Domaine Clarence Dillon company.

The whole domaine is remarkable in that it is very much an urban vineyard. As the southern suburbs of Bordeaux have expanded, they have swallowed up whole tracts of other vines, but the Haut-Brion properties have been saved, the quality of the wine protecting the vines from the developers. Even a wine like Haut-Brion however, is not safe from the national railroad company, S.N.C.F. Both Haut-Brion and La Mission lost vines when railroads were laid through the estates.

> ## TASTING NOTES
>
> ### CHÂTEAU LAVILLE HAUT-BRION 1994
>
> Soft, persisting oak nose and taste, finishes with honeyed coconut. Round with clean, currant fruit acidity, that lasts into the very long, complex seductive aftertaste.
> Rating ★★★★★
>
> SUGGESTED FOOD PAIRING
> Simple, not too spicy food. Full flavored fish like turbot or trout, or roasted or broiled white meats.

The Laville vineyards are interspersed with those of La Tour Haut-Brion in the south east of the domaine. Given over to Sémillon and Sauvignon Blanc, the entire 18 acres are for white wine. Viticulture is textbook Bordeaux, low training makes vineyard work backbreaking, while the 10,000 vines per 2.5 acres (approximately 3 feet between vines in each direction) ensure low yields per vine.

Winemaking too, is traditional, but here modern fashion has caught up with tradition. Barrel fermentation at around 68°F in new barrels is now international best practice. The wines spend 15 months in cask before bottling.

CHÂTEAU MUSAR (UK) LTD

All enquiries to: 25 High Street, Hampton, Middlesex, UK
Tel: (44) 181 941 8311 Fax: (44) 181 941 7843
Visitors: By appointment only

*T*he Australian winemakers have a word all of their own, "mog," an acronym for "matter other than grapes." This usually means bits of the vine that have fallen into the harvester, or insect pests caught up with the grapes. It can even include general vineyard litter, and the odd wire staple from a trellis post. At Château Musar "mog" can be far less prosaic. Making wine in a war zone, as Serge Hochar does, gets you fame, but it can also result in your having to extract shrapnel from your grapes before you press them.

The Bekaa valley sits between Mount Lebanon and the Anti Lebanon, east of Beirut. Here, in a war-torn area, Serge Hochar and his team produce a range of remarkable wines. The red is the best known–Cabernet Sauvignon-based, but with about 20 percent Cinsault blended in. Earlier vintages also have a percentage of Syrah. This has long been one of the more affordable classics, a wine whose quality far exceeded its price.

FACT BOX

WINEMAKER: Charbal Abighanem
SIZE OF VINEYARD: 335 acres
PRODUCTION: information not available
GRAPE VARIETIES: Obaideh, Merwah
RECOMMENDED VINTAGES: 1995, 1993, 1990

White Château Musar is less well known. The grapes used are the Obaideh and Merwah, hardly internationally famous varieties. Musar has in the past claimed that these are in fact the Chardonnay and the Sémillon respectively. It has even been claimed that these are the originals and the French varieties were taken there from Palestine by the Crusaders. These are certainly native grapes, and there is a certain resemblance to the French varieties. The vines are grown at an altitude of 500–1,000 feet above sea level, which reduces the temperatures to an average of about 77°F. The region enjoys some 300 days of perfect sunshine per year, the perfect climate to ripen grapes. The soils are gravel over limestone, irrigated by water from the snow-capped mountains.

Harvesting is by hand, and is early, as might be expected this far south. Typically the vintage starts in August here, the political climate permitting. There have been years when the war has interrupted production, but normally the wine is made in spite of the conflict. Fermentation is in temperature-controlled tanks. These were installed some years ago but between 1987 and 1992 they were not used because Serge Hochar wanted to make a fuller wine for long aging rather than concentrating on primary fruit. Oak maturation follows. Like all good wineries this is not done according to a recipe–the length of time will vary from vintage to vintage.

The cellars of Château Musar.

Château Pape Clément

33600, Pessac, Bordeaux, France
Tel: (33) 5 56 07 04 11 Fax: (33) 5 56 07 36 70
*Visitors: By appointment only–Monday–Friday 9:00AM–12:00
NOON and 2:00PM–5:00PM; sales are only through Bordeaux
merchants and brokers, no cellar-door sales*

*C*hâteau Pape Clément, Grand Cru Classé of the Graves, is perhaps best known for its clarets, but white wine is also produced on the estate, a white wine of unusual quality. Unlike the Médoc, north and west of the city of Bordeaux, here the Appellation permits the cultivation of both black and white grapes, even for the district and commune appellations. (In the Médoc any white wines produced can be sold only under that most humble of appellations, Bordeaux Blanc.) Being in the northern part of the Graves, just south of the city of Bordeaux, Pape Clément comes into the Pessac-Léognan Appellation. This AC was created in 1987 to differentiate this better area from the general, and large, Graves Appellation further south. As of right, however, the château retains its classification as a Graves estate.

FACT BOX

WINEMAKER: Giles Paquereau, with consultant Ribéreau-Gayon

SIZE OF VINEYARD: 84 acres total, 6 acres for white grapes

PRODUCTION: 500 cases of white

GRAPE VARIETIES: Sauvignon Blanc, Sémillon, Muscadelle

RECOMMENDED VINTAGES: 1996, 1995, 1994

TASTING NOTES

CHÂTEAU PAPE CLÉMENT BLANC 1995

Very pale-lemon yellow, youthful and cool-climate appearance. Light, fresh, and youthful nose of honeydew melon, limes, and lemon blossom overlaid with a smoky character. Dry with very crisp acidity, very clean fresh taste, again melons and smoky oak. Good long finish. Not much hint here of the Sauvignon, except perhaps in the acidity. This wine was, when tasted, still very immature, even at three years old. Given another two or three the wine will be a more integrated whole.

Rating ★★★★

SUGGESTED FOOD PAIRING
Ideal with lobster.

Pape Clément gets its name from its most famous owner, Pope (or Pape) Clément V, born in the Gironde Département in the thirteenth century. Pape Clément was the first of the Avignon Popes, of Châteauneuf-du-Pape fame, who refused to move to the Vatican. In 1309, Clément gave his vineyard to the Archbishop of Bordeaux. It remained in the charge of the bishopric until the French Revolution in 1789. This makes it one of the oldest estates in Bordeaux. The present owners, the Montagne family, have owned the château since 1939.

The estate comprises 90 acres, of which some 84 are given over to vines. The vast majority of these are currently black varieties, the Cabernets and Merlot needed to make the Cru Classé red Bordeaux (claret) for which the area is so famous. A paltry six acres are given over to white varieties, a measure of the

The impressive exterior of Château Pape Clement.

relative importance of red and white wines in the Bordeaux marketplace today. Not that long ago white wines represented the majority in the region.

The classic three white varieties are grown, Sauvignon Blanc, Sémillon, and Muscadelle. The first two are almost equal in the vineyard, representing 90 percent of the planting between them, with Muscadelle being about 10 percent. All percentages should, however be taken with a word of warning. The proportions in the vineyard may or may not represent the proportions in the wine. Different weather conditions, different ripening, and so on will affect the wine's composition, so, for example, the 1995 vintage shows very little sign of Sauvignon influence at all.

All the grapes are picked by hand, crushed and pressed, then about 30 percent of the clarified must is fermented in new barriques, the remainder being in stainless-steel vats. Subsequent maturation is also carried out in wood, the period in oak depending on the vintage. Tasting has shown that further bottle-maturation is to be recommended.

CLOUDY BAY VINEYARDS

PO Box 376, Blenheim, New Zealand
Tel: (64) 3572 8914 Fax: (64) 3 572 8065
Visitors: Daily 10:00AM–4:30PM

*I*f there is one wine from New Zealand that has captured the hearts and minds of wine writers and drinkers throughout the world, and in doing so done more to promote New Zealand's wine in general than any other, it is Cloudy Bay Sauvignon Blanc.

Established in 1985, Cloudy Bay is a joint venture between Cape Mentelle, one of the top Western Australian producers, and the champagne house Veuve Clicquot. Sited in the Marlborough region in the north of New Zealand's South Island, Cloudy Bay's vineyards are in the valley of the Wairau river, bounded by the Cloudy Bay itself–named by the explorer, Captain Cook in 1770– by the Richmond Hills (whose peak, Mount Riley, is pictured so graphically on

FACT BOX

WINEMAKER: Kevin Judd
SIZE OF VINEYARD: 150 acres supplies 40% of needs
PRODUCTION: (all types) 75,000 cases
GRAPE VARIETIES: Sauvignon Blanc, Chardonnay, Pinot Noir, Cabernet Sauvignon, Merlot–sold as varietals
RECOMMENDED VINTAGES: Cloudy Bay Sauvignon Blanc is best drunk young but good recent vintages have been 1997, 1996, 1994, 1991
LOCAL RESTAURANT/HOTEL: Hotel d'Urville, Queen Street, Blenheim

the label), and by the hill ranges that form the Hawkesbury, Waihopai, and Bancroft valleys. Each of these has recently been recognized as an individual sub region of Marlborough.

Marlborough has the ideal climate for producing fine, elegant wines. A cool region, roughly the same average temperature as Burgundy in France, it has the greatest number of sunshine hours of any region in New Zealand. Since sunshine causes photosynthesis, this results in fully ripe grapes, but the cool climate allows for a long growing season, promoting fuller flavors. Added to this, the soils are easy to work and fertile. The terrain is relatively flat, the Wairau river valley resulting from glacial movements which have, over the millennia

Cloudy Bay's Sauvignon Blanc vineyards ...

deposited deep alluvial gravels. Snow melting in the hills provides a plentiful supply of ground water so the vines grow well.

In such conditions it is all too easy for the vines to produce lots of vegetative growth at the expense of fruit ripeness. Careful control of the vines and the crop through innovative training systems are the order of the day at Cloudy Bay. In contrast to somewhere

... and their high-tech winery.

TASTING NOTES

SAUVIGNON BLANC 1997

Very pale, almost water-white. Medium intensity, very youthful green, grassy aromas. Catty and herbaceous. This vintage has no signs of oak on the nose. Dry with very high zingy acidity; green apples. Medium weight and noticeable alcohol. Very good length. Excellent wine, benchmark Sauvignon, but needs a few months to settle down.

Rating ★★★

SUGGESTED FOOD PAIRING

Goat's cheese salad, fish, chicken, or veal.

like Bordeaux, where about 4,000 plants per acre would be grown, each small and compact, here only 750 per acre have been planted, pruned on the Scott Henry system so that each length of vine hedge has two productive branches rather than just one.

The Cloudy Bay estate provides about 40 percent of the grapes needed, the balance coming from local vineyards with which Cloudy Bay had long-term contracts. Strict quality controls are applied to the contract growers. Machine harvesting is normal on the easy terrain, followed by crushing and destemming to avoid bitter tannins from the stalks. As might be expected from a new winery with a pedigree such as this, the equipment is all state-of-the-art, with gleaming stainless steel throughout.

Most of the must is fermented in stainless steel but a small proportion is fermented in new French oak barrels to add body and an extra degree of complexity to the finished wine. It is this that sets Cloudy Bay apart from the masses of other simple, fruity Sauvignon Blancs that come out of New Zealand. Many Sauvignons show well in tastings, but are one-dimensional. The winemaker, Kevin Judd, is determined not to overdo the oak, but a little adds just the right amount of seasoning to balance the wine.

As well as Sauvignon Blanc, Cloudy Bay produces Chardonnay, Pinot Noir, and Cabernet Sauvignon. However, it is the Sauvignon for which they are justly famed.

CLOUDY BAY

SAUVIGNON BLANC 1996

COLLARDS BROTHERS LTD

303 Lincoln Road, Henderson, Auckland, New Zealand
Tel: (64) 9 838 8341 Fax: (64) 9 837 5840
*Visitors: Store open Monday–Saturday 9:00AM–5:00PM,
Sunday 11:00AM–5:00PM*

*C*ollards is a fairly small, family-owned company that specializes in premium-quality varietal wines. The emphasis here is on clear varietal definition, Sauvignon that shouts "Sauvignon," Riesling that shouts "Riesling" and so on.

The two Collard brothers who now run the company are continuing a tradition of horticulture that has been in the family for virtually all of this century. The original estate was founded by an Englishman, J.W. Collard, in 1910. He married a local girl from the Averill family who were, by 1920, grape-growers and winemakers. It was natural that Collard should start to grow grapes, which, from the first harvest until 1963, were all processed at the Averill winery. In 1963 the winery was purchased by Penfolds of Australia, at which point the decision was taken to

FACT BOX

WINEMAKER: Bruce Collard
SIZE OF VINEYARD: 25 acres at Rothesay and 5 acres at Henderson—between them supply 40% of needs
PRODUCTION: approx. 25,000 cases
GRAPE VARIETIES: Chardonnay, Sauvignon Blanc, Cabernet Sauvignon, Semillon, Cabernet Franc, Merlot, Riesling—mostly used as varietals
RECOMMENDED VINTAGE: 1994

build a Collard winery. Since that time the company has been at the forefront of innovation in New Zealand, being among the first companies to plant Riesling, make a dry Chenin Blanc and commercialize a Cabernet Sauvignon/Merlot blend.

The second Collard vineyard was established by Geoffrey and Bruce Collard in 1979. Northwest of Auckland, this plot is planted on feed-draining loam soil. The fruit from here is used for the flagship wines, the Rothesay label.

Grapes here are Chardonnay, Sauvignon Blanc, and Cabernet Sauvignon. The original Henderson vineyard is given over to Semillon, Cabernet Franc, Merlot, and Riesling. In all, the company-owned vineyards only supply about 40 percent of their requirements, the remaining 60 coming from contract growers in Waikato, Hawkes Bay, and Marlborough.

Geoffrey is the viticulturist. His driving principle is that to make good wine you need good grapes. Ensuring the health of his vineyards is more than a mere job for Geoffrey: he has turned it into an obsession. The reputation of the vines in both Collard vineyards is famed throughout the New Zealand wine industry and cuttings are much in demand for new plantings elsewhere in the country.

Winemaking is mainly in the hands of Bruce, but both brothers get involved. Geoffrey is an excellent taster and is a regular show judge as a result. As meticulous when making his own wines, Bruce prefers to use traditional winemaking techniques, always maintaining the varietal character rather than adding flavors from the techniques used. So, for the Sauvignon Blanc, the fermentation temperatures are kept cool to retain volatile flavors, but not too cold, avoiding the estery effect this can have.

TASTING NOTES

MARLBOROUGH CHARDONNAY 1995

Pale lemon-gold color with some green tinges. Quite full buttery nose with some spice and toast from the oak and rich tropical-fruit flavors of guava and pineapple. Dry with a streak of fresh acidity holding the fruit flavors together. Medium weight and quite light in alcohol for a wine of this type. Only a medium length of finish, surprisingly so after the initial attack.
Rating ★★

SUGGESTED FOOD PAIRING
Shellfish dishes with wine-based sauces, chicken in creamy sauces, but also goes very well with Mediterranean vegetarian dishes like hummus and pita bread.

COOPERS CREEK

PO Box 140 Kumeu, Auckland, New Zealand
Tel: (64) 9 412 8560 Fax: (64) 9 412 8375
Visitors: Store, sales, and picnic area with barbecue facilities
Monday–Friday 9:00AM–5:30PM, Saturday–Sunday
10:30AM–5:30PM

*C*oopers Creek winery, a relative newcomer in the youthful New Zealand wine industry, is about half a mile north of Huapai, half an hour's drive out of central Auckland along Highway 16. It was started in 1980 by Andrew and Cynthia Hendry. Their aim was to capture the best of the New Zealand wine styles, the new drier styles that were just becoming popular.

Coopers Creek has a number of vineyards. An advantage of starting relatively late is that they have learned from other people's experience regarding site selection. Thus grape varieties are planted where they are known to perform best–Cabernet and Merlot at Huapai, Chardonnay at Hawke's Bay, Sauvignon Blanc at Marlborough, and so

FACT BOX

WINEMAKER: Kim Crawford
SIZE OF VINEYARD: 35 acres–grapes also bought in from contract growers
PRODUCTION: 50–60,000 cases total, including 2,000 of Swamp Chardonnay, made in good years only
GRAPE VARIETIES: Chardonnay, Sauvignon Blanc, Riesling, Semillon, Pinot Noir, Merlot, Cabernet Sauvignon–mostly used as varietals
RECOMMENDED VINTAGES: 1996, 1994, 1992

on. This sort of knowledge needed generations to develop in Europe, but in New Zealand it took a matter of a few years.

Winemaking is under the control of Kim Crawford. He trained at Roseworthy in Australia and joined Coopers Creek in 1988. He is the only winemaker to have been awarded the accolade of Champion Winemaker in two consecutive years, 1995 and 1996, at the New Zealand Royal Easter Show. Kim is a hands-on winemaker. Not content to take control of the grapes on arrival at the winery, he is a firm believer in going out into the vineyard in the weeks before the harvest, and tasting the grapes to assess the optimum harvest date.

Swamp Reserve Chardonnay is the company's top wine. The fruit comes from Hawke's Bay, prime Chardonnay country. The soils here are mostly river silts, rich and fertile. All the fruit for the Swamp Reserve comes from company-owned vineyards, hand-picked to select only premium fruit.

Fermentation is cool and slow. The clarified must is fermented at the rate of half a degree of alcohol per day until about half the sugar is converted into alcohol. At that point two-thirds of the fermenting must is run off into casks, half new and half second-fill French oak, to complete the fermentation. The remaining third ferments to dryness in stainless steel before being matured in wood. The wine spends a total of up to one year in cask before bottling.

TASTING NOTES

HAWKE'S BAY 1995 SWAMP RESERVE CHARDONNAY

Medium depth of color, with noticeable legs on the glass. Smoky spicy nose with caramel and toffee from the oak, vanilla and stem ginger. Ripe melon fruit, cream and butter with a lime-juice hint as well. Dry with a shaft of steely acidity balancing the ripe fruit. Full palate, quite alcoholic but in balance with the fruit intensity. Long finish.

Rating ★★★

SUGGESTED FOOD PAIRING

Full-flavored salad such as chicken liver cooked in sage, served over a bed of salad leaves.

HAWKES BAY 1996

CHARDONNAY

750ML   ALC.13%VOL.
PRODUCT OF NEW ZEALAND

DE BORTOLI PTY LTD

De Bortoli Road, Bilbul, New South Wales, Australia
Tel: (61) 2 69649444 Fax: (61) 2 696498411
Visitors: Cellar-door sales Monday–Friday 9:00AM–5:30PM;
Saturday–Sunday 9:00AM–4:00PM;
public holidays 10:00AM–4:00PM

*D*e Bortoli wines have been made in Australia since 1928, four years after the founder, Vittorio De Bortoli, emigrated to Australia from northern Italy. He and his wife started making wines from their 55-acre farm near Bilbul in New South Wales.

The company is still run by a De Bortoli, now Darren, grandson of the founder. Darren, like most Australian winemakers, trained at Roseworthy, graduating in 1982. He joined the family firm and took over as chief winemaker of De Bortoli wines in the mid-1980s, and has since become the managing director. While studying winemaking at Roseworthy, Darren was introduced to the great French sweet wine, Sauternes, and by his own admission, fell in love with the style.

FACT BOX

WINEMAKER: Steve Webber
SIZE OF VINEYARD: variable depending on botrytis infection
PRODUCTION: total of 3 million cases
GRAPE VARIETY: Semillon
RECOMMENDED VINTAGES: 1994, 1987
LOCAL RESTAURANT: Bassano's

No longer restricted to 55 acres, the company buys in grapes from a large number of growers around the Riverina region, and grows grapes in the famous Yarra Valley in Victoria. As a result the company now produces some 3 million cases of wine annually, of all styles from sparkling (Emeri Champagne on the domestic market) through reds, whites, and fortified to the wine for which they are justly most famous, Noble One.

Colorful artwork used by De Bortoli.

This wine came about in the 1982 vintage. This was a large harvest, with some grapes remaining on the vines unpicked. Inevitably, these became rotten with, the growers assumed, brown rot. Darren De Bortoli recognized it as the beneficial form of *Botrytis cinerea*, noble rot, and, much to the relief, and no doubt amazement, of the growers, bought the entire crop. Released to great acclaim, the wine was originally sold as De Bortoli Sauternes but quite rightly the company chose to drop this name in advance of a bilateral trade agreement with the European Community which sought to protect the Appellation Contrôlée name. The wine has been made in every vintage from 1982 except 1989, when rain ruined the crop.

Grapes are grown both on the De Bortoli estate and by contract growers. Because botrytis is unreliable, the area of vineyard used for this wine will vary from vintage to vintage. Hand-

Giuseppina De Bortoli (left) and friends sample
ripening grapes prior to the harvest.

harvesting has been the norm until recently, although experiments
with machine-picking are looking promising. Pressing is a long,
slow business with high must weights like these. Fermentation, too,
is long, taking about three weeks to complete because of the high
sugar levels. After fermentation, which is in tank, the wine is
transferred to French oak barrels from the Seguin Moreau
cooperage for a year of maturation, giving the wine more of a
French feel than many New World sweet wines.

Over the years Noble One has picked up a whole wallful of
diplomas, cups, and trophies, to the extent that the company
publishes a leaflet simply listing the awards, eight columns of
minute print for a mere 12 vintages.

DIRLER

13 Rue d'Issenheim, 68500 Bérgoltz, Alsace, France
Tel: (33) 3 89 76 91 00 Fax: (33) 3 89 76 85 97
Visitors: Monday–Friday 8:00AM–12:00 NOON;
Saturday 2:00PM–5:00PM

*D*irler is a very small Alsace producer, specializing in the wines from the village of Bérgoltz, at the southern end of the finest part of the Alsace vignoble. The firm was established in 1871 and has been passed from father to son ever since. Throughout that time the emphasis has been on maintaining the image and reputation of the wines from their own village. Thus Dirler wines are as much from the village of Bérgoltz as they are from Alsace in general.

Bérgoltz is on the flat between the Vosges and the Rhine, the border with Germany. Behind the village are the Vosges mountains and specifically the Grand Cru Alsace vineyards of Saering, Spiegel, and Kessler, perhaps three of the most famous of all Grands Crus in Alsace. These steep hillside vineyards are home to Riesling, Gewürztraminer, and Muscat. Maison Dirler, despite their diminutive size overall, owns a very

FACT BOX

WINEMAKERS: Jean and Jean Pierre Dirler
SIZE OF VINEYARD: 19 acres
PRODUCTION: 5,000 cases
GRAPE VARIETIES: All the Alsace varieties, Gewürztraminer, Pinot Blanc, Riesling, Pinot Noir, Pinot Gris, Muscat, Chasselas, Sylvaner. Generally sold as varietal wines, although a little of the blended Edelzwicker is made
RECOMMENDED VINTAGE: 1990
LOCAL RESTAURANT: Restaurant Philippe Bohrer in Rouffach

significant area of Grand Cru, about one-third of the company's total vineyards.

The Dirler house in Bérgoltz.

Dirler use grapes only from their own vineyards, of which they have some 19 acres in production, out of a total area of 21 under vine. The remainder is too young, the vines having recently been planted. Vines are productive only after the third year. On the steep hills of the Grands Crus there is no choice but to hand-pick, for no machine has yet been designed to work on terrain like this. The grapes are pressed and fermented in either stainless steel or wood, but, as with most Alsace wood, these are large old wooden casks that have long since given up any oaky flavors. Temperature control was introduced with the stainless-steel vats in 1984.

No Dirler wines are sold until at least a year after the vintage–sometimes they are not released for 18 months. This is an attempt on the part of the company to encourage consumers to drink their wines with a little bit of bottle age. As well as the Grand Cru a full range of Alsace wines is made, from the basic blended Edelzwicker to Grands Crus Sélection de Grains Nobles. Edelzwickers are usually a blend of the least interesting grapes of the region, but Dirler makes an interesting exception to the rule in the Edelzwicker Reserve, a blend of Pinot Blanc and Muscat which is well worth seeking out for interest's sake.

TASTING NOTES

GRAND CRU SPIEGEL RIESLING 1995

Pale lemon-yellow straw color with an aromatic, floral nose of spring blossom and crisp fruit. A touch of apple and some citrus hints. Full ripe and rich palate, with the piercing acidity that Riesling is famous for being balanced by concentrated flavors. Medium weight and good lengthy finish. A wine to keep for a few years before it can be called really ready.

Rating ★★★★

SUGGESTED FOOD PAIRING
White fish and pork work very well with the Riesling, the acidity cutting through any creaminess in the fish sauce. Also good with choucroute.

DOMAINE BONNEAU DU MARTRAY

21420 Pernard-Vergelesseses, Bourgogne, France
Tel: (33) 3 80 21 50 64 Fax: (33) 3 80 21 57 19
No visitors

*T*he hill at Corton is one of the most recognizable parts of the landscape in Burgundy. To students of wine throughout the world the Corton hill is the epitome of the complex and little-understood concept of "terroir." This tree-topped hill is home to some of the most sought-after Grand Cru red and white wines in the world, yet a few yards downhill from the Corton and Corton-Charlemagne vineyards the vines yield basic generic Bourgogne blanc and Bourgogne rouge.

Among the most prestigious of the growers on the best sites is Domaine Bonneau du Martray. Legend has it that the present Domaine Bonneau du Martray Corton estates are on the same site as the Clos Charlemagne, the vineyard owned by Emperor Charlemagne himself before 775 AD when he gave it to the collegiate church.

FACT BOX

WINEMAKER: M. le Bault de la Morinière
SIZE OF VINEYARD: 23½ acres
PRODUCTION: maximum of 3,500 cases of this wine
GRAPE VARIETY: Chardonnay
RECOMMENDED VINTAGES: 1996, 1995, 1992

It remained with the church until the French Revolution when, like all church lands, it was handed over to local families. The Bonneau du Martray family, descendants of Nicolas Rolin (1376–1462), founder of the Hospice de Beaune, took it over and ran the vineyards until 1969 when René Bonneau du Martray died leaving no children. He left the vineyard to his niece, Countess Jean le Bault de la Morinière.

Such is the estate's reputation that Domaine Bonneau du Martray Corton Charlemagne regularly fetches the highest prices in the annual Hospice de Beaune auction. This sale, which is held in aid of the hospice each November, sets the general prices for Burgundies for the year ahead.

Burgundy's vineyards are very fragmented, so that most wine exported comes from the négociant houses, who buy wines or grapes from a number of growers. The wines from the Domaine

M. le Bault de la Morinière at the entrance
to the site.

TASTING NOTES

CORTON-CHARLEMAGNE GRAND CRU 1994

Pale golden color with a still youthful nose of butter and honey, with cinnamon spice and vanilla coming through from the oak. The nose has an elegance that is difficult to describe, but unmistakable— a combination of intensity and subtlety at the same time. Dry, with typical Burgundian fresh acid backbone. Powerful flavors on the palate, backed up with quite high alcohol, which is in perfect balance. The flavor lingers for ages. A very youthful wine, still too young, needing another two to three years before it starts to show its true worth.

Rating ★★★★★

SUGGESTED FOOD PAIRING

Lobster or crayfish, or poached white fish. Avoid smoked fish where the flavor would overpower the subtleties of the wine.

Bonneau du Martray vines were sold this way until 1972, when the decision was made to sell directly, under the Domaine label rather than anonymously under the négociant's brand.

Domaine Bonneau du Martray produces wine only from its own vineyards. All of the Bonneau du Martray vineyards are Grand Cru, classified as such by the Appellation rules. The 40-year-old vines grow in vineyards facing south and southwest, giving exposure to the afternoon sun. Vines are planted close together, and trained low to maintain quality, albeit at the expense of backbreaking picking. Fermentation begins in temperature-controlled stainless-steel vats but is completed in new oak barrels. Malolactic fermentation and maturation occur in the casks, the wine staying there for two winters before blending and bottling.

DOMAINE COURBIS

Les Ravieres, 07130 Châteaubourg, France
Tel: (33) 4 75 40 32 12 Fax: (33) 4 75 40 25 39
*Visitors: Monday–Friday 8:00AM–12:00 NOON
and 2:00AM–6:00PM*

*T*he Rhône Valley is most famous for its red wines. Typically full-flavored and full-bodied, they are among the biggest of the world's fine red wines. A little white and some rosé wine is also made but it is not nearly so well known.

The valley divides neatly into two, each part very distinctive and very different from the other. The south is relatively flat with a Mediterranean climate. Here a vast range of wines is made from a large number of permitted grapes, on many different soils. Oranges and olives thrive here. Most of the wine from the south is generic Côtes du Rhône, while only a small percentage is sold under a Cru label like Châteauneuf-du-Pape or Gigondas.

The north is one narrow hillside, so steep that the vineyards are mostly terraced. The climate is cooler, particularly

FACT BOX

WINEMAKERS: Laurent and Dominique Courbis

SIZE OF VINEYARD: 10 acres of white grapes–total estate 50 acres

PRODUCTION: 6,500 cases

GRAPE VARIETIES: Marsanne, Rousanne

RECOMMENDED VINTAGES: 1995 (particularly recommended), 1994, 1990

LOCAL RESTAURANT: Pic, in Valence

when the mistral, a cold wind from the Alps, blows. The soil is more homogeneous, schistose slate being universal. Grape varieties, too, are more restricted: all the red wines are made from Syrah, the white from Marsanne and Rousanne, or Viognier. Here the Crus dominate: very little northern Rhône wine ends up in an anonymous blend. Between the northern and southern parts lies the town of Montélimar, known for its nougat, not its wines.

Among the most dynamic growers in the area are the Courbis brothers, Laurent and Dominique. Based at Châteaubourg, they own vineyards in Saint-Joseph and Cornas, two of the top Crus of the Northern Rhône. The Courbis family have been working the steep hillsides of the region for generations, and have recently expanded 'into other regions, establishing vineyards in the Ardèche, an up-and-coming locality to the east of

The dramatic terraced vineyards of St Joseph.

the Rhône in an area better known for its simple vins de pays, but where good, unexploited sites exist. They are also founder members of the Rhône Vignobles, an association of premium estates dedicated to the concept of terroir–emphasizing the vineyard as well as the Appellation wherever appropriate.

White-wine production here needs great care. Grapes have to be picked by hand because of the terrain, and have to be treated with great care because, in this heat, oxidation can occur all too soon. They are pressed as soon as possible and fermented in cooled tanks, kept below 62°F to preserve the fruit. Part of the fermentation is in wood, followed by a long period in cask before bottling. Depending on the vintage this can be from 12 to 24 months. About one-fifth sees new wood, one-fifth one-year-old wood, and the rest stay in tank.

DOMAINE DE CHEVALIER

33850 Léognan, France
Tel: (33) 5 56 64 16 16 Fax: (33) 5 56 64 18 18
Visitors: Weekdays, by appointment only

*D*omaine de Chevalier lies in the western extreme of the Pessac-Léognan appellation, southwest of Léognan itself. This area was once part of the Graves appellation, the foundation of Bordeaux wines. Grapes were grown here before the Médoc was planted. The name Graves comes from the free-draining gravel soil of the region.

Originally laid planted in about 1770, the vineyard has always been surrounded by pine forests, giving it a remote atmosphere, somehow separate from its neighbors. Although the wine's reputation grew, the vineyards were dug up at the beginning of the nineteenth century and it was 60 years before they were replanted, when it was bought by Jean Ricard, whose father owned Château Haut Bailly. The family ran the property until 1983 when Claude Ricard, who took over in 1948, was forced by family pressures to sell to the present owner, Olivier Bernard.

FACT BOX

WINEMAKER: Daniel Billaud (consultant enologist Pascal Ribereau-Gayon)

SIZE OF VINEYARD: 12 acres devoted to white grapes

PRODUCTION: 1,000 cases

GRAPE VARIETIES: Sauvignon 70%, Sémillon 30 %

RECOMMENDED VINTAGES: 1997, 1996, 1995

GRAND VIN DE BORDEAUX

DOMAINE DE CHEVALIER
GRAND CRU CLASSÉ DE GRAVES

1970

APPELLATION GRAVES CONTROLÉE

JEAN RICARD, PROPRIÉTAIRE A LÉOGNAN (GIRONDE)

MIS EN BOUTEILLE AU CHATEAU

In contrast to the great houses of the Médoc, the château here is a modest single-story affair, but the winery is a splendid circular building, fitted out with the latest in temperature-controlled stainless steel vats.

Domaine de Chevalier produces both red and white wine under the Pessac Léognan Appellation–sold under Graves Appellation until the late 1980s when this higher quality district within Graves was granted its own AC. This explains why the wines are still, as of right, within the Grand Cru Classé system of Graves.

The vineyard here is small, the total estate is only 86 acres, 12 of which are given over to white grapes. Picking is done by hand, not because of the terrain, which is almost flat, but for selection. Pickers traverse the rows up to five times, choosing only the ripest grapes each time, leaving others to ripen further.

Fermentation takes place in wood. One quarter new French oak is used each year, the other barriques all being less than five years old. Fairly high temperatures are permitted to give the wines body and aging potential at the expense of the green, grassy characters of cold fermented Sauvignon. Chevalier Blanc spends quite a long time in barrels, typically two winters after the harvest, being bottled in the spring of the third year. It deserves long bottle maturation too. Generally the wines show at their best between five and ten years after the vintage.

TASTING NOTES

DOMAINE DE CHEVALIER 1994

Pale lemon-yellow, vividly bright in the glass. Delicate notes of vanilla, peach, and almonds on the nose. The Sauvignon characters are very restrained here. This wine is the epitome of elegance. It demands attention to get the best out of the glass. Dry yet ripe on the palate with a firm backbone of acidity. Medium weight with a very fine, elegant finish that seems to go on for ever.

Rating ★★★★★

SUGGESTED FOOD PAIRING
A wine like this deserves the finest food. Scallops, very gently steamed, or another light seafood would be ideal.

DOMAINE DES COMTES LAFON

Clos de la Barre, 21190 Meursault, France
Tel: (33) 3 80 21 22 17 Fax: (33) 3 80 21 61 64
No visitors

*S*outh of the town of Beaune, not far from the main N74 road, lies a village that is probably the most famous of all the white-wine communes in the Côte d'Or: Meursault. The marl and limestone soils here are ideal for the Chardonnay, making some of the finest white wines in the world. More white wine is made in this commune than in any other in the Côte d'Or, and it is the whites for which they are justly famous. A little red is also made from the Pinot Noir, but this is rarely seen.

Meursault has no Grand Cru, a fact that surprises many wine connoisseurs. However, the Les Perrières vineyard has always been considered the best of the Premiers Crus, a whisker away from Grand Cru status in the hierarchy. The premier producer of Les Perrières is Domaine des Comtes Lafon.

FACT BOX

WINEMAKER: Dominque Lafon
SIZE OF VINEYARD: 33 acres
PRODUCTION: 5,300–7,300 cases
GRAPE VARIETIES: Chardonnay (Pinot Noir also grown)
RECOMMENDED VINTAGES: 1996, 1995, 1992, 1990, 1989
LOCAL RESTAURANT: Le Vieux Moulin at Bouillard

The vineyards after winter pruning.

As befits a wine of this quality, all the grapes are hand-picked, a worthwhile expense considering the price asked for the wine. The Chardonnay grapes here are among the most precious in the world, and are handled accordingly. Winemaking is the Burgundian standard, now copied by so many around the world, of barrel fermentation followed by long cask maturation with lees stirring, or battonage, as it is called. Temperature control in barrels can be difficult so the must is cooled before it is placed in them. After that, it is the cool ambient temperatures of a northern district that keeps things in check, not high technology. This far north, temperatures can be controlled by the simple expedient of opening the doors and letting the cold air in.

Domaine des Comtes Lafon will always be associated with feasts as well as the wine. An earlier Comte Lafon, Jules, is credited with reviving an old Burgundian tradition, the Paulée de Meursault. In the third week of November Burgundy holds three feasts, *les trois glorieuses*. In the Meursault Paulée, 600 local wine producers and their guests sit down to a grand banquet. The festivities start at noon and continue well into the early hours of the following morning, helped by the fact that each grower has brought along a bottle (or two) of their finest and oldest wines.

TASTING NOTES

MEURSAULT-PERRIÈRES 1994

Mid-gold hue with startling highlights. A little green showing the youth of the wine. Very dumb nose at present, fine and restrained with toasty, almondy notes from the oak, and fat, rich, buttery hints, too, but nothing overt or powerful. The palate is a different story. Dry, of course, with the fresh, crisp backbone of acidity that marks good white wines. Full, broad, and creamy palate with appley hints and a long, elegant yet rich finish.
This is a wine for long-term aging, despite not being a stunning vintage.
Rating ★★★★★

SUGGESTED FOOD PAIRING
This wine demands good food, simply cooked. Lobster or premium smoked salmon.

DOMAINE HUET

L'Echansonne-11, 13 Rue de la Croix Boisée,
37210 Vouvray, France
Tel: (33) 2 47 52 78 87 Fax: (33) 2 47 52 66 74
Visitors: Open 9:00AM–12 NOON and 2:00PM–6:00PM

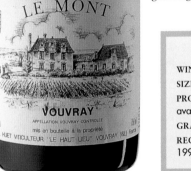

*V*ouvray, on the north side of the River Loire in northern France, can produce some of the country's greatest wines. Here the gentle south-facing slopes are planted with Chenin Blanc, a grape that can give very high natural acidity, enabling great aging in the best of vintage years.

Among the most highly reputed of the producers here is Domaine Huet. Gaston Huet, the man in charge of the operation, first made wine at Domaine du Haut-Lieu in 1929, a year after his father had bought the estate. The following year was a disaster: hail destroyed the crop. But things looked up after that and soon he had to start a négociant business to keep up with the demand for his wines. This continued until 1965 when the decision was reached that the firm should return to growing all its own grapes. Gradually

FACT BOX

WINEMAKER: Noel Pinguet
SIZE OF VINEYARD: 86 acres
PRODUCTION: information not available
GRAPE VARIETY: Chenin Blanc
RECOMMENDED VINTAGES: 1997, 1996, 1995

Huet produces sparkling wine made in the
traditional method, like champagne.

the vineyard had been expanded as neighboring plots came on the market, and in the 1950s two further vineyards were added, Le Mont and Le Clos du Bourg.

The original vineyard has quite heavy soils, with a relatively high clay content. The wines from here are soft and supple. Le Mont is on the hillside bordering the Loire itself, with clay and silica soil. Clos du Bourg is behind the church in Vouvray, enclosed by stone walls as the name implies. Three hundred years ago this vineyard was owned by the church. The soil here is shallow so the vines can get their roots down into the underlying limestone. About half of the vines are between 30 and 50 years old.

In 1987 the Huet family decided to experiment with biodynamic viticulture. So successful was the trial that

in 1992 the entire vineyard holding was turned over to this means of cultivation. Biodynamic farming not only respects nature and the soil, like organic farming, but takes into account the positions of planets and the constellations. Some chemicals are permitted–sulfur and Bordeaux mixture are used against rots–but plant-based sprays made from nettle and yarrow are preferred. No herbicides or insecticides are used here.

The Vouvray Appellation is one where a whole range of wines is made, depending on the vintage. In a poor year all the wine is made as dry or sparkling. Average vintages produce some sweeter wines with better vintages producing a higher proportion of semisweet and even very occasionally sweet wines. The ideal then is to have fully ripe grapes with some noble rot, obviously not an annual occurrence.

Huet still use wood for some of the fermentation, although they also have stainless-steel vats. Malolactic fermentation is avoided and fermentation is stopped when required by the addition of sulfur dioxide, the only cellar chemical used.

CLOS DU BOURG

VOUVRAY
APPELLATION VOUVRAY CONTROLEE
12 % Vol.   mis en bouteille à la propriété   750 ml
S.A. HUET VITICULTEUR "LE HAUT LIEU" VOUVRAY (I&L) France

DOMAINE JOSMEYER

76 Rue Clèmenceau, 68920 Wintzenheim, Alsace, France
Tel: (33) 3 89 27 91 99 Fax: (33) 3 89 27 91 90
*Visitors: Monday–Friday 8:00AM–12 NOON and 2:00PM–6:00PM;
Saturday 8:00AM–12 NOON
afternoons by prior arrangement*

*D*omaine Josmeyer is in the Haut-Rhin Département, in the picturesque village of Wintzenheim, about three miles west of Colmar. The firm is now currently run by Jean Meyer, the fifth generation of the family to be in charge since they were established in 1854.

The Domaine owns 42 acres of vineyard, supplying a little over half the total requirements. The balance is bought in from about 30 smallholders. All the grapes are bought very locally, from vineyards in Turkheim and Wintzenheim. The finished wines not only have the Alsace regional character, but a very specific "Turkheim/Wintzenheim" character, perhaps firmer and more structured than some from the Bas-Rhin further north. Many of the growers from whom Josmeyer buy, own very small plots, not financially viable on their own. These are part-time farmers, working their vines in their free time or during the weekend.

FACT BOX

WINEMAKER: Jean Meyer

SIZE OF VINEYARD: 42 acres–supplies just over half of requirements

PRODUCTION: 29,000 cases total

GRAPE VARIETIES: Gewurztraminer, Pinot Blanc, Riesling, Pinot Gris, Muscat, Chasselas, Sylvaner; used unblended

RECOMMENDED VINTAGES:
1996, 1995, 1993, 1992, 1990

The company vineyards are on four separate sites. Herrenweg is on alluvial soil, near the Fecht river between Turkheim and Wintzenheim. Warstein, southwest of Wintzenheim, has a more granitic soil. These vineyards produce good-quality wines with moderately firm structure, but the best Josmeyer vineyards are the two Grand Crus, Hengst in Wintzenheim and Brand in Turkheim. When used unblended, the last two are sold as Grand Cru wines, but the brands "les Folasries" and "les Archenets" enable Josmeyer to blend the products of a number of different vineyards.

Jean Meyer is convinced that Alsace produces, or at least is capable of producing, the finest dry white wines in the world. Working to this philosophy, the Josmeyer wines, except for Sélection des Grains Nobles, are dry–drier than many others produced in the region. Vinification is simple. The grapes are hand-harvested when fully ripe, but the emphasis is on fruit maturity rather than sugar levels. Pressing is in a modern pneumatic press and the must is settled and fermented in old oak casks. Some of these casks are a hundred years old, making them effectively inert, although very slightly porous, so there is no pick-up of oak flavors. Being relatively small, between 260 and 1,580 gallons, and in a cold climate, heat readily dissipates, so temperature control is not needed. Natural yeasts are used, Jean Meyer being convinced that part of the individuality of each wine comes from the microflora of the vineyard and winery.

TASTING NOTES

LES ARCHENETS GEWURZTRAMINER 1992

Deep golden yellow with flecks of green around the edges. Pungently aromatic nose. Tropical fruit salad with ripe, almost oily character of litchis and rose petals. Quite developed and mature now with sweet spices coming through as well. The ripeness and richness of the very intense flavors, combined with the moderate acidity and noticeably high alcohol give this wine an almost sweet character, despite its dryness. Full weight in the mouth with a long, perfumed finish.

Rating ★★★

SUGGESTED FOOD PAIRING

The spiciness and richness make this the ideal partner for mildly spiced and sweet and sour flavored Asian cuisine.

DOMAINE PHILIPPE PORTIER

Bois Gy Moreau, 18120 Brinay, France
Tel: (33) 2 48 51 09 02 Fax: (33) 2 48 51 00 96
Visitors: By appointment during office hours

The Quincy Appellation is perhaps the least well known of the Loire's Central Vineyards' wines. Smaller than, and consequently not as famous as, Sancerre and Pouilly Fumé, both Quincy and the neighboring Reuilly use the same Sauvignon Blanc grape variety, offering similar but rather more exclusive wines.

The vineyards here date back at least as far as the Middle Ages when the Bénédictine monks of Beauvoir Abbey planted vines on the left bank of the Cher river between Brouges and Vierzon. This later became the Quincy Appellation, one of the earliest ACs, being granted AC status in 1936, very soon after Appellation Contrôlée was set up. The whole Appellation is only 420 acres, so these wines will always be in short supply. The climate here is temperate with continental, cold winters and cool rather than hot summers. In marginal climates

FACT BOX

WINEMAKER: Philippe Portier
SIZE OF VINEYARD: 14 acres
PRODUCTION: 3,700 cases
GRAPE VARIETY: Sauvignon Blanc
RECOMMENDED VINTAGES:
1997, 1996
LOCAL RESTAURANT: l'Irne Alieu in Vierzon

vintages can vary considerably but the small Quincy Appellation is less prone to vintage differences than most Central Vineyard areas. This is because the east- and southeast-facing slopes are better exposed to the sun than some other parts.

Domaine Philippe Portier comprises 14 acres in the Appellation. The soil is sandy over clay subsoil and of course all the grapes grown are Sauvignon, but are carefully selected clones of the variety. The family-owned estate enjoys a southern exposure, maximizing the amount of sunshine, and thus the grape ripeness. The winery, equipped with all the latest white-wine-making equipment, is a restored historical farm, the Berry Farm.

Yields are reduced in the vineyard by thinning the crop partway through the season. This green harvest has to be timed perfectly. The aim is to concentrate the vines' energies on ripening a few bunches well. If the green harvest is too early, the vine will try to increase yield by expanding the grapes remaining. Too late and the effort will be wasted, since the vine will already have used energy on the sacrificed grapes. If the harvest is timed well, the improvement in flavor can be outstanding. This far north a late harvest, often well into October, is normal.

Vinification is in stainless steel, with a long period (about six months) of lees aging after fermentation to give extra palate structure. The wines are given a period of bottle maturation too before release so they should be in perfect condition when sold. They are ideally drunk young while still full of the vibrant youthful fruit.

TASTING NOTES

QUINCY 1996

So pale it is almost water-white, brilliantly clear and bright. Pronounced nose of youthful fruit. Tropical fruit like guava and mango mingles with citrus and blossom. Very different from the pungent green flavors of a New Zealand Sauvignon, this is more complex than most, and more gentle. Dry with marked fresh acidity but a full, broad texture in the mouth and some weight. Great length.

Rating ★★★★

SUGGESTED FOOD PAIRING

The intensity and the acidity make this the ideal partner for pork, as well as seafood and white fish, especially in a creamy sauce.

DOMAINES SCHLUMBERGER

100 Rue Théodore Deck, 68500, Guebwiller, Alsace, France
Tel: (33) 3 89 74 27 00 Fax: (33) 3 89 74 85 75
*Visitors: By appointment only—Monday–Thursday 8:00AM–12:00
NOON and 2:00PM–6:00PM; Friday 8:00AM–12 NOON and
2:00PM–5:00PM*

*G*uebwiller is probably the most industrial of the Alsace wine villages, dominated by a textile industry, whose mills are owned by the Schlumbergers, who are also the most influential vine growers in the town. As well as factories, the village boasts some of the finest vine-growing sites in Alsace, a vast hillside with vines planted on the east, southeast and southwest faces. At 350 acres, the Schlumberger holding is remarkable. One of the largest in France, let alone Alsace, it stretches over 3 miles of hillside. There are over 530 miles of vines, in neat rows on the steep hills, the southern foothills of the Vosges. About half the Schlumberger vines are in Grand Cru sites.

Viticulture was introduced to the family, a dynasty of manufacturers and traders, nearly 200 years ago, in 1810, by Nicolas Schlumberger. The present incumbents are the

FACT BOX

WINEMAKER: Jean Paul Sorg
SIZE OF VINEYARD: 350 acres–170 acres of which is Grand Cru
PRODUCTION: 84,000 cases
GRAPE VARIETIES: Gewurztraminer, but also the full range of Alsace varieties except Chasselas
RECOMMENDED VINTAGES: 1994, 1991, 1990, 1989, 1988

seventh generation of the family to run the vineyards. Initially, the vineyard holdings were small but gradually expanded, in particular after phylloxera struck, when Ernest Schlumberger took advantage of the opportunity presented to group a large number of small vineyards together as he replanted them.

The house style is typically rich and full-flavored, even in youth, a testament to the exposure of the vines and to the care taken in the vineyards.

Nicolas Schlumberger.

TASTING NOTES

CUVÉE CHRISTINE

Medium gold in color with the amazing polish that top Alsace wines seem to have, brilliantly clear. Fine, elegant nose of honey and beeswax with concentrated soft spice and tropical fruit. Distinctly botrytic. Full, ripe palate. Sweet but not fully sweet. Ripeness of flavors far more evident than the sweetness. Soft acidity that is typical of the variety, but fully balancing the flavors.

Interestingly, Cuvée Clarisse seems drier than Cuvée Christine, although analysis shows them to be the same sugar level. This demonstrates the way acidity confuses the palate.

Rating ★★★★★

SUGGESTED FOOD PAIRING

This is too dry to balance most dessert courses, but is perfect with foie gras and will even stand up to many of the local cheeses.

The hills are difficult to work, the slope in some places being as steep as one in two, and the soil is a poor sandstone. These together lead to the wine quality being outstanding and to the number of Grands Crus designated here. Schlumberger is the leading producer of Grand Cru Alsace wines.

Yields are kept low, and most of the vineyard work has to be done by hand, especially picking for the top wines where very careful selection is required. Fermentation is carried out in very large, very old wooden casks. After the wine is made, it is racked into clean casks where, unusually for Alsace, it is given a period of time to mature before bottling. The total capacity of the cellars is equivalent to over two good crops. There is no formula for deciding how long the wines stay in wood–it all depends how the particular wine is maturing.

Schlumberger produce some of the most appealing of all Alsace wines at all levels–from the "basic" range through to their top products, the Grands Crus and the outstanding Cuvées Christine and Clarisse. Cuvée Clarisse is the rarest and finest of all Alsace wines. Like vintage port and champagne,

it is made only in exceptional vintages. Unlike these two, the vintages can be a quarter of a century apart. The current vintage is the 1989, the previous one was 1964. More frequent, but still only in the best vintages, is Christine. These two are both Sélection des Grains Nobles wines–that is, they are made from grapes infected with noble rot. As in Germany, on the other side of the Rhine, this happens only in certain vintages.

Large, old oak casks are used to mature the wine.

DOMAINE VACHERON SA

Cave St Père, 1 Rue du Puits Poulton B.P. 49,
18300 Sancerre, France
Tel: (33) 248 54 09 93 Fax: (33) 248 54 01 74
Visitors: Caves open 10:00AM–12 NOON and 2:30PM–7:00PM

The family-run Domaine Vacheron comprises over a dozen individual vineyards spread over 84 acres on the hillsides of Sancerre in France's Loire Valley, two-thirds planted with Sauvignon Blanc, the only variety permitted under Appellation Contrôlée regulations for Sancerre Blanc. The remaining third is dedicated to Pinot Noir for the production of red and rosé wines. With white Sancerre the wine of choice for lunches around the globe, and the Central Vineyards of France still considered by many to produce archetypal Sauvignon Blanc, it comes as a surprise to many to learn that, before phylloxera arrived at the end of the nineteenth century, most Sancerre was red, in the style of light Burgundy wines.

FACT BOX

WINEMAKER: Jean Dominque

SIZE OF VINEYARDS: 84 acres: 27 Pinot Noir, 57 Sauvignon Blanc–used unblended, wines are varietals

PRODUCTION: 13,500 cases

GRAPE VARIETIES: Pinot Noir, Sauvignon Blanc

RECOMMENDED VINTAGES: 1997, 1996, 1995, 1990, 1989

LOCAL RESTAURANTS/HOTELS: Restaurant la Tour, Restaurant la Pomme d'Or, Hotel Panoramic

The vineyards are on two distinct types of soil. Sauvignon Blanc vines planted on the calcareous soil–pebbly chalk from the Jurassic period–tend to produce the gooseberry notes for which it has

become so famous. Those planted on the other soil, a flint-rich earth called silex, are said to produce gunflint characters in the wine and a long-lasting bouquet. Vacheron do not sell these as single-vineyard wines, preferring judiciously to blend the two styles to add complexity to the final wine.

Climate has a positive effect in the Loire. Cool growing conditions result in elegance and a rather more restrained character than might be found in warmer

The rooftops of Sancerre.

parts of the world. The negative side of this is that vintages are far more important, since in some years the grapes fail to ripen. Domaine Vacheron's vineyards are on south-facing hillsides facing into the sun, giving them the best chance even in poor years, and perfect ripeness in the best vintages.

Although not entirely organic, the Vacheron family are, like many top estates, reducing the chemical input in both the vineyard and winery. To this end only organic fertilizers are used.

All the grapes are picked by hand to ensure only healthy fruit is chosen, and pressed without skin contact to avoid excessive herbaceousness and oxidation of the must. Natural yeasts are used and the wine fermented at 64–68°F, cool but not cold fermentation.

> ## TASTING NOTES
>
> ### LES ROCHES SANCERRE BLANC 1996
>
> Pale-lemon yellow with a pungent nose, fruity and minerally. Flinty with fine grassy, asparagus and gooseberry hints. Bone-dry with the marked spine of acidity that one expects for a cool-climate Sauvignon. Intense, but elegant with a long finish.
> Rating ★★★
>
> ### SUGGESTED FOOD PAIRING
> Shellfish, especially with a rich creamy sauce, goats' cheese, or as an apéritif.

Vacheron's fifteenth-century cellar, Cave St Père, with its picturesque conical-roofed tower, is situated in the ancient narrow streets of the old part of Sancerre. Visitors are welcome here or at the nearby Le Grenier á sel, where they can taste the wines.

DOMAINE ZIND HUMBRECHT

Rte. De Colmar, 68230 Turkheim, France
Tel: (33) 3 89 2 70205 Fax: (33) 3 89 2 72258
*Visitors: By prior arrangement; sales open daily
8:00AM–12:00 noon and 2:00PM–5:00PM*

Zind Humbrecht of Wintzenheim was created in 1959 by the union of two long-established wine growing families, Zenon Humbrecht of Gueberschwihr and Emile Zind of Wintzenheim. The Humbrechts have been growing vines in Alsace since the middle of the seventeenth century when Sonntag Humbrecht founded the firm. The present head is Olivier Humbrecht, the twelfth generation of direct descendants to be in charge. Although they have been growers for centuries, it was not until 1947 that the family started making and bottling their own wine for sale, since which time only wine grown on their estates has been sold under the Domaine label.

As is common in France, the vineyard holding is not all in one place. Altogether Zind Humbrecht owns 10 separate plots of vineyards, in 10 different locations within five

FACT BOX

WINEMAKER: Olivier Humbrecht
SIZE OF VINEYARD: 98 acres
PRODUCTION: 10–15,000 cases total
GRAPE VARIETIES: Riesling, Gewurztraminer, Muscat, Pinot Noir, Pinot Gris—each used unblended as varietals
RECOMMENDED VINTAGES: 1995, 1994, 1990, 1989
LOCAL RESTAURANTS: l'Homme Sauvage and Auberge Dubrand in Turkheim

different communes. The total area of vineyard is just 98 acres. A great range of wines is produced, each single vineyard being sold as such rather than blended.

Zind Humbrecht has a powerful portfolio of single estates, and parcels of four different Grands Crus. The largest of these is Clos Saint Urbain in the Rangen Grand Cru just outside the village of Thann.

Rangen has volcanic soils and long, cool ripening seasons, ideal for Riesling. The River Thur at the base of the hill allows, in the best vintages, for the formation of noble rot so some excellent Sélection des Grains Nobles wines can be made.

Although Zind Humbrecht are on record as innovators, they were among the first, for example, to use temperature control in fermentation. Olivier Humbrecht is very modest and understates the attentiveness and

> ## TASTING NOTES
> ### 1996
> ### CLOS HÄUSERER
> ### RIESLING
> Very pale colored wine as befits a cool climate Riesling, with an aromatic, floral nose, still quite closed. Full flavored palate with the steely acidity that is the mark of a good Riesling. Enormous length. Still very young, this wine would benefit from a number of years of bottle maturation before pulling the cork.
> Rating ★★★★
>
> ### SUGGESTED FOOD PAIRING
> Fine flavored foods, in particular fine seafood such as lobster or crayfish. Also excellent with asparagus.

concern for detail that makers of fine wine must have. When asked about malolactic fermentation his simple reply was "sometimes the wine wants to do it!"

Some of the vines are over 70 years old, but the average is about 25. Harvesting is by hand and pressing is slow and gentle. Whole bunches are pressed. As in Champagne the grapes are not crushed first so only the finest juice is extracted. Barrels are used, but Alsace is not a great believer in new oak. Here the traditional barrel is a large oval one, so old that it has become encrusted with tartrates, effectively making them inert vessels. Zind Humbrecht prefer the drier styles of

Alsace wines, rather than the off-dry so popular elsewhere in the region. Their Riesling Grand Cru is typical of this.

ENATE (VIÑEDOS Y CRIANZAS DEL ALTO ARAGON, SA)

Ctra de Barbastro a Naval, Km 9,200, 22314 BAJAS,
Huesca, Spain
Tel: (34) 974 30 23 23 Fax: (34) 974 30 00 46
Visitors: Daily 8:30AM–1:00PM and 3:00PM–7:00PM

*T*he sleepy region of Somontano had hardly changed in decades, certainly not as far as wine production was concerned, until, that is, the late 1980s. The growers cultivated a handful of local grapes, none very exciting, most of which went to the local cooperative cellars to be made into drinkable, but ultimately boring wines, most of which were of strictly local appeal. Somontano has the ideal climate for fine-wine production; warm dry summers and wet winters, guaranteeing enough water reserves.

The revolution started after Spain joined the European Community (now the European Union) in 1986. Presented with the incentive of EC funding and the threat of a flood of better, cheaper wine from other European states, the local Aragon government did all they could to promote the development of higher-quality winemaking.

FACT BOX

WINEMAKER: Jesus Artajana
SIZE OF VINEYARD: 580 acres
PRODUCTION: 2 million bottles
GRAPE VARIETIES: Chardonnay for this wine, but also Cabernet Sauvignon, Tempranillo, Macabeo (Viura)
RECOMMENDED VINTAGES: 1993, 1992

Considerable investment initially went into the vineyards, with large, financially sufficient vineyards taking over from the smallholders of yore, and new varieties being introduced from France. No longer Garnacha and Morisel, but better grapes like Cabernet Sauvignon, Merlot, and even Chardonnay, Sauvignon Blanc, and the ubiquitous Tempranillo were introduced.

Most of the investment was done by three companies, one of the most impressive being Viñedos y Crianzas del Alto Aragon, SA, who, fortunately for us all, trade under the simpler brand name of Enate. The vineyards are immaculately tended, not a weed in sight, so all the available soil moisture is available for the vines. Vine training here, like in many of the "newer" areas in Spain, is along wires, a contrast to most of the country, where bush training is usual. Visitors often comment on the sprawling nature of the vines' shoots, quite unlike the regimented hedges in France or the New World. The reason is the climate: sprawling shoots means more shade. This is an area with an abundance of sunshine: ripening grapes is not a problem, but sunburn of the fruit and drying of the soil can be.

All the picking is done by hand, partly for reasons of quality–selection of only fully healthy grapes–and partly for social reasons. The terrain here is quite flat, ideal for mechanization, but manual harvesting gives paid employment to scores of workers who might otherwise be unemployed. Vinification owes more to the New World than to Spanish tradition. The grapes are pressed and the must fermented in new French oak barrels. American oak, which is cheaper, is far more normal in Spain. This oak-influenced fermentation, along with the long wood maturation, typically eight months, results in a full, toasty wine whose complexity is enhanced by the malolactic fermentation and battonage (stirring of the dead yeast lees).

> ## TASTING NOTES
> ### 1996
> ### CHARDONNAY
> Deep golden color, brilliantly clear. Rich, ripe nose initially dominated by nutty, toasty oak but fruit flavors coming through afterward. Melon and pineapple with a touch of citric character as well. Dry but so mouth-filling it seems sweeter than it really is, partly from the sweet oak flavors. Full-bodied and buttery on the palate with a broad and intense flavor.
> ### Rating ★★★
> #### SUGGESTED FOOD PAIRING
> Broiled fish or smoked salmon.

F.E. TRIMBACH

15 Route de Burgheim, 68150 Ribeauvillé, Alsace, France
Tel: (33) 3 89 73 60 30 Fax: (33) 3 89 73 89 04
Visitors: Monday–Saturday 9:00AM–6:00PM

*T*rimbach produces some of the finest of all Alsace wines, although the style, one of finesse coupled with a magnificent level of austerity, means they are not as immediately appealing as some of the richer, fuller houses. Perhaps Trimbach is a bit of an acquired taste, but it is a taste well worth the effort of acquiring; these are some of France's finest wines. Significantly, this is a view held even by their competitors in Alsace.

A full and typical range of Alsace wines is made by Trimbach. The basic wines, if they can be called that, are the straightforward varietal wines. Better grapes from better sites will be labeled "Reserve" while the "Reserve Personnelle" range is made in top vintages only, fuller and richer than the Reserve wines. Three premium cuvées top the dry-wine range, Cuvée Frédéric-Emile, Clos Sainte Hune, both Rieslings, and Seigneurs de Ribeaupierre, a Gewurztraminer. If conditions

ALSACE
APPELLATION ALSACE CONTROLÉE

Clos Ste Hune

RIESLING 1993

FACT BOX

WINEMAKERS: Bernard and Hubert Trimbach

SIZE OF VINEYARDS: 75 acres supplies 30% of needs. Clos St Hune is 3 acres

PRODUCTION: 80,000 cases total, 7,000 bottles of Clos Sainte Hune annually

GRAPE VARIETIES: Riesling for this wine, but also Pinot Blanc, Pinot Gris, Gewurztraminer, Muscat, Pinot Noir

RECOMMENDED VINTAGES: 1997, 1996, 1995, 1990

are right Vendange Tardive (late-harvest) and Sélection des Grains Nobles (noble-harvest) wines are also made.

The company can trace its roots back to 1626, the present owners being the eleventh generation to be in charge. The firm became internationally famous when in 1898 Frédéric-Emile Trimbach showed his wines at the international fair in Brussels. The wines won all the most coveted of prizes, making the name for the company. Cuvée Frédéric-Emile, a choice Riesling from old vines, harvested late to get greater alcohol and flavor testifies to the importance to Trimbach of this.

Even finer than Cuvée Frédéric-Emile, however, is Clos Sainte Hune. This vineyard near Hunawihr has been the jewel in the Trimbach crown for over 200 years. A tiny vineyard, under 3½ acres, this is technically a Grand Cru wine, but Trimbach believe the reputation of the vineyard is even greater than that of the Grand Cru Appellation, so omit the words on the label. Only about 7,000 bottles are made each vintage, never enough to meet an ever-increasing world demand since this is almost universally recognized as the finest of all Alsace, and therefore the finest of all French Rieslings.

Ribeauvillé in the heart of Alsace.

Trimbach's main aim at every stage of winemaking is the preservation of the fruit characters of the wine. Adamantly against the use of new wood, they even spurn the old oak barrels still used by many in the region, the argument being that if the wine is in any vessel that is not totally inert there may be some loss of quality. Similarly, malolactic fermentation is not allowed, since it would add unnecessary and unwanted flavors to the wine. Despite this, fermentation is at fairly high temperatures, about 68–71°C, high for an aromatic wine. The wines are bottled young and will continue to improve in the bottle. Clos Sainte Hune is said to normally need seven years after the vintage to reach its peak; for fine vintages even longer would be recommended.

TASTING NOTES

CLOS STE HUNE RIESLING 1993

Very pale-lemon yellow with a watery rim at the moment. Fragrant, floral, spring-blossom nose, still very youthful at four years old. Just an almost imperceptible hint of the steely, minerally characters that come to this wine with a little more bottle age. Dry, classic Trimbach style. Full-flavored but firm almost to the extent of being hard and austere, but experience shows that will mellow in a further three or more years. Excellent wine needing time, and this from a less than great vintage.

Rating ★★★★

SUGGESTED FOOD PAIRING

A wine of this quality needs fine but simple food. Poached trout or salmon, served simply with melted butter, and boiled potatoes is ideal, and will not swamp the flavors of the wine, which deserve to be accessible.

F.X. PICHLER

A-3601, Oberloiben 27, Austria
Tel and Fax: (43) 27 321 85315
*Visitors: Monday–Friday 7:00AM–6:00PM and Saturday
7:00AM–6:00PM*

*F*ine wine is often in short supply. The best wines, like the best of anything, are made in small quantities so that demand will always outstrip supply, at whatever price. Some producers give in to the temptation to increase prices to limit demand, often to short term advantage but long term loss. Others maintain a fair price, based on the value of the wine in the marketplace but without being greedy, and restrict availability through allocations instead. Customers are not upset, and so remain loyal.

The most strictly allocated wine in Austria is that of Weingut Franz Xavier Pichler of Loiben in Wachau. Like Weinguten Knoll and Prager, Pichler is based in the heart of the Wachau region, in the town of Oberloiben. Here the Danube takes a dramatic right-angled turn from north-south to east-west, around a steep hill. This results in a perfectly exposed hillside for grape cultivation, with sun from morning to dusk during the ripening period.

FACT BOX
WINEMAKER: Franz Xavier Pichler
SIZE OF VINEYARD: 20 acres
PRODUCTION: 5,000 cases
GRAPE VARIETIES: Grüner Veltliner, Riesling, but also small amounts of Sauvignon Blanc, Muskateller
RECOMMENDED VINTAGES: 1995, 1994, 1993, 1990

The Pichler family have been growing grapes here for five generations. Riesling and Sauvignon, even a little Muskateller are grown, but the main variety here, as in the rest of the Wachau region, is Grüner Veltliner. For half a century the Pichlers have been studying the clones of Grüner Veltliner, taking cuttings from the best plants and propagating from them. This clonal selection means that the particular clone of Grüner Veltliner grown here has much smaller berries than most, giving lower yields but with greater concentration of flavors than might be found elsewhere. This concentration is particularly noticeable on the wines from the steepest parts of the vineyard, Loibenberg and Kellerberg. Here the crystalline soils and terraced vineyards combine with the low yields to give some of the greatest dry wines Austria produces.

Like Knoll and Prager, Pichler is a member of the Vinea Wachau Nobilis Districtus. This group, founded in 1983, consists of winemakers who have created one of the strictest quality classifications in Europe, over and above that set by Austrian national wine law. The top category, Smaragd, denotes wines only from the best vintages from perfectly ripe grapes. The name comes from the emerald-colored lizards that bask in the sunshine amongst the vines on the terraces, choosing only the warmest sites.

TASTING NOTES

LOIBNER LOIBENBERG GRÜNER VELTLINER 1992 (SMARAGD)

Very pale straw yellow, with large tartrate deposits noticeable in the bottle—a sign of natural winemaking. Vibrantly clean nose. Steely and fresh, just beginning to show some of the development that maturity brings. Spice and stone fruit nose, peaches and apricots with the faintest hint of sweet spice and a little of the floral character of a young Riesling. Fine elegant palate that shows the same firm structure of the nose; clean, dry with crisp acids and fine flavors. An unusual, and valuable combination of concentration with restraint. Great length.
Rating ★★★★

SUGGESTED FOOD PAIRING
Fine flavored, simply cooked fish dishes. The wine is undoubtedly fine and should be allowed to express itself, so full flavored foods should be avoided.

GEORGES VERNAY

69420, Condrieu, France
Tel: 474 59 52 22 Fax: 474 56 60 98
Visitors: Château has a tasting room and a store

*I*f reputations are anything to go by, the Northern Rhône produces most of the region's finest wines, despite being fairly small in terms of production volume. Very little basic Côtes du Rhône comes from here, almost all the wines being sold are under one of the superior Cru appellations. There are eight crus. The red wine areas have really captured the world's attention in recent years, with appellations like Hermitage and Côte Rotie, but the region also has three crus devoted to white wine production, St. Peray, Condrieu, and Château Grillet.

Of these, Condrieu is perhaps the best known, although it is one of the rarest of all French white wines. The small town of Condrieu, with its impossibly narrow streets, sits in a bend of the river, on a small piece of flat land hemmed in by the Rhône and the steep hillsides that are

FACT BOX

WINEMAKER: Luc Vernay
SIZE OF VINEYARD: 17 acres of Condrieu (also own land in other areas)
PRODUCTION: 2,500 cases
GRAPE VARIETY: Viognier
RECOMMENDED VINTAGE: 1996
LOCAL RESTAURANT: Beau Rivage

Georges Vernay.

home to the terraced vineyards that are the Appellation. Only one grape is grown here, the Viognier, a shy bearer. Low yields are a fact of life for growers here. Not much more than a decade ago it was calculated that, because of the low yields, there were only about 89 acres of this vine throughout the world, a figure that has changed dramatically as growers on all continents discover its unique qualities.

Among the finest wines from this tiny area are those of Georges Vernay. Georges Vernay has, through years of practical experience, become the undisputed master of Viognier, and of Condrieu. Growers of this pernickety grape come from all over the world for his advice. He started with just 2.5 acres of vines in 1952, now increased to 17 acres, the best being a plot called Coteau de Vernon.

The vines here are planted on terraces hugging the hillside. Each vine is trained separately in a strange wigwam shape to protect it from the cold mistral blowing off the Alps. Hand viticulture is the only option. After pressing, the must is cooled and allowed to settle for 12 hours or so before being put into barrels. Both large and small are used, the best grapes getting the benefit of the smaller wood. New oak is only used for replacement of worn-out casks, don't look for new oak vanilla notes here, barrels are here for complexity, not flavoring.

The time in wood varies from vintage to vintage—but one year is normal, followed by further aging in stainless steel. Bottling is delayed until the wine is deemed ready, often after an extended period maturing. Further bottle maturation is often valuable too.

GOLAN HEIGHTS WINERY

PO Box 183, Katzrin, Israel 12900
Tel: (972) 669 62001 Fax: (972) 669 62220
Visitors: Daily 9:00AM–4:00PM; tours of winery store and
museum (welcomes approximately 70,000 visitors per year)

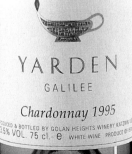

YARDEN

GALILEE

Chardonnay 1995

PRODUCED & BOTTLED BY GOLAN HEIGHTS WINERY KATZRIN ISR
13.5% VOL. 75 cl.- e   WHITE WINE   PRODUCE OF ISRE

*A*lthough we tend to think of wine as a European drink, it should not be forgotten that the vine came to Europe via the Middle East, and Israel has had a tradition of winemaking and drinking since Old Testament times.

The volcanic soils and high altitude of the Golan Heights were first identified as being suitable for premium viticulture as recently as 1976. The soil provides good drainage while the altitude keeps the temperatures down, giving the long and relatively cool growing season so often associated with fine wine production. As important in this generally dry part of the world, water from the mountains can be used to irrigate the vineyards, reducing the stress of the vine.

The first vineyards were planted by moshavs (cooperative farms) and kibbutzes

FACT BOX

WINEMAKER: Victor Schoenfeld
SIZE OF VINEYARD: Almost 1,000 acres
PRODUCTION: 270,000 cases
GRAPE VARIETIES: mainly Cabernet Sauvignon, Merlot, Chardonnay, Sauvignon Blanc, but also Pinot Noir, Cabernet Franc, Riesling, Muscat, Gewürztraminer
RECOMMENDED VINTAGES: 1993, 1990, 1985

(collective farms) in 1976. Initially the grapes were sold to existing cooperative wineries on the coast, which meant a loss of control and individuality. In 1982 some experimental vinifications were carried out using the estate fruit, the results of which showed that there was a clear need to harness the potential quality of the grapes. The following year a new state-of-the-art winery was built to handle the winemaking.

High-tech winemaking equipment is essential in a hot climate.

Grapes come from the four kibbutzes and four moshavs that own the company. They manage the vineyards, which are spread from the edge of the Sea of Galilee to the foot of the snow-capped

TASTING NOTES

YARDEN CHARDONNAY 1995

Remarkably pale color for a wine from such a southerly latitude. Moderately intense nose of butter and lemon with some youthful grassiness as well. Oak very well integrated and not in the least bit overpowering. Dry with soft acidity and medium weight. Fine, clean palate, with a good finish.
Rating ★★

SUGGESTED FOOD PAIRING
This is a fairly light flavored wine which makes it very versatile. Try it with salads, chicken, or fish dishes. It is particularly good with Mediterranean appetizers

Mount Hermon. Altitudes vary from 1,300 to 4,000 feet. The vineyard managers get very detailed instructions from the winemakers about the day-to-day running of the vineyards to ensure the winery gets the grapes it needs come harvest time.

The winery has continued to invest in the latest equipment, so the latest in pneumatic presses and the gentlest of pumps are there as, of course, are stainless-steel vats with temperature control, most important in this climate. Winemaking here is supervised by Victor Schoenfeld, a graduate of the University of California, Davis, as are his two assistant winemakers.

The company's top range of wine, Yarden, was first launched in 1984, since when it has picked up a large collection of international awards.

GRANJA FILLABOA SA

Plaza de Compostela, 6 ent., 36201 Vigo, Spain
Tel: (34) 437000 Fax: (34) 432464
Visitors: Daily 9:00AM–1:00PM and 4:00PM–7:00PM

*L*a Fillaboa is an estate in the relatively newly demarcated Rias Baixas region in the northwest of Spain, north of Portugal. A Roman bridge at the entrance to the estate bears witness to the antiquity of the manor here, and the wines were held in high esteem at the turn of the last century. As we approach another century's end, the reputation of the wines is again notable.

Here in Galicia, between the Miño that forms the border with Portugal and the River Tea, rainfall is high, and the land lushly green, in contrast to the arid nature of most of Spain. As with the Vinho Verde region to the south, the wines here are light and at best elegant. Unlike those of its Portuguese neighbor, Rias Baixas wines are highly fashionable in the best restaurants of Madrid.

Despite a history of winemaking in the area that goes back centuries, and historical

FACT BOX

WINEMAKER: Tomas Santacruz
SIZE OF VINEYARD: 62 acres
PRODUCTION: 18,000 cases
GRAPE VARIETY: Albariño
RECOMMENDED VINTAGES:
drink youngest available, but 1995 and 1996 were both highly rated
LOCAL RESTAURANT: Puesto Piloto in Vigo

records that show the estate was a wine producer in the later part of the nineteenth century, Fillaboa became a commercial producer of Albariño as recently as 1986. It was then that the estate grubbed up all the old vines and replaced them all with Albariño. Albariño is the grape of Galicia, widely acknowledged as the best variety

among the many in the area. A delicately flavored grape, it needs careful handling if the wine is to show its true characters.

The stone walls of the Fillaboa bodega conceal a winery equipped with all the very latest in vinification technology. Grapes, which have been hand-picked and sorted to remove any unhealthy fruit, are destemmed and gently pressed. Only the first pressings are used for the finished wine. The must is treated with pectolytic enzymes, which help break down the solid matter and speed settling, which is carried out in refrigerated tanks. Centrifuging the must would be quicker, but would result in a loss of some of the already delicate flavors.

Fermentation is in stainless-steel vats. No oak is used at all in this winery. Temperatures are kept cool but not cold, typically 63°F. This helps add palate structure, while not losing too many volatile components. The wine is released in the new year following the vintage, as a young wine. Albariño generally is a wine to be drunk young and fresh, so do not keep it too long.

TASTING NOTES

1996 ALBARIÑO

Pale golden color with a nose which at first seems simply vinous, without any one particular character coming through but closer study reveals a remarkable range of very subtle flavors. Slightly herbal with a hint of coriander, yet floral at the same time with even a hint of spiciness. Dry with moderate acidity and medium weight, this wine is fuller-flavored than might be expected, with a good, medium to long finish.

Like the best Italian dry whites, and fine young Chablis, this is a wine that needs careful study; not all upfront and obvious, it is far more subtle.

Rating ★★★

SUGGESTED FOOD PAIRING
Lightly flavored seafood and white fish, simply cooked

HAMILTON RUSSELL VINEYARDS

Hemel-en-Aarde Valley, PO Box 158, Hermanus, Cape 7200,
South Africa
Tel: (27) 283 23595 Fax: (27) 283 21797
*Visitors: Monday–Friday 9:00AM–5:00PM; Saturday
9:00AM–1:00PM*

*T*he Hamilton Russell estate was the first South African vineyard to make serious ripples in the international wine markets with their Pinot Noir. Now they are causing a similar stir with that other great Burgundian grape variety, Chardonnay.

The vineyard was established by Tim Hamilton Russell, the son of an anti-National Party South African MP, in 1975. With a lifelong interest in wine, Tim had read geology and climatology at Oxford, so was in an ideal position to choose the perfect vineyard site. One hundred and twenty miles southeast of Cape Town, the Hamilton Russell estate is the most southerly vineyard in Africa, and therefore the coolest. The site at Hermanus was chosen for its cool temperatures and water-retentive, shale soil.

FACT BOX

WINEMAKER: Kevin Grant
SIZE OF VINEYARD: 160 acres
PRODUCTION: 25,000 cases
GRAPE VARIETIES: Pinot Noir, Chardonnay, Sauvignon Blanc–used as varietals
RECOMMENDED VINTAGES: 1996, 1995, 1993, 1991
LOCAL RESTAURANT: the Burgundy in Hermanus–great for fresh fish and specialties like ostrich and crocodile!

The ocean is only a couple of miles away but the vines are protected from the strong southerly winds, and from saline deposits, which can be very damaging to the leaves, by the Raedna-Gael mountains.

The Atlantic influence is far greater here than in most of the rest of the Cape, with the possible exception of Constantia. The breezes mean the maximum temperatures rarely go over 86°F, and the summer average is nearer 70°F. At these temperatures the grapes can ripen slowly.

The estate is now run by Tim's son, Antony. His passion is not simply purity of varietal flavor, but individuality. A vigorous exponent of the notion of "terroir," he is determined that his wines should not just be good Pinot Noirs or good Chardonnays, but typical of Walker

Hamilton Russell is in the cool, fertile Walker Bay area.

Bay. Varietal definition is important, but the elusive, almost mythical concept of terroir is what makes the world's great wines stand out.

Certainly the techniques used should emphasize the locality. Higher-than-average vine density in the vineyard, coupled with lower-than-average yields of fruit, means that each vine is giving all the concentration it can. Fermentation is in small (Burgundian-sized, 60-gallon) French oak barrels, using the naturally occurring yeasts as much as possible. Temperatures are allowed to go fairly high for white wine, up to 79°F. For Chardonnay it allows for greater weight on the palate. Post-fermentation, a proportion of the wine goes through malolactic fermentation, and all the wine is matured for up to nine months in cask, depending on the quality of the fruit.

> **TASTING NOTES**
> ### 1996 WALKER BAY CHARDONNAY
> Very pale color. Toast and lime flavored nose with some yeasty character as well. Dry with moderate acidity and medium weight and intensity on the palate with a reasonable length. (The 1995 is reputed to be a more serious wine)
> Rating ★★
>
> SUGGESTED FOOD PAIRING
> The light flavors make this a very useful wine. It will partner white meats and fish with almost any sauce.

HERDADE DO ESPORÃO

Office address: Finagra S.A., Rua Duarte Pacheco Pereira, 8,
1400 Lisboa, Portugal
Tel: (351) 1 301 99 01 Fax: (351) 1 301 99 68
Visitors: Open weekdays 9:00AM–5:00PM, by arrangement

*I*n the heart of the Alentejo, in inland
Portugal, toward the Spanish frontier lies the
Esporão Estate. One of the oldest in Portugal, the
estate has been in existence without major changes
to the boundaries since 1267, not long after the
Portuguese state was created. It is also one of
the largest winemaking estates in Portugal, with
almost 1,000 acres of vines out of an estate total
of almost 5,000 acres.

In contrast to the coastal areas, here in the
south away from the sea the climate is dry in
the summer, with plentiful rain in the winter,
although in the early 1990s there was a very
long-running drought here. Anyone used to
Douro scenery will be astonished by the
landscape here–vast expanses of virtually
flat land make large-scale agriculture of all
types, including viticulture, feasible.

FACT BOX

WINEMAKER: David Baverstock

SIZE OF VINEYARD: 1,000 acres total,
predominantly for red wine production

PRODUCTION: 464,000 cases per
year

GRAPE VARIETIES: Antào Vaz, Arinto,
Roupeiro, Mantendo, Diagalves, Perrum,
Sémillon, Sauvignon Blanc

RECOMMENDED VINTAGES:
1996, 1995, 1994, 1991

The estate is owned by Finagre, an agricultural holding company in turn owned by Joaquim Bandeira. He bought the estate in 1973, just before Portugal's revolution. For five years from 1974 it was taken over by the workers but eventually returned to the rightful owners. Serious viticulture and winemaking came later, in the mid-1980s. By 1986 the recently planted vineyards were producing grapes and a winery was needed.

Built in time for the 1987 vintage, the remarkable winery is constructed with huge underground cellars to help keep temperatures down. Aided by all the latest technology, winemaking here is carried out by the Roseworthy-trained but Portuguese-resident winemaker, David Baverstock. He has a wide selection of grape varieties to work with, both native Portuguese and international. Unsurprisingly the winemaking is very modern, although a small amount of red wine is made by treading– a small reminder that David's first

job in Portugal was with a port producer. The white is partially fermented in American oak barrels.

Like Mouton Rothschild, each vintage of the top Esporão wines is decorated with the work of a different contemporary Portuguese artist. The commissions are highly thought of, and much sought after.

TASTING NOTES

REGUENGOS D.O.C. RESERVA 1996

Pale lemon with considerable spritz. Pungently oaky nose with banana and melon fruit characters behind it. Dry with balanced acid, medium weight, and concentrated oaky flavors. Good length. Very much a modern "New World" style of wine designed to appeal to drinkers of Australian and Californian Chardonnays.
Rating ★★★

SUGGESTED FOOD PAIRING
This wine needs a full-flavored food accompaniment such as smoked or broiled fish.

HOUGHTON WINES

Dale Road, Middle Swan, Western Australia
Tel: (61) 619 274 5100 Fax: (61) 619 274 5372
Visitors: Cellar-door sales daily 10:00AM–5:00PM

*H*oughton Wines has long been the mainstay of Western Australian wine production. This, the largest state in Australia, has only a small proportion of the country's vineyards, located in an isolated pocket in the extreme southwest corner of the state. Currently a very small contributor to the Australian total, Western Australia accounts for as little as 1.5 percent of the country's total. The main region here is the Swan Valley, now responsible for about a quarter of Western Australian production. In the early 1970s, the Swan valley accounted for virtually all the state's wine, but other areas like Margaret River and Great Southern have since been developed.

Most Houghton wine comes from the Swan Valley, some 35 miles northeast of Perth. Most Swan Valley production is controlled by Houghton, hence the two swans on the labels.

FACT BOX

WINEMAKER: Paul Lapsley
SIZE OF VINEYARD: 314 acres, of which 123 are currently under vine
PRODUCTION: 34,000 cases (company total)
GRAPE VARIETIES: Chenin, Muscadelle, Chardonnay, Verdlho, Semillon
RECOMMENDED VINTAGES: 1996, 1995, 1994

The estate was first created in 1836 when a syndicate of three British army officers bought the land. Commercial grape growing and winemaking did not start until they sold the property to Dr John Ferguson in 1859. The firm is now the largest producer in Western Australia and Houghton's have recently made a multimillion dollar investment in the area, which will strengthen this position further. They now have vineyards in Swan, Margaret River, and Frankland.

The Houghton winery surrounded by its vineyards.

The first vintage for Houghton was a mere 25 gallons; they are now one of the larger Australian producers, making some 925,000 gallons each vintage. Houghton makes a range of wines. The mid-range Wildflower series, each label illustrated with an example of local flora, and the Gold Reserve range, a collection of premium-quality wines, have recently joined the company's greatest success, HWB.

HWB is the new name for what can only be described as one of the most successful branded wines in Australian history. For most of the last 60 years the wine has been sold as Houghton's White Burgundy, one of the country's biggest-selling wines. Such labeling has been perfectly legal for the domestic market but with Australia looking ever more to the export markets they have had to bring many of their wine laws into line with other countries', in particular with those applying to European Union (EU) wine. Burgundy is, of course, a region in France so the name has had to be dropped as part of a bilateral agreement between the EU and Australia.

TASTING NOTES

H.W.B. 1996

Medium depth of color, with some viscosity showing. Medium-intensity, aromatic, perfumed nose of stone fruit and red fruit, peaches, and raspberry juice. Dry with a fairly broad palate. Medium acidity, moderate weight and alcohol, and reasonable length. Very pleasant wine, although it is not in the least like Burgundy.

Rating ★

SUGGESTED FOOD PAIRING

Any white meat, simple chicken or pork dishes, and white fish.

HOUSE OF NOBILO

Station Road, Huapai, Auckland, New Zealand
Tel: (64) 9 412 9148 Fax: (64) 9 412 7124
e-mail:nobilo@ibm.net
*Visitors: Monday–Friday 9:00AM–5:00PM; Saturday
10:00AM–5:00PM; Sunday and public holidays 11:00AM–4:00PM*

*N*obilo is the fourth-largest wine producer in New Zealand, and the biggest of all the family-owned concerns. Nobilo was established over 50 years ago by a Croat immigrant, Nikola Nobilo. His family came from the Adriatic island of Korcula, off the Dalmatian coast. Winemaking can be traced back through the family for at least 300 years. In the last 30 years the firm has been at the forefront of innovation in the New Zealand industry.

In the late sixties Nobilo took the brave decision to replant and expand the vineyards with noble European *vinifera* varieties,

FACT BOX

WINEMAKER: Greg Foster

SIZE OF VINEYARD: 74 acres at Huapai with a further 173 acres operated in joint ventures; grapes also bought in

PRODUCTION: a total of 4,430 tons of grapes is crushed each vintage; about 9,000 cases of Tietjen Chardonnay is made each year

GRAPE VARIETIES: Chardonnay, Sauvignon Blanc, Pinot Noir, Merlot, Cabernet Sauvignon, Pinotage–all used in varietal wines

RECOMMENDED VINTAGES: information not available

LOCAL RESTAURANT: Grace Hills, Pomona Road, Kumeu

Chardonnay, Cabernet Sauvignon, and Pinot Noir. This move, which seems so obvious now, was very controversial at the time.

The first vintage for Cabernet and Pinotage was 1970, a South African variety Nikola Nobilo had also planted in a small way. The young wine was matured in new barrels, the first recorded instance of any New Zealand wine seeing new oak. By 1973 the wines were ready to be shown, and the Pinotage was judged best wine at the

Nobilo's winery and visitors' center.

National Wine Competition that year. Ever since, Nobilo has been highly regarded on the domestic market for its red wines.

TASTING NOTES

TIETJEN VINEYARD 1995 GISBORNE CHARDONNAY

Vivid pale gold in color with a buttery, spice nose. Cinnamon toast from the French oak over layers of sharp fruit and butterscotch. Dry with crisp acidity but a very ripe palate (this is one of the best recent vintages in New Zealand) medium to full weight and long finish.

Rating ★★★

SUGGESTED FOOD PAIRING
Broiled fish or white meats; the crisp acid would make this a good partner for pork dishes.

A couple of years later Nobilo launched the first medium-dry Müller-Thurgau wine. Extremely popular on the home market, this easy-drinking style now accounts for half the wines drunk in New Zealand.

More recently the emphasis has been on drier styles with the premium varietals, the noble Chardonnay, Sauvignon, and Pinot Noir. Nobilo's best Chardonnay comes from the Tietjen estate in Gisborne. Just as Marlborough is considered the best area for Sauvignon, Gisborne is the best area for Chardonnay in New Zealand. This estate is owned by a Dutchman, Paul Tietjen, not by Nobilo.

The 1996 Tietjen Chardonnay was machine-harvested and processed at Nobilo's winery in Auckland. Gentle pressing and separation of the free-run juice from the press was followed by part-cask and part-tank fermentation. Casks were French, only a proportion of new oak being used. Maturation was in cask for seven months.

HUGEL & FILS

68340 Riquewihr, France
Tel: (33) 39 47 92 45 Fax: (33) 39 49 00 10
Visitors: Sales daily; tours Monday–Friday by appointment only

*O*f all the Alsace producers the yellow labels of Hugel & Fils are probably the best known in all of the major export markets. Over 80 percent of Hugel's wines are exported to over 100 countries worldwide, yet the wines are still regarded as archetypal Alsace, benchmark wines by which others are judged.

The firm is family-run. Five family members led by "Johnnie" are the only shareholders in the company, which has been in the family since 1639–12 generations of Hugels. Hans Ulrich Hugel settled in Riquewihr in 1639 and soon took charge of the powerful Association of Vine Growers. In 1672 his son built a house in Rue des Cordiers. Over the door was the family crest, still used as the company's logo. The family stayed in that house until the early years of the twentieth century when Frédéric Emile

FACT BOX

WINEMAKER: Marc Hugel
SIZE OF VINEYARD: 67 acres owned by Hugel, 300 acres under long-term contracts
PRODUCTION: 100,000 cases
GRAPE VARIETIES: (Hugel Estate) Riesling, Gewurztraminer, Pinot Gris, Pinot Noir
RECOMMENDED VINTAGES: 1996, 1995, 1990, 1989*, 1988, 1985, 1983 (* for Vendange Tardive)

Hugel moved to new premises in the center of Riquewihr, premises still in use today.

By this time the family had already established its reputation for meticulous viticulture and winemaking. By this stage, however, the historically high reputation of the region had declined. Alsace had been one of the most highly regarded wine-producing regions in the Germanic Holy Roman Empire but the effect of wars, pest, and diseases, as well as the burgeoning reputations of other areas, had taken their toll. By the end of World War I the situation was desperate.

After the return of Alsace to France in 1919 a few growers, most notably Frédéric Hugel, turned their attention to quality production, believing that the wines were capable of being the finest white wines in the world. This was at a time when the wines were considered cheap and simple, but their efforts paid off, as can be seen by the wines made here today.

Hugel owns about 67 acres of vineyard, only in the Riquewihr district. These are mostly in prime sites, on the steepest terrain with the greatest exposure to the sun. No fertilizers are used as this will increase yields. Hugel yields are, on average, 30 percent lower than the Alsace average, which comes through in far greater concentration in the finished wine. These vineyards supply only a small proportion of the firm's needs. The remainder is bought from some 350 smallholders, owning a total of some 300 acres. The production is bought in the form of grapes only, so Hugel can control the winemaking.

Alsace wines are almost invariably varietal, which here means 100 percent of that variety, not the 85 percent common elsewhere.

TASTING NOTES

1995 TOKAY PINOT GRIS JUBILEE HUGEL

Medium depth of color, still looking quite young. Full aromatic nose of spice and very ripe tropical fruit. Not quite the litchi character of Gewürztraminer, but close. Perfumed and rich. Dry to the taste with quite high acidity, a feature that distinguishes Pinot Gris from Gewürztraminer. Full weight and flavor, and quite high alcohol. Enormous length and wonderfully ripe, rich finish. Still very young though. This is a wine to keep until it is at least five, and preferably ten, years old.

Rating ★★★★★

SUGGESTED FOOD PAIRING

The intensity of this wine means it works well with rich foods like pâtés and charcuterie.

In order to preserve the best of the varietal character the Hugel philosophy is to avoid oak and to bottle very young. Thus, the flavors are trapped in the bottle to develop there. Equally important, each type of wine, and Hugel make a large range, is bottled in one batch. If, for instance, you buy a bottle of Hugel Tradition Riesling from a particular vintage you know that all the other bottles of the same wine were bottled at the same time, so they should be consistent. Not all wine companies do this.

Hugel's historic house in Riquewihr.

At the top of the range are the rare Jubilee, Vendange Tardive, and Sélection de Grains Nobles wines. Sélection de Grains Nobles are made from grapes affected with noble rot, not common in this part of France so made only in exceptional vintages. Vendange Tardive are late-harvest wines, not necessarily affected with botrytis. They may be vinified to dryness, but most producers prefer some sweetness. Jubilee wines are dry wines of outstanding quality, again only made in exceptional

The famous 200-year old, ornately carved St Catherine cask.

vintages. In Hugel's case these three are made only from their own vineyards, and only from Grand Cru sites, although Hugel chooses not to use the term Grand Cru on the label.

Do not be misled by the word Tokay on the label of the wine tasted, this wine has nothing to do with the Hungarian Tokaji, or with the Australian Tokays. Tokay has long been an Alsace synonym for Pinot Gris.

HUNTER'S WINES

PO Box 839, Rapaura Road, RD3, Blenheim, New Zealand
Tel: (64) 3 572 8489 Fax: (64) 3 572 8457
Visitors: Visitors center and wine store open Monday–Saturday
9:00AM–5:00PM; Sunday 10:30AM–4:00PM

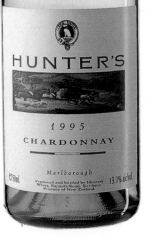

*H*unter's wines started out inauspiciously, with borrowed equipment in a disused cider factory, yet within a very short period of time the awards started to flood in, and have continued to do so ever since.

Jane Hunter, now managing director of Hunter's Wines, started with her late husband Ernie in 1983. She had previously worked for New Zealand's biggest wine company, Montana, and came from a viticultural family, her father being a grape grower in Australia's Riverland. Academically, too, Jane is well suited to her chosen profession, having trained in viticultural science at Adelaide. The period at Montana must have been invaluable, organizing research, dealing with contract growers, and with management budgets. Even so, it

FACT BOX

WINEMAKER: Gary Duke, consultant winemaker Dr Tony Jordan
SIZE OF VINEYARD: 44 acres
PRODUCTION: 35,000 cases total
GRAPE VARIETY: Sauvignon Blanc, Chardonnay, Riesling, Gewürztraminer, Cabernet Sauvignon, Pinot Noir, Merlot—mostly used unblended in varietal wines
RECOMMENDED VINTAGES: 1997, 1994, 1991

must have been something of a culture shock to find, after the tragic death of Ernie, four years after founding Hunter's, that she was at the helm. Undaunted, Jane continued the work they had started together and has now accumulated over two dozen gold medals for her wines, not to mention the many other medals and trophies.

The Hunter's vineyards, 100 acres in the Wairau valley of New Zealand's Marlborough region, at the north of the South Island, supply less than a third of the company's needs. The remaining fruit is bought, only from local growers so the wine is true to its Marlborough roots. Here the stony soil gives good drainage and the cool climate, in conjunction with the long hours of sunshine, gives ideal conditions for the grapes to accumulate flavor components, without getting overripe, which can cause the acidity to fall. Indeed, crisp natural acidity is one of the hallmarks of New Zealand's wines.

Winemaking here is totally modern. Most of the grapes are machine-harvested, after which anaerobic

TASTING NOTES
1995
CHARDONNAY

Subtle oak at first on the nose, followed by butter and lemon characters. Dry, but with ripeness to round off the spine of crisp acidity. Oak more obvious on the palate than the nose, giving greater weight and an intense palate to the wine. Long, clean finish.

It will be interesting to see how this wine develops with age. It has all the hallmarks of one that will gain great complexity and roundness with a few years' bottle age.

Rating ★★★

SUGGESTED FOOD PAIRING
This wine is full enough in flavor to work well with milder game dishes as well as rabbit and broiled chicken.

winemaking is the norm. The fruit is carefully handled and processed as quickly as possible to avoid oxidation. Long cool fermentation is preferred. Many winemakers chill their musts to between 59 and 64°F, but Jane and her team go down to 54°, which slows the reactions, and retains as much of the fruit as possible. The wines take 28 days to ferment. Hunter's Chardonnay spends nine months in French oak barrels, 45 percent of which are new each vintage. French oak is more expensive than American but gives more subtle flavors. Malolactic fermentation is encouraged in 40 percent of the wine to add a little of the buttery diacetyl character, and to tone down the fruit acids, but without overdoing it.

INNISKILLIN WINES INC.

RR #1 Line 3, Niagara-on-the-Lake, Ontario, Canada
Tel: (1) 905 468 2187 Fax: (1) 905 468 5355
Visitors: Daily for sales; guided tours twice a day

*T*o outsiders Canada's image is one of cold climates, fir trees, and snow–lots of snow. In fact the country enjoys a range of climates and in the south the cool, continental climate is, in places, ideal for grape production. Inevitably the choice of grape varieties is somewhat limited, but a number of French hybrid vines–that is vines developed by crossing *Vitis vinifera* with American species– have been developed specifically for such cold areas. One such is Vidal Blanc, a hybrid developed from Ugni Blanc and a Seibel variety. The advantage of Vidal Blanc here is its tolerance to extremely low winter temperatures when it is dormant.

Canada has a remarkably long history of vine cultivation and winemaking, starting in 1811, but until relatively recently this was mostly high-alcohol, sweet wines from native varieties. In recent years, mostly since the seventies, two

FACT BOX

WINEMAKER: Karl J. Kaiser
SIZE OF VINEYARD: 113 acres
PRODUCTION: 150,000–200,000 cases total per year (Icewine is a small part of this)
GRAPE VARIETIES: Vidal, but also Chardonnay, Riesling, Auxerrois, Pinot Gris, Pinot Noir, and Cabernet Sauvignon
RECOMMENDED VINTAGES: 1994, 1995, 1996, 1997 an excellent year for Chardonnay and Riesling

Harvesters picking grapes in the early hours.

areas, British Columbia in the west and Ontario in the east, have developed very high-quality wine industries.

Inniskillin is one of these, founded in 1975 by a fruit nursery-man, Donald J.P. Ziraldo, in conjunction with an Austrian expatriate, Karl J. Kaiser. The Canadian wine industry, like the retail trade in Canada, is very strictly controlled but fortunately for the pair the chairman of the local Liquor Control Board was in favor of a premium vineyard in the region.

The vineyards are on the Niagara Peninsula where the topography buffers the vines against the worst of the winds off Lake Ontario, and reduces the incidence of spring frosts. Severe weather at this time of the year will destroy the crop, yet paradoxically, extreme cold in the fall is the making of Inniskillin's rarest and finest wine.

Ontario claims to have the world's most reliable climate for Icewine production. The fully ripe, healthy

TASTING NOTES

1995 VIDAL ICEWINE

Medium gold color with a pronounced, perfumed richness on the nose, slightly floral and distinctly fruity. Sweet, of course, but with high acidity which perfectly balances the sweetness so there is no hint of cloyness. Concentrated fruit flavors with a very long and elegant finish.
Rating ★★★★

SUGGESTED FOOD PAIRING
This is a wine for desserts, but sweets that are too sweet will make it seem a little dry and tart. Medium-sweet desserts, especially those involving fruit, work very well.

The Brae Burn visitors center.

grapes are left on the vine until the temperature drops to 19°F, or lower, freezing the grapes. As they freeze it's the water content that solidifies first, concentrating the sugar and flavor content of the remaining liquid. Harvesting is done in the bitter cold and the press yields hugely concentrated must. The fermentation, which can be difficult with such high sugar concentrations, is done in stainless steel, and the flavors are so concentrated that no additional characters are required.

Inniskillin's Icewines have won many awards internationally, rightly so, as one of the world's newest "classic" styles of wine.

KLEIN CONSTANTIA

PO Box 375, Constantia 7848, Republic of South Africa
Tel: (27) 21 794 5188 Fax: (27) 21 794 2464
*Visitors: Monday–Friday 9:00AM–5:00PM; Saturday
9:00AM–1:00PM*

*T*he Klein Constantia estate, some 20 minutes' drive from the center of Cape Town, is one of the country's most beautiful vineyard locations. It was originally part of the estate granted to the Dutch Governor Simon van der Stel in 1685, and grape growing has been practiced here for 300 years. The original estate has been divided into two. Groot Constantia is a national monument, and a working vineyard; Klein, or Little Constantia, is a privately owned concern.

In the eighteenth and nineteenth centuries the wines of Constantia became legendary. The sweet, Muscat-based Constantia was the wine requested by Napoleon, when exiled to St Helena. Klein Constantia has reintroduced this classic wine as Vin de Constance. Made from late-harvest but

FACT BOX

WINEMAKER: Ross Gower

SIZE OF VINEYARD: 182 acres, 54 acres Sauvignon Blanc

PRODUCTION: 45.000 cases total

GRAPE VARIETY: Sauvignon, Chardonnay, Riesling, Sémillon, Muscat, Chenin, Cabernet, Merlot, Shiraz, Pinot Noir, and Pontac—mostly used as varietal and in a "Bordeaux blend" red

RECOMMENDED VINTAGES: 1996 Chard Reserve, 1997 Riesling, Sauvignon Blanc, and Chardonnay

not botrytic Muscat de Frontignan grapes, this wine is sold in half-litre replicas of the original bottles. Although highly regarded it is unlikely that this is as good as the original Constantia is reputed to have been.

Today the estate's best wines are dry light whites.

Classic Cape Dutch architecture of the Constantia house.

About half the total estate, 183 acres, is under vine, with three-quarters being white grapes. Much of the rest of the land is in the Constantia mountains, which provide the dramatic backdrop to the Cape-Dutch homestead. The vineyards are in two distinct parts. The lower, warmer, north-facing vineyards are planted with black varieties, while the higher, cooler plots are given over to Chardonnay, Sauvignon Blanc, Riesling, and Muscat.

Because the estate is on a narrow peninsula, breezes off False Bay and the influence of the Atlantic Ocean behind the mountains keep the climate cool, with no extremes of temperature, while the heavy winter rains ensure that plenty of ground water is available.

The Sauvignon Blanc grapes are crushed and given overnight skin-contact to maximize the aromatic content in the wine. After settling for 24 hours the must is fermented reductively in stainless steel. Temperatures are kept down to about 55°F, which keeps in the volatile components and means a total fermentation period of about 10 days. Because the crisp acid of Sauvignon is part of its appeal, no malolactic fermentation is allowed. The wines are allowed to mature in bulk for four months before release.

TASTING NOTES

1996 SAUVIGNON BLANC

Very pale, almost water-white. Medium-pronounced, youthful, grassy, and elderflower nose, with some green bell pepper. Dry with moderately crisp acidity and medium weight. Full floral flavor, alcohol in balance, not noticeably high or low. Good length of finish.

Rating ★★★

SUGGESTED FOOD PAIRING
The winemaker recommends this wine with crayfish caught in the estate dam.

KUMEU RIVER WINES

550 Highway 16, PO Box 24, Kumeu 1454, New Zealand
Tel: (64) 9 412 8415 Fax: (64) 9 412 7627
*Visitors: Monday–Friday 9:00AM–5:00PM; Saturday
11:00AM–5:30PM*

*K*umeu River Wines was established in 1944 by Mick and Katé Brajkovich, immigrants from Yugoslavia who had first settled in New Zealand in 1938. Initially they worked in the far north of the country, digging kauri gum, but soon moved to Henderson in West Auckland to work in vineyards and orchards. Eventually they saved enough money to buy their own plot of vines and founded San Mario Wines.

By this time Mick had died, but his son Maté continued his work, along with his wife, another Dalmatian immigrant, Melba. Their four children soon set to work in the family business and still do. Michael is the winemaker, Marijana is the sales director. Milan is the company viticulturist, running all the company's vineyards, and

FACT BOX

WINEMAKER: Michael Brajkovich

SIZE OF VINEYARD: 62 acres–supplies 90% of needs

PRODUCTION: 20,000 cases total

GRAPE VARIETIES: Chardonnay (65%), Sauvignon Blanc, Merlot, Malbec, Pinot Noir, Cabernet Franc–mostly sold as varietals

RECOMMENDED VINTAGES: 1996, 1994

LOCAL RESTAURANT: Gracehill

Paul took a degree in marketing and took over the company's sales and marketing after a stint working in the wine trade in England.

Maté, who died in 1992, was one of the most highly respected of all New Zealand's winemakers. Heavily involved in the wine industry's organizations throughout his life, he was chairman of the Wine Institute of New Zealand from 1982 to 1985. He was awarded an OBE in 1985 for services to the industry.

San Marino Wines became Kumeu River Wines in 1986 to emphasize the changes that had taken place in the preceding few years. The company had moved toward premium varietals such as Chardonnay and Sauvignon Blanc, Pinot Noir, and Merlot, all grown at the newly developed vineyards in the Kumeu river valley.

> ## TASTING NOTES
> ### 1996 KUMEU CHARDONNAY
> Medium golden color with a ripe, fruity nose. Oak quite evident in the nose, coming across as toasty and cedarwood-like but with full buttery, lemony fruit character behind that. Dry, with medium weight and very crisp acidity. Good long finish.
> Rating ★★★
>
> SUGGESTED FOOD PAIRING
> Broiled scallops, poached salmon with dill sauce, crayfish.

The Kumeu River winemaking philosophy is simple, and can be summed up in the words "Great wine is made in the vineyard." Enormous care is taken to grow healthy fruit, which is then treated gently to turn it into wine. The vineyards are "lyre"-trained, a system that gives maximum exposure to the sun and plenty of ventilation to reduce the incidence of rot. Pressing for the white wines is whole-cluster, time-consuming but, as Champagne's Dom Perignon discovered, it gives the finest musts. Natural yeasts are used, and barrel fermentation is the norm for the white wines. Michael's French experience shows through in the wines, which are not as heavily oaked as some, the oak being there to support and complement the fruit, not overpower it.

The Maté vineyard.

LAKE'S FOLLY VINEYARD

Broke Road, Pokolbin 2321, New South Wales, Australia
Tel: (61) 49 987 507 Fax: (61) 49 987 322
Visitors: Cellar-door sales Monday–Saturday 10:00AM–4:00PM

*S*tephen Lake, the proprietor, describes Lake's Folly as a hobby that got out of hand. Hobby it may have been, once, but now it is a hugely successful family business making some of the finest Chardonnays in the Hunter Valley. Max Lake, founder of Lake's Folly, was one of Australia's most eminent surgeons, specializing in hand reconstruction, and an expert in flavors and scents, before he turned his attentions to wine.

It all started when Max first tasted an old Australian red wine, a wine that sparked a passion for wines that led to the purchase of a small estate in the Hunter. At the time there were very few surviving Hunter vineyards. The wine that had kindled the interest came from a vineyard that had been grubbed up in the 1930s.

FACT BOX

WINEMAKER: Stephen Lake

SIZE OF VINEYARD: 30 acres, 5 acres of which are Chardonnay

PRODUCTION: 4,000 cases total, 1,000 of which are Chardonnay

GRAPE VARIETIES: Cabernet Sauvignon, Merlot, Petit Verdot, Shiraz, Chardonnay

RECOMMENDED VINTAGES: for Chardonnay, 1996, 1995, 1994, 1992, 1986, 1974

LOCAL RESTAURANT: Il Cacciatore

When Lake arrived he was virtually alone. Much of the soil in Hunter is unsuitable for vines, and when the soil is right, it is often in the sunniest spots. In Germany that would be welcomed, but here the temperatures are high anyway, so the vines need shelter. It took Max Lake six months to fine a suitable patch of deep volcanic soil, facing south, on which to plant. The first vines were planted in 1963 and the first vintage, a Cabernet, was the 1966–some one-and-a-half barrels' worth.

The white wines came later. Max started getting interested in Chardonnay in the seventies, an interest that soon became an obsession. Lake's Folly Chardonnays are distinctive. Whereas many New World Chardonnays are full of very upfront fruit and buttery character with masses of oak but often lacking acidity, Lake's Folly wines are crisper, more subtly oaked and made for the long term.

Stephen Lake places enormous emphasis on the quality of his fruit. All the Chardonnay is hand-picked. Cold fermentation at 54–59°F starts in tank and once going well the must is transferred into barrel. Allier oak from central France and oak from the Vosges forest are used. About one-third of the casks are replaced each year so the oak influence is kept balanced. After fermentation Lake's Folly Chardonnay is allowed to mature in cask for approximately seven months, a period that varies from vintage to vintage.

TASTING NOTES

1996 HUNTER VALLEY CHARDONNAY

Medium gold, with a youthful nose of cedar and spice behind a fresh fruity, citrus character, lemons and lime juice. Dry, truly dry in a way that few Australian Chardonnays are, with intense fruits and a Burgundian-like streak of crisp, cleansing acidity holding the flavors together for a long finish.
Rating ★★★★

SUGGESTED FOOD PAIRING

The intensity and the crisp acids of this wine demand a firm flavor in the food. Broiled chicken or fullish-flavored fish like trout or turbot.

Marqués de Murrieta sa

Ctra. Logroño–Zaragoza Km5, 26080 Logroño, Spain
Tel: (34) 41 25 8100 Fax: (34) 41 25 1606
Visitors: Vineyards not open to public

*A*s one drives into Logroño from the east one cannot miss the spectacular stone-built cellars of Marqués de Murrieta, constructed on the hillside so that each of the six subterranean levels has access at ground level. Within the thick stone walls, away from the Spanish sun, is a unique stock of wine, over 15,000 barrels and 2½ million bottles of wine at any one time, a total of eight times the average annual sales.

Marqués de Murrieta is one of the few remaining producers making totally trad-itional white Rioja, aged for astounding periods of time in barrel and bottle prior to release. Not for them the vagaries of fashion, these are wines that retain their

FACT BOX

WINEMAKER: Francisco Mª Moreno Camacho

SIZE OF VINEYARD: 500 acres

PRODUCTION: 125,000 cases (15% white) (NB production figures are total for the estate, red and white)

GRAPE VARIETIES: Viura 85%; Garnacha Blanca 10%; Malvasia (used blended) 5%

RECOMMENDED VINTAGES: Reserva–1993, 1992, 1991; Castillo Ygay white–1975–70

LOCAL RESTAURANTS: Restaurant Egöes, Logroño, Restaurant Chuchi, Foenmayor

own personality—not to everyone's taste, but true to themselves.

The Ygay estate, southeast of Logroño and home to Murrieta wines, was established by Luciano Murrieta García Ortiz Lemoine, Marqués de Murrieta, in 1870. He had previously been making wines in a leased cellar taking his inspiration from Bordeaux winemakers. Like them, he aged his wines in oak barrels, which, he believed, would enable them to travel well. Luciano Murrieta is reputed to have been the first person to ship dry unfortified wine from Spain. The first wine was made on the Ygay estate in 1877; within a year the first international exhibition awards had arrived.

The dim lighting in the Ygay cellars.

On Don Luciano's death in 1911 the estate passed on to his heirs until, in 1983, three generations later, it was bought by Don Vicente Cebrián Sagarriga, Conte de Creixell. Vicente Cebrián was born in Madrid but his roots were in Galicia, the northwest corner of Spain, north of Portugal. The company have another estate there, Pazo de Barrantes, producing the young fresh Albariño wines for which the area is famous. Having bought Ygay, Vicente moved his family into the Castillo away from the city and into the vineyard. Vicente died in 1996 and the wineries are now run by his son, Vicente, and his daughter, Cristina.

Winemaking mixes tradition with innovation, the latter only where appropriate. The grapes, most Viura,

TASTING NOTES

YGAY RESERVA 1991

Don't be misled by the deep golden color, this is not a sweet wine. Pungent, oxidative nose but with honey and dried-fruit nose, too. Bone-dry with marked acidity that will cut through olive oil or fat in most dishes. Full, intense flavor gripping the palate and a long, lingering finish.
Rating ★★★★

SUGGESTED FOOD PAIRING
Strong cheese, full-flavored fish dishes, and pasta dishes, especially if the sauce is tomato-based.

The spectacular Castillo Ygay.

are crushed but not destemmed. This allows for a certain amount of tannin in the finished wine. Pressing is in wooden basket presses, made to a design that goes back to before Ygay was founded. These release the juice slowly, but produce a low yield so only the best juice goes to the modern, temperature-controlled, stainless-steel fermenters. After the 15 days or so that fermentation lasts, the wine is allowed to settle and is then racked into old American oak barrels (new wood is not used for the white wines). The white Murrieta Reserva is aged for between 30 and 36 months in wood, followed by two years of bottle age. White Castillo Ygay, released only in exceptional vintages, will spend up to 20 years in wood and bottle before sale.

MATUA WINES

Waikoukou Road, Waimauku, Auckland, New Zealand
Tel: (64) 9 411 8301 Fax: (64) 9 411 7982
Visitors: Monday–Friday 9:00AM–5:00PM

The Matua wine company has grown up with the modern New Zealand industry. At 21 years old it is the same age as modern New Zealand winemaking. At the time Matua was starting up, the whole industry was changing and a sense of identity was just beginning to form. Matua has been a part of forming that identity.

The leaders of Matua are Bill and Ross Spence (no relation of the author). Their father was also a winemaker, but neither wanted to follow his lead. Ross studied at Fresno, California, while Bill took his degree at Massey, the New Zealand wine university. Both came away knowing that the country was not achieving its potential, that it could produce wines of world-beating standards. Twenty-one years later there are no doubts.

FACT BOX

WINEMAKER: Mark Robertson
SIZE OF VINEYARD: 500 acres
PRODUCTION: 120,000 cases
GRAPE VARIETIES: Sauvignon Blanc, Chardonnay, Cabernet Sauvignon, Merlot, Pinot Noir, Malbec—mostly used in varietal wines
RECOMMENDED VINTAGES: 1996, 1994
LOCAL RESTAURANT: The Hunting Lodge, owned by Matua

The Spence brothers started in a corrugated-iron shed near Auckland in the mid-1970s. Right from the start they were innovators. The first crop included Chardonnay and Tienturier, both unusual in those days. It also included Sauvignon Blanc, the first time this grape had been used in the country. Little did they know that within the next 15 years New Zealand was going to become internationally famous for the quality of its Sauvignon.

Needing capital to expand, the Spences went into partnership with the Margans, another Auckland family, to form Matua Wines Limited in 1976. The new company established a vineyard in the Waikoukou Valley, 22 miles from Auckland. A stylish new winery and visitors' center was built–visitors were seen as vital to the success of the venture from the start.

Matua is one of the larger of the small companies. As a high-quality, low-yield operation it is often seen as a boutique winery, but if so, it is the largest boutique winery in the country. However it can hardly be called a large company. It is very much a hands-on business for its founders.

Not all Matua grapes are grown in the company's own vineyards. A little over a third are bought in from contract growers, particularly those for the red wines. The Matua vineyards are on four sites. Waimauku in Auckland is the original. Established in 1976 this is a subtropical, high-rainfall region where black grapes and Chardonnay do very well. The Judd estate in Gisborne and the Smith Dartmoor estate in Hawkes Bay were both established in 1980. Chardonnay, Semillon, and the black grapes are grown here, along with a little Sauvignon. The Shingle Peak vineyard in Marlborough is the premium Sauvignon vineyard. It is smaller than the others but the cooler climate here is ideal for preserving the aromatic and tropical-fruit flavors of this grape.

> ## TASTING NOTES
>
> ### 1996 JUDD ESTATE CHARDONNAY
>
> Vivid green-gold color with a restrained oak and butter note. Quite complex with hints of vanilla and cinnamon with lemon and lime as well as some butterscotch character. Dry with a Burgundy-like streak of fresh acidity which acts as a backbone for the complex if understated fruit. Medium weight and alcohol, clean texture.
>
> Rating ★★★★
>
> #### SUGGESTED FOOD PAIRING
>
> Broiled trout or poached salmon in a butter sauce, or simple broiled chicken.

M CHAPOUTIER

18, Avenue du Doctor Paul Durand, 26600 Tain, France
Tel: (33) 4 75 08 28 65 Fax: (33) 4 75 08 81 70
Visitors: Le Caveau, convenient for Tain station, has a shop, puts on film shows, and offers visits, courses, and conference facilities. Phone for details.

The house of Chapoutier is one of the oldest in Tain l'Hermitage in the northern section of the Rhône valley. In recent years it has come out of relative obscurity to become one of the best known and most respected firms in the area. This metamorphosis has come about during the tenure of the present generation of Chapoutiers, the brothers Michel and Marc.

Since their father's retirement in 1977 they had noticed a change in consumer attitudes. Buyers had become increasingly exacting, and, more important, increasingly willing to pay premium prices for really good Rhône wines. In 1986 they decided to turn the company into a superior producer, with every possible effort being expended to reach that aim.

FACT BOX

WINEMAKER: Michel Chapoutier
SIZE OF VINEYARD: 200 acres in the Rhône, also owns vineyards in Côteaux d'Aix en Provence and Banyuls
PRODUCTION: 200,000 cases
GRAPE VARIETIES: Marsanne for this wine, but also Syrah, Grenache Noir, Viognier
RECOMMENDED VINTAGES: 1996, 1995, 1992, 1991 for white wines; 1996, 1995, 1990 for reds

Michel Chapoutier is the viti-culturist. He is passionate about terroir. He limits yields, pruning to leave only a few buds, and therefore few potential bunches of grapes. For the same reason old vines are kept longer than they might in other vineyards. Generally old vines produce lower yields of finer fruit. The Chapoutier vines are an *average* of 40 years old–most other growers replace their vines at between 25 and 35 years. The Marsanne vines in the Hermitage Appellation are a staggering 70 years old.

Chapoutier is an exponent of bio-dynamic viticulture, a philosophy that takes organic standards to the extreme. The timing of spraying programs is set by the position of the planets and the phases of the moon. This may seem like hocus-pocus but Chapoutier claim to suffer a fraction of the normal rot problems in wet years.

The northern Rhône is mostly a steep east-facing hillside, with the Hermitage and Crozes Hermitage vineyards on a hill on the west bank of the Rhône with an equally steep aspect to the south and southwest. Terraced vineyards are not uncommon, so all the vineyard work, including picking, has to be done by hand. Only naturally occurring yeast is used for fer-mentation. For the Marsanne it is done partially in large, inert vats and partly in new French oak.

The wine is oddly labeled. The official Appellation is Hermitage but for this wine the brothers choose the old-fashioned spelling, Ermitage, without, it seems, yet encountering the wrath of the officials from the INAO in the Champs Elysées.

TASTING NOTES

1994 "DE L'ORÉE" ERMITAGE

Polished golden color with a nose reminiscent of white peaches and apricots, just beginning to develop some characters of age. Some slightly sweet earthy aromas. Dry with balanced acidity and full flavor. Medium- to full-bodied with a touch of oak still evident on the back of the palate. Very long finish. A very young wine needing a few years yet to be at its peak.
Rating ★★★★★

SUGGESTED FOOD PAIRING
The full soft flavor of this wine makes a good partner for lobster and crayfish.

MICHELE CHIARLO AZIENDA VITIVINICOLA SRL

Strada Nizza Canelli, 99–14042 Calamandrana AT, Italy
Tel: (39) 141 75231 Fax: (39) 141 75284
Visitors: Monday–Friday office hours, by appointment only

Among the many excellent wine producers in Piemonte in the northwest of Italy, Michele Chiarlo, a native of Monferrato in the heart of the region, is one of the best. Tall and slightly stooped, he comes across as a quiet, unassuming man, yet beneath the calm exterior there must be a will of iron. His aim is simple: to produce the best wine that Piemonte is capable of, not easy in an area renowned for the quality of its wines.

Michele Chiarlo's family had been grape growers for five generations, but did not have an estate winery. The Michele Chiarlo winery was initially founded in 1956 but it was many years before the investment began to pay off enough that he was able to expand. As soon as he could, he bought vineyards in the best sites in Barolo,

FACT BOX

WINEMAKER: Stefano Chiarlo

SIZE OF VINEYARDS: 90 acres owned in Barolo and Asti, grapes for Gavi from contract growers

PRODUCTION: 92,000 cases total

GRAPE VARIETIES: for Gavi, Cortese, but numerous other grapes grown for other wines

RECOMMENDED VINTAGES: 1996, but drink youngest available

LOCAL RESTAURANT: Ristorante Violetta in Calamandrana

1996 ROVERETO GAVI
DENOMINAZIONE DI ORIGINE CONTROLLATA
di GAVI
MICHELE CHIARLO

Barrique maturation in the Chiarlo cellars.

and built cellars in which to age his wine, and in Gavi he established a modern winery able to turn the Cortese grapes of the region into one of Italy's finest white wines.

Here in the foothills of the Alps the best vineyards are amphitheater-shaped, giving the ideal exposure on all sides to the sun. The best sites in the center of the region are given over to Nebbiolo for Barolo production but in a narrow strip some nine miles long and three wide in the south of the region, close to the Ligurian border, Cortese is highly prized. This lightly flavored grape was first popular as a quaffing wine made to quench the thirst of visitors to the Ligurian coastal resorts, but soon the inherent qualities became apparent, largely through the work of the premium estates in the area. By the 1960s and early 1970s the wine's reputation had been made.

Most of the grapes used by Michele Chiarlo, and all those for the Rovereto Gavi, come from contract growers. Very firm control is exercised over the

viticulture and grapes not reaching the required standards will not be used. Fertilizers are used very sparingly, only when soil analysis shows it is needed, and herbicides are now avoided completely. The DOC discipline for Gavi allows quite high yields but, in common with so many producers of high-quality wine, Chiarlo carries out crop thinning halfway through the season to concentrate the vines' efforts into ripening a few clusters well. Many growers spray their vines according to a standard time-table. Here careful monitoring of the meteorological conditions, through thermometers, rain gauges, barometers, and hygrometers in the vineyards indicates when disease is most likely, thus limiting spraying to only when it is likely to be most effective.

Winemaking, too, is gentle. Because it's thought that every treatment takes something away from the wine, the musts and wines are handled as little as possible. Grapes are pressed using the gentlest, softest presses possible. Whole bunches are pressed for the white wines so as not to damage the skins too much. Cool temperatures are used for the Gavi, but chilled to only about 63°F, so as not to get the estery, bubblegum flavors that can result from going colder. Cortese is naturally not very aromatic, so the fewer additional flavors the better. Pumping, fining, and filtering are all kept to a bare minimum, but sterile filtration is used before bottling, which is done under a blanket of nitrogen, the ideal way to keep the wine from oxygen.

All this care results in a wine that shows immense refinement. No big, blowsy flavors here. Like so many Italian whites, Rovereto is a fundamentally delicate wine which, if tasted quickly in a flight of bigger wines, could easily be overlooked. It is well worth taking the trouble to study this wine in greater depth, though, because a little work and a little thought will reveal a myriad subtle flavors.

TASTING NOTES

1996 ROVERETO GAVI DI GAVI

Very pale-lemon color with small green highlights. Intriguing, almost ethereal nose. Slightly spicy with a hint of vanilla, but also lime juice and lemon peel and almost licorice notes. Dry with refreshing acidity and medium weight. Great, long refined finish.

Rating ★★★★

SUGGESTED FOOD PAIRING

Fine on its own as an apéritif, and with the finest, very fresh fish and seafood dishes served simply, without sauces.

MIGUEL TORRES SA

Apartado 13, Vilafranca de Penedés 08720, Barcelona, Spain
Tel: (34) 3817 7401 Fax: (34) 3817 7444
Visitors: Visitors' center open office hours; includes restaurant

*I*f there is one area of Spain known for innovation, it is Penedés. This reputation is largely the result of one man, the indefatigable Miguel Torres Jnr, now head of Miguel Torres SA.

The Torres company was originally founded in 1870, the capital coming from the proceeds of a successful investment in a Cuban oil company. The Spanish Civil War almost destroyed the business twice—first when the local republican workers' committee confiscated the business, and later when a stray bomb landed on the winery. Legend has it that wine was flowing through the gutters of Vilafranca del Penedés that day.

The bodega was rebuilt and in 1950 Miguel Torres took the brave step of

FACT BOX
WINEMAKER: Miguel Torres
SIZE OF VINEYARD: total 2,570 acres—supplies 50% of needs; Milmanda plot 25 acres
PRODUCTION: 2 million cases, including 2,000 cases of Milmanda
GRAPE VARIETIES: (for Milmanda) Chardonnay, also Parallada, Garnacha, Cariñena, Tempranillo, Cabernet Sauvignon, Pinot Noir, Muscat, Gewürztraminer, Merlot, Sauvignon Blanc
RECOMMENDED VINTAGES: 1997, 1996

stopping the trade of wine in barrel, insisting that all his wines should be sold in bottle, with his brand. This may seem an obvious move today, but was unusual for Spain in the fifties. Perhaps even more important for the long-term health of the company was the decision of Miguel Torres Jnr, younger son of Miguel Torres, to study enology in Dijon in 1959. On his return dramatic changes were instigated. New grape varieties, "foreign" ones like Chardonnay and Sauvignon Blanc, Cabernet and Merlot, began to make an appearance. A laboratory was built, and stainless-steel vats complete with temperature control were installed.

Vineyards of the Milmanda castle by Waltraud Torres, 1987.

Philosophies changed, too. The Spanish traditionally value long aging, often to the detriment of fruit flavors. Torres introduced earlier bottling, and the notion of assessing the wines regularly, and bottling when ready, rather than after a set period. Such actions were unheard of in Spain at the time.

All of this would have remained little known, but for a wine competition in France in 1979. Miguel Torres entered his top red wine, Gran Coronas Black Label 1970, in a line-up that included such greats as Château Latour 1970 and Château La Mission Haut-Brion. Judged by a jury of 60 experts, the Torres wine was a clear winner. The company's reputation was made and since then they have been able to grow consistently without having to advertise. Significantly, a majority of the Michelin-starred restaurants in France stock at least one Torres wine.

MIRANDA WINES

57 Jondaryan Avenue, PO Box 405, Griffith, New South Wales, Australia 2680
Tel: (61) 69 62 4033 Fax: (61) 69 62 6944
Visitors: Cellar-door sales only, daily

*M*iranda Wines was started by Francesco Miranda, a Neapolitan immigrant to Australia, in 1938. His brother had already started a new life in the settlement of Griffith, and Francesco–called "Pop" around the winery–brought his wife, Caterina, out to join him. At that time the Riverland area of New South Wales was just being developed. It is now one of the greatest fruit-producing areas in the country, responsible not only for grapes and wine but also citrus and stone fruit as well as vegetable and cereal production.

"Pop" Miranda had three sons, all of whom are now involved in the company and oversee the production of the wines. The company now has two production sites, one in New South Wales, the other in the Barossa in South Australia. Between them they make some 1½ million cases of wine each year, making them one of the largest family-owned wine producers in the country.

FACT BOX

WINEMAKER: Jim Miranda
SIZE OF VINEYARD: information not available
PRODUCTION: 1.5 million cases
GRAPE VARIETY: Semillon for this wine
RECOMMENDED VINTAGES: 1995, 1993

TASTING NOTES

1993 GOLDEN BOTRYTIS

Deep-orange golden wine with a full honey and beeswax nose. Hints of orange marmalade and a hint of sweet spice make for a complex nose. Sweet with balanced acidity and full weight with quite light alcohol and a long finish.
Rating ★★★★

SUGGESTED FOOD PAIRING
This needs light desserts such as fruit salads or meringues to balance the sweetness without overpowering the wine. Alternatively, the French would drink a wine like this with foie gras.

The Barossa operation, Rovalley Estate, was bought in 1991, having been founded in 1919. This is a premium wine-growing region and Miranda felt the acquisition was necessary if they were to continue to compete in an ever-more quality-conscious marketplace. International recognition has already been forthcoming with the Rovalley Ridge Grey Series having won a number of awards, including a much coveted International Wine & Spirit Competition award.

The Griffith winery is in Riverina, New South Wales. This has long been thought of as a bulk-wine area–responsible for something like one-fifth of Australia's total wine output. Much of this is sold on the domestic market only and includes Australian "port" and "sherry," poor imitations of the Iberian originals. Popular locally, the Miranda range is blessed with dubious names like Cobweb Port and Pop's Crocks. Bag-in-box wine is also an important part of the production here, drunk in large quantities at the ubiquitous "barbies." The region is, however, becoming increasingly well respected for its botrytisized Sémillons, a new style of wine to the region.

Miranda Golden Botrytis is one such. Only five vintages of the wine have so far been released. Sémillon is blended with a small amount of Rhine Riesling, the true Germanic Riesling, to add acidity to the Sémillon, which is naturally a low-acid grape even when grown in cooler areas than this.

Montana Marlborough Winery

Main Road South, State Highway 1, Riverlands, (PO Box
331), Blenheim, New Zealand
Tel: (64) 3 578 2099 Fax: (64) 3 578 0463
*Visitors: Store open Monday–Saturday 9:00AM–5:00PM;
Sunday 11:00AM–4:00PM; tours Monday–Saturday
10:00AM–3:00PM on the hour; Sunday by prior
arrangement only*

*B*y international standards Montana is big. By
the standards of the relatively small New
Zealand wine industry, it is a giant. With vineyards in
Marlborough, Auckland, Gisborne, and Hawkes Bay,
totalling almost 2,500 acres, Montana alone accounts
for 16 percent of the country's vineyard area.

Montana was founded by Ivan Yukich, a market
gardener of Dalmatian origins. Immigrants from
the Slav states were responsible for starting a

FACT BOX

WINEMAKERS: Andy Frost and
Patrick Materman

SIZE OF VINEYARDS: Montana own
almost 2,500 acres, 1,500 of which are
in Marlborough

PRODUCTION: information not
available

GRAPE VARIETIES: Sauvignon Blanc for
this wine. Chardonnay, Riesling,
Semillon, Müller-Thurgau, Pinot Noir,
Cabernet Suavignon are also grown in
Marlborough, with Gewürztraminer and
Muscat grown elsewhere

RECOMMENDED VINTAGES:
drink youngest available

LOCAL RESTAURANTS: Rocco's
Restaurant Blenheim, Château
Marlborough, Peppertree Cottage

number of New Zealand's wine companies. Yukich planted a small plot, just half an acre, in the Waitakere Ranges and named his vineyard Montana, Croatian for "mountain." The first Montana wine was sold in 1952. During the 1960s the company expanded rapidly, planting new vineyards and building a winery at Gisborne. At the time this had the capacity to bottle four times the country's total production, a gesture of confidence in the industry they now dominate.

MONTANA WINES LIMITED
New Zealand's Leading Winemaker

Much of the early production was Müller-Thurgau-based, medium-dry white wine, referred to as Kiwi-milch, so similar was it in style to the German Liebfraumilch. During the seventies and eighties Montana made two decisions which have had far-reaching consequences for the whole of the industry. In 1973 they were the first company to plant vineyards in Marlborough. In 1980 they were the first to plant Sauvignon Blanc in the area. Marlborough is now considered to produce Sauvignon of world-beating quality.

Since then Montana has continued to innovate. Joint ventures with Champagne Deutz to develop their sparkling wine, and Cordier of Bordeaux to improve their red, will ultimately help the whole industry.

The Montana Sauvignon Blanc is made from fruit grown on the Brancroft estate, just outside Blenheim. After crushing, the grapes are allowed a few hours of skin contact so the flavor components, mostly just under the skin, are released into the juice. Cool fermentation in stainless steel follows—no oak here because the winemakers want the fruit to show through. The wine is usually bottled young, within three months of the harvest, and should be drunk within a year or two of the vintage.

TASTING NOTES

MARLBOROUGH SAUVIGNON BLANC 1996

Pale-lemon yellow with a few lazy bubbles at the bottom of the glass. Aromatic gooseberry, elderflower, and green-bell-pepper nose. Just off-dry with crisp cleansing acidity and medium body. Good length.
Rating ★

SUGGESTED FOOD PAIRING
Good as an apéritif and with mildly spicy cuisine such as Thai and Chinese food.

NAUTILUS ESTATE
NEW ZEALAND

Blicks Road, Renwick, Marlborough, New Zealand
Tel: (64) 9 366 1356 Fax: (64) 9 366 1357 (Auckland offices)
Visitors: Daily 10:00AM–5:00PM in summer;
daily 10:30AM–4:30PM in winter

*N*autilus was created in the mid-1980s. Robert Hill-Smith wanted to import a New Zealand wine into Australia and needed a brand. In contrast to the vast, mostly arid continent of Australia, New Zealand is made up of small islands, and nowhere is far from the sea. This thought combined with sea life resulted in the brand, and Barrie Tucker developed the supporting design of pink shellfish, which has become one of the most recognized symbols in New Zealand wine.

The first wine, a Sauvignon Blanc, was the 1985 vintage, exported in 1986. Three years later Chardonnay was added to the range, soon followed by Cabernet Sauvignon/ Merlot and a Pinot Noir/Chardonnay sparkling wine.

FACT BOX

WINEMAKER: Matt Harrop
SIZE OF VINEYARD: 35 acres—supplies 10% of requirements
PRODUCTION: 20,000 cases
GRAPE VARIETIES: Sauvignon Blanc, Chardonnay, Cabernet Sauvignon, Merlot, Pinot Noir/Chardonnay sparkling wine—mostly used unblended
RECOMMENDED VINTAGES: 1997, 1996, 1994, 1991

Only 10 percent of the fruit comes from Nautilus's own 35-acre vineyard at the western end of the Wairau Valley in Marlborough. The bulk is sourced locally from contract growers. It is all machine-harvested, mostly at night when the cool temperatures preserve the freshness of the grapes.

The Chardonnay is fermented in French oak barrels, first, second, and third fill being used. Post-fermentation further aging in oak occurs, but not new wood. This adds complexity and maturity without causing excessive oak flavors.

They treat Sauvignon Blanc differently. Once at the winery, the grapes are crushed and gently pressed. The must is allowed to settle before being inoculated with cultivated yeast strains. The strains chosen are those that emphasize the aromatic properties of the grape, bringing them out more in the glass.

Fermentation for the Sauvignon is long and cold, entirely in stainless steel. The must is chilled to 46–54°F, one of the coolest temperatures possible, to preserve the fresh gooseberry and passion-fruit notes in the wine. At this temperature the fermentation takes up to four weeks to complete. No malolactic fermentation is allowed so the wine retains its fresh natural acidity. The result is a classic New Zealand Sauvignon, squeaky-clean with a pronounced fruity and flavorsome, crisp palate.

TASTING NOTES

MARLBOROUGH SAUVIGNON BLANC 1996

Almost water-white. Medium-intensity perfumed gooseberry fruit. A little grassy with hints of passion fruit (grenadilla). Dry, crisp acidity with moderate fruit. More fruity on the palate than grassy. Good, long, clean finish.

Rating ★★

SUGGESTED FOOD PAIRING
Any shellfish (perhaps the label is influential here); very good with mussels in a light sauce.

Nautilus

MARLBOROUGH
SAUVIGNON BLANC
1 9 9 6
750mL   12.5% Alc/Vol

PENFOLDS WINES LIMITED

78 Penfold Road, Magill, South Australia 5072, Australia
Tel: (61) 301 5569 Fax: (61) 301 5562
Visitors: 10:30AM–4:30PM; tours on the hour

*P*enfold Wines was started by Christopher Rawson Penfold, born in 1811 in Sussex, England. He studied, and practiced medicine in London and Brighton before emigrating to Australia in 1844, setting up home at Magill in the foothills outside Adelaide. They called their cottage "the Grange," a name that has subsequently gone down in history as one of the greats of the wine world.

Dr Penfold was a firm believer in the medicinal properties of wine. As a result he planted a vineyard at the homestead, a vineyard that turned out to be so successful that wine sales soon became the main source of the family income. In doing so he gave birth to one of the four great Australian wine companies.

Until the 1970s the most successful wine styles in Australia were fortified

FACT BOX

WINEMAKER: John Duval

SIZE OF VINEYARD: total for Southcorp–14,820 acres

PRODUCTION: information not available

GRAPE VARIETIES: Chardonnay with 10% Sauvignon Blanc

RECOMMENDED VINTAGE: only 1994 so far available

LOCAL RESTAURANT: Magill Estate Restaurant (five-star rating)

wines, mostly imitations of port and sherry. So much so that the great Penfolds winemaker, the legendary Max Schubert (1915–1994), kept his unfortified wine production a secret from his bosses for many years. What Schubert was working on, at the company winery at the Magill estate, was a red table wine made from Shiraz, modeled on the great wines of Bordeaux that he had tasted when traveling in Europe. This, in the eyes of the management, was a waste of time, and of valuable fruit that could go into the "ports." The wine eventually saw the light of day as Grange Hermitage, now simply called Grange–without doubt the best red wine made south of the equator.

Grange has always been labeled as Bin 94, so when Penfolds decided to bring out a white wine as a partner to Grange they initially called it Bin 94a. The first commercial release, the 1995 vintage, will be called Yattarna; this is an Aboriginal word meaning "little by little".

In true Australian style, the wine does not come from one vineyard. This goes against everything the European legislators believe in, but the quality of wines like this must surely give them food for thought. Cool sites have been selected for Bin 94a. Adelaide Hills, Eden Valley, Tumbarunba, and Macedon were used for the 1994 vintage but there is no guarantee that the same vineyards in the same proportions might be used in any following year. Selection for this wine was made when the wine was in the barrel. All the wine had been barrel-fermented in new and second-fill French oak. Both barriques and the slightly larger hogsheads were

TASTING NOTES

RESERVE BIN 94A CHARDONNAY 1994

Medium-gold wine, the brilliant deep yellow of a warm-climate Chardonnay. Very oaky nose but nutty and spicy oak rather than smoky. Behind the oak there are complex flavors of tropical fruit, pawpaw, and mango with lime and melon too. Some buttery notes from the malolactic fermentation. Dry and very full-flavored. Full-bodied for a white with some tannin from the oak. Great long finish. Good now but it will be interesting to see how this wine develops.
Rating ★★★★

SUGGESTED FOOD PAIRING
Poached salmon with a dill and butter sauce.

The original Grange cottage.

used. After fermentation the wine stayed in contact with the yeast lees for about 10 months before bottling. Nine-tenths went through malolactic fermentation to add complexity to the finished wine. A long bottle-maturation period followed before release in February 1998.

Penfold's modern winery.

PETALUMA LTD

Spring Gully Road Piccadilly, South Australia
PO Box 33a, Crafers SA 5152
Tel: (61) 8 339 4122 Fax: (61) 8 339 5253
Visitors: By appointment only

*I*n every wine-producing country one or two people stand head and shoulders above the rest, leaders who show the way for others to follow. Brian Croser of Petaluma is one such leader. Passionate and highly qualified, Croser is a technocrat. He wants to know everything there is to know about what is going on in the wines, and yet, simultaneously, he is perhaps Australia's most committed "terroirist"–always looking for the perfect vineyard site.

Some wines get their identity from the vineyard, while others are created brands. Petaluma *is* Brian Croser. After studying enology at the University of California, Davis, he returned to Australia to work for Hardy's. In 1978 he teamed up with another great name in modern Australian winemaking, Tony Jordan, to form the wine consulting firm Oenotech. It is claimed that almost every successful winery

FACT BOX

WINEMAKER: Brian Croser
SIZE OF VINEYARD: information not available
PRODUCTION: information not available
GRAPE VARIETIES: Chardonnay, Cabernet Sauvignon, Riesling, Merlot
RECOMMENDED VINTAGES: 1996, 1995, 1994

PETALUMA

1996 CHARDONNAY
PICCADILLY VALLEY

13.5% vol PRODUCE OF AUSTRALIA
BOTTLED AT PICCADILLY SA 750ml

in the country has used their services at some stage. At the same time he set up what was to become Petaluma.

The vineyards are spread over three districts, Clare, Coonawarra, and the Adelaide Hills. The winery is at Piccadilly in the Adelaide Hills. All of these are, by Australian standards, cool, essential for the development of fine flavors and preservation of the natural acidity in the grapes. The Chardonnay was once a blend of Clare and Piccadilly wines; before that Coonawarra and warmer-climate Cowra fruit went into the blend. It is now entirely made from Piccadilly fruit. A wine with fruit and body certainly, but also one with finesse, perfume, and elegance. Grapes from six separate vineyards are used, each adding its own character and structural element.

Petaluma Chardonnay is not necessarily made straight after the vintage like most wines. To give the wine the attention it deserves, they sometimes delay the fermentation for months. The grapes are crushed and pressed when picked but the juice is then chilled to just below 32°F to settle, and then racked into clean refrigerated vats, until Brian is ready.

Fermentation is in new Vosges oak barriques (60-gallon barrels) and for the 1996 vintage, which was colder than average, full malolactic fermentation was encouraged. The wine was matured in oak, on the yeast lees for nine months before bottling.

TASTING NOTES

1996 PICCADILLY VALLEY CHARDONNAY

Medium to deep golden color, very noticeable legs when the glass is swirled. Intense nose of vanilla oak with butter and cream, and a slight smell of cloves. Soft, overripe rocha pears and honeydew melon notes but also a crisper fruit, quince or very green apple. Dry but so ripe it comes across as off-dry, sweet smoky oak flavors with fine balancing acidity. Very full-bodied and concentrated but with an elegance that is so often missing from big, upfront Chardonnays. A wine that can be kept for five years or so, if you can be patient.
Rating ★★★★

SUGGESTED FOOD PAIRING
Fine wines deserve fine foods. Lobster or salmon, or other full-flavored seafood work well with this wine, as would wild duck or other game fowl.

PILTON MANOR VINEYARD

Pilton, Shepton Mallet, Somerset, BA4 4BE, UK
Tel: (44) 1749 890325 Fax: (44) 1749 890262
Visitors: July–September daily 11:00AM–5:00PM;
otherwise by appointment

*P*ilton Manor was one of the first vineyards to be set up during what is called the Modern Revival of English viticulture. Many commentators claim that viticulture came to England with the Romans, although there is little evidence for this. Certainly grape growing and winemaking were long established by the Middle Ages, and by the time of Henry VIII (1491–1547) many vineyards had been established, often by English religious communities who needed wine if only for the sacrament. These fell into disuse after the dissolution of the monasteries and the formation of the Church of England, and viticulture effectively stopped in Britain until the 1950s (the great vine at Hampton Court being an exception).

The vineyards at Pilton Manor were planted in 1966. However, records show a

FACT BOX

WINEMAKER (AND PROPRIETOR):
Jim Dowling

SIZE OF VINEYARD: 10 acres

PRODUCTION: 1,600 cases total

GRAPE VARIETIES: Huxelrebe, Seyval blanc, Baccus, Reichensteiner, Pinot Noir

RECOMMENDED VINTAGES:
1994, 1993, 1990, 1989

LOCAL RESTAURANT: Blostins in Shepton Mallet

vineyard was established here in 1189 by the Abbot of Glastonbury, who had a summer palace at Pilton.

Local legend has it that the child Jesus was brought here by Joseph of Arimathea–as recorded in the rousing hymn "Jerusalem"–so the history of the area goes back a lot further. Christ's first recorded miracle, of course, was turning water into wine. In the view of many it is a miracle that English viticulturalists even *ripen* grapes, let alone turn the result into fine wine. The vineyard is small by world standards, only 10 acres of vines. The soil is a clay marl over limestone and the aspect a southwest-facing falling slope. This gives good exposure to the sun and drains away frost, which can be an enormous problem for English vineyards in the spring. The vines are trained in an open canopy using the French Guyot system to ensure plenty of air circulation, keeping diseases at bay in the damp Somerset climate.

TASTING NOTES

1992 WESTHOLME LATE HARVEST

Deep burnished copper color with strong legs forming on the glass. Intense bouquet of orange peel and honey, with apricots; a perfumed richness. Just beginning to show a little maturity. Sweet, but with the sweetness balanced by a fine acidity and mouth-filling fruit flavors. Honey and Seville orange, almost marmalade characters. Great long, clean finish that is not in the least cloying, despite the sweetness.
Rating ★★★★

SUGGESTED FOOD PAIRING
Light desserts, these should not be too sweet or the wine will seem dry, or cheese soufflé.

A range of grape varieties is grown–grapes like Huxelrebe, Bacchus, and Reichensteiner. Most are crosses developed in Germany specifically to ripen well in cold, damp climates. Pinot Noir is grown for sparkling wine production–Pilton Manor was one of the first to make Traditional Method sparkling wines in Britain–and the ubiquitous hybrid vine, Seyval Blanc, represents one vine in five. This is a particular favorite with English producers although the European Union bureaucrats do not encourage it.

Noble rot is no more reliable in England than it is anywhere else. The Westholme Late Harvest is not produced every vintage. Only when the rot attacks the Huxelrebe is it possible. Hand-picking is vital, as with all noble-rot wines, followed by pressing and a long, slow fermentation. The choice of an aromatic variety and the effect of noble rot give this wine an unusually scented character.

ROBERT MONDAVI WINERY

(Visiting) 7801 St Helena Highway, Oakville CA 94562, USA
(Mailing) PO Box 106, Oakville CA 94562, USA
Tel: (1) 707 259 9463
Visitors: 7 days a week (telephone for times)

*R*obert Mondavi has probably done more to improve the quality and, perhaps more important, the quality *image* of the wines of California than anyone else in the industry. Like the Gallos, Robert's father, an Italian immigrant from the Marche in Eastern Italy, grew grapes in California for shipment "back East" to the home winemakers during prohibition. When prohibition was repealed the family left the hot Central valley to plant grapes in the much cooler Napa valley, where today Mondavi has an enormous investment. This move, away from the bulk production of sweet fortified

FACT BOX

WINEMAKER: Tim Mondavi

SIZE OF VINEYARD: 1,500 acres of Napa owned by RMW but grapes also bought in

PRODUCTION: Oakville 400,000 cases; Coastal 700,000 cases; Woodbridge 5 million cases; Byron 52,000 cases

GRAPE VARIETIES: Chardonnay for this wine, but also Sauvignon Blanc, Sémillon, Pinot Noir, Zinfandel–used as varietals

RECOMMENDED VINTAGES: Chardonnay Reserve 1995, 1994

LOCAL RESTAURANT: own restaurant but also recommended is Mustards in Oakville

The Mondavi winery is one of the most famous
landmarks of the Napa Valley.

wines, so popular at the time, to vineyards that had the potential to produce high-quality light wines was to prove crucial to the future of the company.

After his father's death in 1959, Robert left the family firm to set up on his own. His Hispanic-styled landmark of a winery building, on the St Helena Highway near Oakville, was built in 1966. Since its establishment the Robert Mondavi company has been a trail-blazer for the rest of the California industry. The Mondavi experiments with oak in the 1970s changed California's, and arguably the whole New World's, attitude to oak maturation. The research continues. Yeast strains, high- or low-density cultivation, and natural farming are all currently being studied.

The Robert Mondavi Winery makes wines at many price-points. The basic range consists of sound if unexciting wines–all very well crafted but lacking depth. At the top end, however, the wines can, and do, take on anything the rest of the world can produce. The Reserve range includes some of the finest wines made anywhere.

Testament to the pursuit of quality is in the joint venture with the Rothschilds of Châteaux Mouton Rothschild in Bordeaux. In one of the first such international ventures, Mondavi was able to team up with one of the best red-wine makers in Europe.

Chardonnay for the Reserve Chardonnay is selected from a number of different locations. Each premium vineyard is harvested at the optimum time and each block fermented and aged individually before the selection is made. The cherry-picking from only the best sites and batches is one of the advantages size brings. For the 1994 vintage, 86 percent of the grapes came from the Carneros district in the south of the Napa, the balance from a vineyard at Santa Maria. Both of these areas are cooled by maritime influences, helping the grapes develop rich fruit characters.

After hand-picking, the fruit was whole-bunch-pressed to retain maximum fruitiness, and barrel-fermented in French oak. Malolactic fermentation and long oak maturation, a little over a year in wood, with regular lees-stirring, has added extra structure and complexity to the wine.

TASTING NOTES

1994 NAPA VALLEY CHARDONNAY RESERVE

Brilliant yellow color, medium depth and polished appearance. Initially pungent oak on the nose, rather like walking into a sawmill, but under that there are layers of hot butter and spice, cloves and cinnamon with soft fall fruit: apples and sweet pears. Full rich palate, luscious yet dry. Full-bodied and noticeably alcoholic with good balance of acids. Great length. A real mouthful of a wine. One well worth laying down, though great now.

Rating ★★★★

SUGGESTED FOOD PAIRING

A wine like this demands full-flavored foods. Broiled fish or chicken, especially if served with a cream sauce, or any smoked fish or sausage.

Robert Mondavi.

ROSEMOUNT ESTATES LIMITED

Hunter Valley, New South Wales, Australia
Tel: (61) 2 9902 2100
Visitors: information not available

*B*ob Oatley bought the estate, in the Upper Hunter Valley, in the 1960s, having previously been a very successful coffee and cocoa planter. The estate was purchased to graze cattle and breed horses, but since wine was becoming popular, and there were vineyards in the Lower Hunter, he planted a few vines as well. The first wine was made in 1973, the first commercial vintage being 1975–a surprise show success with the Traminer grape variety.

Seeing the success that Chardonnay was having in California, Bob snapped up Penfold's Chardonnay vineyard at Wybong when it came on the market. Along with the vines was a large and modern winery, just the ammunition needed to take on the big players in the market. Shortly afterwards Rosemount was able to buy the Roxburgh Estate from Denham Estates. It is difficult

FACT BOX
WINEMAKER: Philip Shaw
SIZE OF VINEYARD: more than 2,000 acres total over New South Wales and South Australia
PRODUCTION: information not available
GRAPE VARIETIES: Chardonnay, Cabernet Sauvignon, Merlot, Shiraz, Semillon, Sauvignon Blanc–mostly used unblended in varietals
RECOMMENDED VINTAGES: 1995, 1994

to believe today but in the late 1970s no one wanted to buy Chardonnay. Bob Oakley and Chris Hancock, then general manager, realized that Chardonnay had a future. Rosemount was going to be in a position to steal a march on the competition by building up a reputation for the grape.

With fruit from these two vineyards Rosemount was able, in 1980, to produce its first "Show Reserve." In keeping with its name the wine was a great success on the Australian show circuit, getting gold medals from competitions around the country and the globe.

Philip Shaw.

Show Reserve Chardonnay is not a single-vineyard wine. The wines are selected after each vintage from the best barrels as they mature in the winery, and are blended in just the right proportions to achieve the optimum balance of characters.

For the 1995 vintage the grapes were sourced from Roxburgh and Giant's Creek. Not all the wines were made in the same way. The Giant's Creek fruit was handled more gently, with partial crushing and partial whole-bunch pressing, whereas the Roxburgh fruit received a heavier pressing to maximize depth of flavor. The must was barrel-fermented in half Allier and half American oak barrels, followed by 11 months of barrel maturation. Malolactic fermentation was encouraged.

TASTING NOTES

SHOW RESERVE 1995 CHARDONNAY

Brilliantly clear, polished mid- to deep lemon-yellow with a ripe aroma of peach and apricot fruit, still rather overpowered by oak. The palate is outstanding. Big, full flavors of ripe fruit and good balancing acidity. Oak and lees flavors add complexity and texture.

This wine really needs further aging to be at its best, although most bottles will be drunk very young.

Rating ★★★

SUGGESTED FOOD PAIRING
A wine like this needs a full-flavored food. Asian cooking, if not too spicy, works well, as would grilled chicken or fish.

THE ROYAL TOKAJI WINE COMPANY KFT

Rakoczi 35, H-3909, Mad, Hungary
Tel: (36) 47 348 011 Fax: (36) 47 348 359
Visitors: By appointment only

*F*ew other wines can claim to be the Wine of Kings in the way Tokaji can, so christened by Louis XIV after Tokaji was introduced to the French court in the eighteenth century. Subsequently the Czars of Russia took to the wine, having been introduced to it by the Hapsburgs.

The region lays claim to being the first ever demarcated to control quality, a claim it shares with the port producers. It also claims to be the first area to discover the beneficial form of botrytis, a century or more before the earliest record of it in Germany.

This much-prized wine was made throughout the communist period in Hungary–indeed, production doubled because Hungary's main wine export market, the Soviet superpower, was an easy market to satisfy. All of the wine was made centrally by the state-controlled Tokaji Wine Trust by dis-

FACT BOX

WINEMAKER: Peter Vinding Diers
SIZE OF VINEYARD: 200 acres
PRODUCTION: 25,000 cases
GRAPE VARIETIES: Hársleveü 65%, Furmint 20%, Muscat 15%
RECOMMENDED VINTAGE: 1993

interested winemakers. Occasionally a stunning example would emerge, but generally they were blended down to a homogenized sameness. Quality suffered, taking the wine's reputation with it.

When communism collapsed in 1989, most of the vineyards were still in the hands of individual growers. Each holding was, however, very small; winemaking would still have to be centralized. The former State Wine Trust was broken up into seven winemaking enterprises; one remained state-controlled, six were privatized.

The first of the private firms to be formed was the Royal Tokaji Wine Company. Originally a cooperative of 63 growers backed by foreign investors, it was restructured in 1993 when it was bought by an Anglo-Hungarian consortium including the English wine writer and broadcaster Hugh Johnson as figurehead. Royal Tokaji have been making their wine since the 1990 vintage–previous vintages sold under their label were made by the Tokaji Wine Trust.

Controversially the new company decided to change the winemaking practices that had been used during the communist period, and some believe for centuries before that. Tokaji had been aged in untopped-up barrels, "on ullage" as winemakers call it. This results in the wine oxidizing slowly, because of the cold, dark tunnels in which the barrels are kept. The new wines are made "reductively," that is with as little contact with the air as possible. The result is greater fruitiness in the wine and less of the aged caramel and toffee flavors. Royal Tokaji claim this is the return to the original style, others claim the oxidative style has always been part of what makes Tokaji. The truth is probably somewhere between the two views, but Royal Tokaji have made other improvements, too. The yields have been dramatically reduced, and they have reintroduced the classification of the vineyards, so now variety has returned, and Tokaji is no longer one uniform product. The net result is that Tokaji is beginning to regain the recognition it deserves.

Like all other top-quality sweet wines, Tokaji is made from grapes affected by *Botrytis cinerea* in its noble-rot form, here called Aszú. Aszú berries are made into a paste which is added to a base wine and allowed to referment. The quantity of Aszú berries added to the wine was traditionally measured in *puttonyos*, the higher the better and the sweeter. Aszú wines will always give the *puttonyos* figure: 3 to 6 are possible, although 5 is the highest normally seen.

One new piece of information on the label is the vineyard, and its Cru or growth. Peter Vinding Diers, one of the founders of Royal Tokaji, has found a historic classification of Tokaji vineyards which he has resurrected. The top Royal Tokaji wines, therefore, state the vineyard and Cru, first or second, as well as the *puttonyos* level.

The mold covered cellars where Tokaji matures.

SANFORD WINES

7230 Santa Rosa Road, Buellton, California 93427, USA
Tel: (1) 805 688 3300 Fax: (1) 805 688 7381
*Visitors: Tasting room and picnic facilities open daily from
11:00AM–4:00PM*

*S*anford is a "born-again" winery. It was originally founded in 1971 when Richard Sanford teamed up with Michael Benedict to form the Sanford and Benedict Winery. The wines were very well received–so much so that they had to be sold on an allocation basis only. Despite this the two men found their relationship was under some strain, so in 1980 the partnership was dissolved and Richard Sanford set up another operation some four miles away from the original site. More recently Michael Benedict has sold his vineyard to an English couple, Robert and Janice Atkin; they have contracted Sanford to manage the property.

Richard Sanford, a US navy Vietnam veteran, first became interested in Burgundian grape varieties when studying geography at university in Santa Barbara. Looking for something "real" to do after his naval service he turned his mind to viticulture. After studying the area, he

FACT BOX

WINEMAKER: Bruno d'Alfonso
SIZE OF VINEYARD: 131 acres, but grapes bought in from other growers too
PRODUCTION: 40,800 cases
GRAPE VARIETIES: Chardonnay, Pinot Noir, Sauvignon Blanc
RECOMMENDED VINTAGE: 1995

THE WHITE WINE *directory*

Sanford Winery in Santa Barbara.

became convinced that the relatively cool climate of Santa Ynez, brought about by the east-west river valley with openings to the ocean allowing the cooling fogs in, would be ideal. There is supposed to be a temperature increase of 1°F for every mile one travels inland. Santa Ynez is very close to the sea and the fogs are collected by the coastal hill ranges. Certainly the area has become famous for its cool-climate varietals, Sanford grows Pinot Noir and Chardonnay, originally from Burgundy, as well as Sauvignon Blanc, another northern regional varietal.

It took until 1995 for Richard Sanford to get his own winery. In 1995 a purpose-built winery was established. Although the winery is state of the art, the winemaking that goes on within it is as traditional as one could hope for. The Chardonnay must is fermented in French oak barrels and matured in them for between eight and ten months. Full malolactic fermentation is encouraged.

One of the biggest problems facing any wine firm, but particularly a new one, is getting the wine-buying public to notice your product for the first time. If the wine is good, repeat orders will follow, but the first bottle is difficult to sell. The Sanford solution was to employ a local artist, Sebastian Titus, to paint a series of pictures of local wild flowers. The label design incorporates the pictures, a different flower for each wine, each vintage.

TASTING NOTES
1995
CHARDONNAY

Deep golden color with good extract showing noticeable legs. Pronounced ripe fruit and oak on the nose. Strong vanilla and clove spice from the oak overlaying tropical fruits, papaya and guava notes with butterscotch and even some honey. Dry on the palate but so ripe as to seem almost off-dry. Balanced acidity and full bodied. The high alcohol level is well integrated and balanced by the weight and concentration of the fruit.
Rating ★★★★

SUGGESTED FOOD PAIRING
Wines of this intensity can almost be considered as red wines. Fuller flavors are needed, so charbroiled chicken or barbecued fish are ideal.

SELAKS

Selaks Winery Auckland,
15 Old North Road, Kumeu, Auckland, New Zealand
Tel: (64) 9 412 8609 Fax: (64) 9 412 7524

Selaks Winery Marlborough,
Hammerichs Road, Blenheim, Marlborough, New Zealand
Tel & Fax: (64) 3 570 5252
*Visitors: Monday–Friday 9:00AM–5:00PM,
Saturday 10:00AM–5:00PM, Sunday 11:00AM–4:00PM*

*L*ike many New Zealand wineries, Selaks was founded in 1934 by a Croatian, Marino Selak. Foreseeing the war in Europe, Marino brought his 16-year-old nephew, Mate, to New Zealand in 1938. Marino was an accomplished viticulturalist and winemaker, whereas Mate tended to the vines as well as the other crops in the family market garden. Gradually wine became more important and the company can now process nearly a thousand tons of grapes each vintage. Despite the size, Selaks is still a family concern with Ivan Selak

FACT BOX

WINEMAKER: Darryl Woollen
SIZE OF VINEYARDS: 320 acres Marlborough, 62 acres in Auckland, plus contract vineyards
PRODUCTION: 74,000 cases
GRAPE VARIETIES: Sauvignon Blanc, Chardonnay, Semillon, Riesling, Cabernet Sauvignon—sold as varietals—and Sauvignon–Semillon blends
RECOMMENDED VINTAGES: 1997, 1994, but the wine is best drunk young
LOCAL RESTAURANT: on site, open for lunch and dinner daily at Auckland Kumeu estate

in charge of production and Michael Selak the export director.

Selaks control 320 acres in Marlborough, and a further 62 on the North Island around Auckland in the Poverty Bay and Hawkes Bay regions. The Marlborough vineyards, some three miles outside Blenheim town, are close neighbors of both Cloudy Bay and Hunter's, in the "Grand Cru" area for New Zealand Sauvignon. Most of the grapes are machine-harvested, a sensible option in this flat region, and are then cold-fermented in large stainless-steel vats. Selaks are particularly, and rightly, proud of their investment in the latest high tech-

TASTING NOTES

MARLBOROUGH SAUVIGNON BLANC VINTAGE 1996

Very pale lemon-yellow with a pungent herbal and fruity nose of tropical fruits, passion fruit ("grenadilla") and guava with some grassy-ness. Just off-dry with crisp acidity, medium weight and concentration with a moderate to long finish.
Rating ★★

SUGGESTED FOOD PAIRING
Creamy pasta dishes and many vegetarian dishes.

nology, most of which is imported from Europe. The musts are innoculated with cultivated yeast. A neutral strain has been selected to preserve the natural flavors of the grape, the aim here being to make a reliably fruity wine rather than a particularly complex one.

During fermentation the vats are refrigerated to between 54 and 57°F, again to preserve the fruit flavors. No wood is used for the Sauvignon, either in fermentation or maturation. The resultant wine is straightforward, without any pretensions but with particularly forward tropical fruit notes. The green, herbaceous characters that so often come with Sauvignon are kept in check and the wine has reasonable body and weight. This is not a wine to keep, though. Drink it within a year or two years of purchase.

The Selaks winery with a mountainous backdrop.

SONO MONTENIDOLI

53037 San Gimignano, Siena, Italy
Tel: (39) 577 941 565 Fax: (39) 557 942 037
Visitors: By appointment only

*H*ere, in Chianti country, one white wine stands out among the sea of neutral Gallestro: the Vernaccia di San Gimignano. Once considered one of the greatest wines of Italy, San Gimignano was the first to be granted DOC status, the Italian equivalent of the French AC, in the sixties. The area has rightly been promoted to the top grade within Italian wine law, DOCG.

The Montenidoli (which means the mountain of birds' nests) estate overlooks the medieval town, with vineyards spread over half a dozen sites, all within a fairly small area. The hilliness of the area is shown by the dramatically varying altitudes of the vineyards, from 650 to nearly 1,500 feet.

The origins of the estate are lost in the mists of time. There is evidence that the

FACT BOX

WINEMAKER: Elisabetta Fagiuoli
SIZE OF VINEYARD: total estate is 418 acres, of which 45 acres are under vine
PRODUCTION: 8,000 cases
GRAPE VARIETIES: Vernaccia, but Trebbiano, Malvasia, Sangiovese, Canaiuolo also grown
RECOMMENDED VINTAGES: 1994, 1990, 1989, 1988, 1987
RESTAURANT: the estate has its own restaurant, La Fidanza

estate existed under the present name, and with vineyards, in 1404. Furthermore, the records show that the estate was well established even then. The present owner, Elisabetta Fagiuoli, has been in charge only since 1965, in effect for the whole of the time the wines have been DOC.

Soils are mostly crumbly sand and clay, and the climate beautifully temperate, warm, but not too hot. Rainfall is plentiful, but mostly comes in the spring and fall, so the summers are sunny. Fall rain can, however, cause problems if it arrives too early, before the harvest. The vineyards are cultivated along organic lines—no pesticides nor herb-

icides are used. This means lower yields for the company, but this is offset by higher quality.

Not all the wine is made in the same way. Four separate and quite different Vernaccias are made. Vernaccia Tradizionale is made with extended skin contact, giving a fuller flavor and weight to the wine. Vernaccia Fiore is made only from the free-run juice. Highest in sugars and acidity, this gives a light, soft and well-rounded if delicate wine. Vernaccia di Carato is unusual for an Italian white wine in that it is fermented in oak, one-third new. This is the fullest and richest of all the Vernaccias from Montenidoli. The fourth wine, Connubio, is a blend of Vernaccia with Trebbiano and Malvasia. This golden yellow wine is reputed to be more like the traditional style of Vernaccia, as drunk historically by the Popes.

TASTING NOTES

VERNACCIA DI S. GIMIGNANO 1995

Very pale-golden yellow with a rich, yet delicate nose that needs some thought. No upfront fruit characters here. Red apple flavors with something a little herbal about it, perhaps saffron, but may be basil. Dry with crisp acidity and a fuller palate than the nose implied, beautifully balanced flavors but they need to be searched out. Long, clean finish.
Rating ★★★★

SUGGESTED FOOD PAIRING
Italian whites tend to be lighter in flavor than New World wines, making them ideal with finer and more delicately flavored dishes. By Italian standards, Vernaccia is a fullish wine, so mild cheeses work well, as do pastas in simple herb sauces like a fresh basil pesto.

TALTARNI VINEYARDS

Moonambel, Victoria 3478, Australia
Tel: (61) 54 67 2218 Fax: (61) 54 67 2306
Visitors: Monday–Saturday 10:00AM–5:00PM;
there are picnic facilities available and wine can be
purchased at cellar-door prices.

*V*iticulture in Avoca, central Victoria, was historically very important. Before the great depression, this area was renowned for its premium wines. As the stock market fell, so did the demand for top-quality wines, so the area almost lost its viticulture entirely. In the 1940s the boom in wool prices further reduced the area's vineyards until in the 1960s two new estates were established, Château Remy shortly followed by Taltarni.

About this time John Goelet, proprietor of Clos Du Val in California, was looking out for another vineyard in which to invest. In 1972, after a worldwide search for the ideal site, he found Taltarni–an aboriginal word meaning the rich red soil of the area. The

FACT BOX

WINEMAKER: Dominique Portet
SIZE OF VINEYARD: 285 acres
PRODUCTION: approx. 50,000 cases total
GRAPE VARIETIES: Cabernet Sauvignon, Cabernet Franc, Malbec, Shiraz, Pinot Noir, Pinot Meunier, Sauvignon Blanc, Chardonnay, Riesling, Chenin Blanc; only estate-grown grapes used
RECOMMENDED VINTAGES: 1997, 1995
LOCAL RESTAURANT: recommend nearby vineyard resort of Warrenmang, which has an excellent restaurant that showcases the region's wines

climate here in the foothills of the Victorian Pyrenees is not dissimilar to Bordeaux's, temperate with cool nights that help keep a freshness in the grapes and wines. Goelet employed David Hohnen, an American-trained Australian, to develop the vineyards, and Dominque Portet, brother of his winemaker at Clos Du Val. The Portet brothers are originally from Bordeaux, sons of the Régisseur or manager of the First Growth property, Château Lafite-Rothschild.

TALTARNI
SAUVIGNON BLANC
1996
VICTORIA
*Estate grown
produced and bottled*
750ml
WINE PRODUCE OF AUSTRALIA

Dominique, therefore, had winemaking in his blood, but still a formal wine education was required, and the premier French wine school, Montpellier, was the logical choice. After a subsequent degree in law and business he moved to California, where he worked with his brother at Clos Du Val before taking over winemaking at the estate from the first vintage.

The Goelet-Hohnen-Portet team soon set about a massive expansion scheme. The vineyards increased from 90 acres to over 220, while the winery was expanded to cope with the projected increase in production. All of the grapes planted were of French origin, but perhaps Dominique Portet's influence was most important: of the first seven varieties planted, five are from Bordeaux.

Taltarni works very much on the château system of Bordeaux. All the wines made on the estate are sold under the estate name, and only estate-grown fruit is used. No contract growers here–if it is a Taltarni wine then everything from selecting the original rootstock to bottling the wine was done by the estate team.

TASTING NOTES

1996 SAUVIGNON BLANC

Very pale wine, clearly cool climate or very early harvest. Pronounced, very youthful nose of grass and gooseberries, classic Sauvignon characters, with some of the warmer tropical flavors as well, mango and papaya in particular. Dry but with significant ripeness on the palate and only moderate acidity which leads to an impression of some sweetness. Medium weight and good length.

Rating ★★

SUGGESTED FOOD PAIRING

The aromatic qualities of this wine, coupled with the impression of sweetness make it an ideal partner for mildly spiced Asian cooking.

VIGNOBLES GERMAIN & ASSOCIÉS

Château de Fesles, 49380 Thouarcé, France
Tel: (33) 2 41 68 94 00 Fax: (33) 2 41 68 94 01
Visitors: Daily 10:00AM–6:00PM

*B*onnezeaux is an enclave within the Côteau de Layon Appellation in the Anjou subdistrict of the Loire valley. It is particularly well favored, producing riper, more nobly rotted grapes, and therefore sweeter wine, more reliably than Côteaux du Layon itself, and Quart de Chaume to the northwest.

The most important producer in the area is Bernard Germain, who owns vineyards in a number of parts of the Anjou Appellation. The flagship property is Château de Fesles, an elegant two-story property between Thouarcé and Martigné, south of the city of Angers. This eleventh-century, hilltop property takes its name from the iron-rich mineral waters of the area. Château de Fesles accounts for about a quarter of the entire Bonnezeaux Appellation.

The only grape used for Bonnezeaux is Chenin Blanc, but Bernard Germain grows other vines on the property. Cabernet Sauvignon, Cabernet Franc, Grolleau, and

FACT BOX

WINEMAKER: Bernard Germain
SIZE OF VINEYARD: 200 acres total
PRODUCTION: 10,000 cases of this wine
GRAPE VARIETY: Chenin Blanc
RECOMMENDED VINTAGES:
1996 (highly recommended), 1995, 1990, 1989

The château and winery of Château de Fesles.

Gamay are all grown on the flatter parts of the vineyards. The best plots are reserved for Chenin.

Like Riesling, Chenin Blanc has an affinity for noble rot if it is ripe enough and if the vintage conditions are correct. The proximity of the Layon river ensures the humidity needed, encouraging the fungus to grow. As with all fine sweet wines, the harvest has to be done by hand, and Château de Fesles will go through the vineyard up to seven times, harvesting only the ripest and most rotten berries each time. The concentrated must pressed from these shriveled berries is fermented in 105-gallon casks. About a third of these are replaced each year, but the new oak is hardly detectable on the wine, showing itself only as a spicy complexity, rather than a dominant vanilla character.

Because Chenin Blanc has such high acidity, and since the flavors have been

> ## TASTING NOTES
>
> ### CHÂTEAU DE FESLES BONNEZEAUX 1996
>
> Very pale green-gold color. Pungent lanolin and honey character, still undeveloped, very youthful. Medium-sweet rather than fully sweet because of the excellent balance of acidity and fruit. Crisp clean palate, not in the least cloying. The alcohol level is, at 13%, quite high for a Loire wine, giving a full body with a long, lingering finish.
> Rating ★★★★★
>
> #### SUGGESTED FOOD PAIRING
> Desserts that are not too sweet would be needed here. Something including fresh fruit perhaps. Alternatively, this wine is excellent with soft blue cheeses like Roquefort.

concentrated by the botrytis, these wines have a remarkable ability to age. A good vintage of Bonnezeaux will reach its peak at about 10 years old, but will continue to improve from a further decade or so before reaching a plateau of quality.

VILLIERA WINE ESTATE

PO Box 66, Koelenhof 7605, South Africa
Tel: (27) 21 8822002 Fax: (27) 21 8822314
*Visitors: Monday–Friday 8:30AM–5:00PM;
Saturday 8:30AM–1:00PM*

*T*he Villiera Estate is very much a family affair, and has been since the present incumbents, the Grier family, took over in 1983. Simon Grier is the viticulturist. He maintains high-density planting in the vineyard and low yields, so each vine is giving of its best. Immaculate training and trimming ensure the breezes that the Paarl region enjoys are able to penetrate the vines, keeping the humidity down and so avoiding rot problems. Sauvignon Blanc has about 37 acres here, or a little over 10 percent of the estate's total.

Winemaking is in the hands of Jeff Grier, Simon's cousin. Chosen as Wineman of the Year for 1995 by the respected South African wine writer and critic, John Platter, he trained at Stellenbosch, the world-renowned viticulture and enology college in the Cape. Jeff was the first winemaker

FACT BOX

WINEMAKER: Jeff Grier
SIZE OF VINEYARD: 740 acres
PRODUCTION: 80,000 cases
GRAPE VARIETIES: Chenin Blanc, Sauvignon Blanc, Chardonnay, Gewürztraminer, Muscat, Riesling, Cabernet Sauvignon, Merlot, Pinot Noir, Pinotage, Shiraz, Gamay, Carignan—mostly used in varietal wines
RECOMMENDED VINTAGE: 1997

Villiera winery surrounded by the vineyards.

to pass the gruelling Cape Wine Master examination, the South African equivalent of the London-based Master of Wine examination. Cathy Grier, Jeff's sister, passed the examination eight years later in 1995, making them the only brother-and-sister pair of Cape Wine Masters. Cathy handles exports and marketing for the estate, so it is very much a family affair.

Villiera Estate Sauvignon Blanc has consistently done well in South African wine competitions, and since 1990 has never been out of the country's top 10. The vines grow in poor soils, giving low yields, and are picked when the flavors have developed to the required degree, which here means some of the tropical fruit characters in addition to the simple herbaceousness of barely ripe fruit. Winemaking is standard for modern-style Sauvignon. Crushed and destalked fruit is given a period of cold skin contact and then fermented in a totally reductive environment, cool with full protection from oxygen in order to emphasize the fruit flavors, followed by bottling as early as possible. A very small amount of sweetness is left in the wine, so small that it is hardly noticeable. And certainly the wine is technically dry, but, just as a little salt brings out the flavors of savory dishes, this helps to bring out the fruit flavors in the wine.

TASTING NOTES

1997 SAUVIGNON BLANC

Very pale, almost water-white rim with a medium-intensity ripe Sauvignon nose. Note the green, grassy characters but fuller, fruitier hints of grapefruit, guava, and passion fruit. Just slightly off-dry with refreshing acidity and medium weight. The touch of sweetness emphasizes the tropical fruit flavors. Reasonably full flavor and mid-weight on the palate with a medium to long finish. Drinking very well now, but this is not a style of wine that benefits from cellarage, so drink the current vintage.
Rating ★★

SUGGESTED FOOD PAIRING
Fullish-flavored seafood, mussels, and other small shellfish go very well.

VIÑA CONCHA Y TORO SA

Fernando Lazcano 1220, San Miguel, Santiago, Chile
Tel: (56) 2 853 0035 Fax: (56) 2 853 0024
Visitors: Daily guided tour of wineries 10:00AM–5:00PM

Concha y Toro was started in 1883 by Don Melchor de Concha y Toro, initially in the Maipo valley just south of Santiago. He and his wife, Doña Emiliana Subercaseux, were unusual at the time in that they employed a French enologist, rather than rely on local skills. Monsieur Labouchère brought the requisite vines with him from France, and Concha y Toro specializes in still mostly French, and in particular Bordeaux, varieties.

The Maipo has a Mediterranean climate not only good for black grapes but extremely comfortable to live in. Almost inevitably, then, the family were attracted to the area and built the first Concha y Toro estate house, a grand manor house, Casona de Pirque. Classically Chilean and set in an impressive park,

FACT BOX

WINEMAKER: information not available

SIZE OF VINEYARDS: 7,400 acres over 13 different vineyards. Also, contract growers supply some grapes

PRODUCTION: information not available

GRAPE VARIETIES: Chardonnay for this wine, but also Cabernet Sauvignon, Sauvignon Blanc, Syrah, Malbec, Merlot, Riesling, Gewürztraminer–mostly used in varietal wines

RECOMMENDED VINTAGE: 1996

landscaped by the Frenchman Gustave Renner, the house is surrounded by colonnaded verandas, perfect for sitting out on during a quiet afternoon or in the early evening.

Clearly not too much sitting and watching the world go by was done, however, as the reputation and profitability of the estate grew rapidly, and by the time the company was 40 years old it was listed on the Chilean stock exchange. The extra capital that this generated enabled the company to evolve much faster and expand its vineyard holdings into other regions in Chile. The company now owns 13 separate vineyards covering a total of some 7,400 acres, as well as buying in additional grapes from a host of contract growers.

The wineries have not been ignored either. Massive investments mean that Concha y Toro have some of the best, state-of-the-art winemaking facilities. All the latest in stainless-steel equipment is, however, of no use whatsoever if the grapes are not up to standard, so the greater part of the effort is expanded in the vineyard. To this end careful control of the vine canopy is employed to aid ripening, and all the grapes are hand-harvested and then selected by trained workers as they are moved along a conveyor belt. Fermentation for most wines is now in stainless steel with full temperature control.

Although the fashion appears to be for heavily oaked Chardonnays, the Concha y Toro "Sunrise" Chardonnay is unoaked, making a refreshing change from the norm. It is blended from a number of the Concha y Toro vineyards and can therefore only carry the designation of Valle Central, rather than a specific vineyard site.

TASTING NOTES

1997 VALLE CENTRAL CHARDONNAY

Pale-lemon yellow. Very fresh youthful aroma of fruit and even slightly floral. Ripe soft fruit, with a hint of citrus as well. Some butteriness there, too, which implies a degree of malolactic fermentation. Dry with crisp acidity and medium body. Quite high in alcohol but with enough weight to balance it. Medium length.

Rating ★★

SUGGESTED FOOD PAIRING
Not an overtly powerful wine so nothing too strong. Simple fish dishes work very well.

VIÑA ECHEVERRÍA

Av. Américo Vespucio Norte 568, Dpt 701, Las Condes,
Santiago, Chile
Tel: (56) 2 207 43 27 Fax: (56) 2 207 43 28
Visitors: By appointment only

*V*iña Echeverría is a family-owned Chilean wine estate that for most of the twentieth century has been growing grapes for sale to other winemakers and exporters. As recently as 1992 they changed philosophy to become producers as well, making fine wines, bottled on the estate for sale under the Viña Echeverría label.

The estate is in the Curicó district, part of the Maulé region of Chile's Central Valley. Here, 125 miles south of Santiago, the Pacific Ocean currents from Antarctica exert their greatest influence, giving a very cool climate, ideal for the successful production of fine white wine. The soils are loam and clay, of low fertility, and well drained.

The grapes grown on the estate have been propagated from pre-phylloxera vine stock. The vineyard is in one large block, not spread out over a number of plots in different sites as often happens.

FACT BOX

WINEMAKER: Roberto Echeverría
SIZE OF VINEYARD: 173 acres
PRODUCTION: 90,000 cases
GRAPE VARIETIES: Cabernet Sauvignon, Sauvignon Blanc, Chardonnay, Merlot–used in varietals
RECOMMENDED VINTAGE: 1996

This slightly restricts the variety of microclimates available, but has the advantage that all the vines are to hand, so treatments can be given easily at the relevant time. Sprays against rot are most effective if timed according to the weather. If humid conditions persist, rot will form. Having all the vines in one plot means they can all be sprayed at once.

Harvesting is entirely by hand, the fruit being carefully loaded into plastic boxes holding only 30 pounds so as to limit the weight on each bunch. This way the fruit arrives in the winery intact, without the threat of prefermentation or oxidation of the juice. Large grape bins and mechanical harvesting damage the grapes. Harvest here, being south of the equator, is in March and April, the white grapes coming in first.

The winery is conveniently located in the middle of the 173 acres of vines, close so the grapes do not have too long to travel in the heat of a harvest day. As one might expect of a newly established winery, the equipment is state-of-the-art, gleaming stainless steel. Gentle pneumatic presses are installed, along with temperature-controlled stainless-steel tanks. Oak, when used here, is new or second-fill.

Sauvignon grapes are crushed and destemmed on their arrival at the winery, and the pulp given eight hours in contact with the skins at a low temperature to take on the aromatic qualities of the variety. Must clarification is static rather than by centrifuge or filtration. This takes between 24 and 48 hours, but the slowness of the process means no flavors are stripped away. Fermentation takes two weeks at a temperature of about 59°F, cool enough to preserve all the aromatic qualities of the fruit. No oak is used for this wine.

TASTING NOTES

1996 RESERVA CHARDONNAY

Pale youthful lemon yellow. Vanilla nose from the oak backed up with delicate fruit flavors. Lemons and limes with some sweet melon characters as well and a hint of butter. Dry with moderate acidity and medium to full weight. Good balance of flavors and structure with a reasonably long finish.
Rating ★★

SUGGESTED FOOD PAIRING
Chicken or fish dishes with some herb or spice characters to match the vanilla spice on the wine.

VIÑA ERRÁZURIZ

Avenida Nueva Tajamar 481, Torre Sur, Of. 503,
Santiago, Chile
Tel: (56) 2 203 66 88 Fax: (56) 2 203 66 90
No visitors

*E*rrázuriz was founded in 1870 by Dan Maximiano Errázuriz, a Chilean whose family came from the Basque country in northern Spain. The first vineyards were established in the Aconcagua Valley, at the northern end of Chile's vineyard area. Realizing the potential given by good soil, with plentiful water from the Andes and the cooling effects of both altitude and the Pacific, he spared no expense in getting the best vine stock available at the time. Vine clones were imported from France, and Maximiano even employed a French enologist to establish the ideal winery.

Five generations later the company is still entirely in family hands. Eduardo Chadwick is the current president of the firm. A direct descendant of Maximiano Errázuriz, he is anxious to maintain the tradition of the firm of emphasizing the regionality of the wines. Top Errázuriz

FACT BOX
WINEMAKER: Ed Flaherty
SIZE OF VINEYARDS: almost 900 acres total, 190 in Casablanca
PRODUCTION: 352,000 cases
GRAPE VARIETIES: Chardonnay, Sauvignon Blanc, Cabernet Sauvignon, Merlot, Syrah
RECOMMENDED VINTAGES: 1997, 1995, 1993

wines generally boast of their origins, rather than just being labeled as Chilean.

The company still has a vineyard in Aconcagua, now named in honor of the company's founder, but it also has estates in Casablanca and Curicó, and a second vineyard in Aconcagua. The Aconcagua vineyards are ideal for red wines–Cabernet Sauvignon and Merlot ripen well here–whereas Chardonnay does better in the cool climate of Casablanca.

Here, as in the Napa valley in California, morning fogs come off the Pacific Ocean. These and the afternoon breezes keep the temperatures down, which leads to a long ripening season, enabling fine flavors to develop. Errázuriz's estate here is called La Escultura. The soils are well drained and alluvial, quite rich for vineyards. Both Sauvignon Blanc and Chardonnay are grown here.

All the harvesting is done by hand and the grapes are whole- cluster-pressed. Ninety percent of the must for Reserve Chardonnay is barrel-fermented, a percentage of it with natural yeast. The Estate Chardonnay featured here is only partially barrel-fermented, about 15 percent. A quarter of the wood is new each vintage. Post-fermentation, the wine is left in cask for a couple of months before bottling. This careful, perhaps even cautious, use of French oak is ideal for this style of wine. The fruit is now exceptionally full-flavored and could easily be overpowered by oak if it was overdone.

TASTING NOTES

1997 LA ESCULTURA ESTATE CHARDONNAY

Very pale-lemon yellow. Light fresh nose of citrus and cream with just a hint of ginger-like spiciness and a hint of wood smoke. Oak very well integrated and not in the least dominating. Dry with soft balanced acidity and medium weight. Broad flavor profile on the palate, more intense than on the nose. Lingering finish.
Rating ★★★

SUGGESTED FOOD PAIRING
Not a heavyweight, so this is an ideal partner for moderately flavored foods such as scallops, steamed white fish, and simply cooked white meats.

Viñas del Vero sa

Carretera Naval Km 3.7, Barbastro, Huesca, Spain
Tel: (34) 74 302216 Fax: (34) 74 302098
Visitors: By appointment only

*D*riving from Rioja and Navarra one crosses seemingly endless miles of pampas-like scenery. Finally, one reaches the next range of hills, and on the other side the world has changed. Unlike the rest of northern Spain, this looks like a wine-growing area. This is Somontano.

Just as Peimonte means foothills in Italian, so Somontano means the same in Spanish, in this case the foothills of the Pyrenees. Here the climate is cooler, although temperatures in the summer can reach the mid-80s, and for Spain, relatively wet, the average rainfall being about 24 inches. Since the late 1980s, a handful of new vineyards and wineries have been established here, with the assistance of the local Aragon government. One such is Viñas del Vero.

FACT BOX

WINEMAKER: Pedro Aibar

SIZE OF VINEYARD: 1,359 acres in total, 200 acres of Chardonnay

PRODUCTION: 300,000 cases total

GRAPE VARIETIES: Chardonnay, Cabernet, Merlot, Moristel, Tempranillo, Syrah, Garnacha, Pinot Noir, Gewürztraminer, Chenin Blanc, Riesling, Macabeo—used in varietals

RECOMMENDED VINTAGES: 1996, 1995, 1994, 1993

LOCAL RESTAURANT: Flor Restaurant in nearby Barbastro

Viñas del Vero grow both local and international varieties, but it is the latter for which they are famed. Planted on well-draining chalky-clay soil, the vineyards are among the most modern in the world. None of the ubiquitous old bush training here: all the vines are trained along wires for ease of mechanization. Unusually for Europe, the vineyards here can be irrigated– normally banned in the European Union for fear of overproduction adding to the infamous wine lake. Irrigation is carefully used: only when the vines are stressed does the pump start, all controlled by humidity sensors within the vines monitored by computer. Fertilizers are applied by the same pipework, again after instructions from electronic sensors. Viticulture for the techno-freak.

TASTING NOTES

1996
CHARDONNAY

Medium lemon-yellow, with a pungent toasty and oaky nose overlying a pure lemon and butter fruit character. Dry, moderate to high alcohol, with oak and butter dominant. Medium weight and finish.

Rating ★★★

SUGGESTED FOOD PAIRING
Any fish or simply cooked chicken dish.

The winery, too, is state-of-the-art. A wide variety of wine-making techniques are employed, different temperatures for different grape varieties to get the optimum balance, use of oak, or not, depending on the variety, and even differently shaped fermenting vats for the Pinot Noir–a notoriously difficult grape to work with.

Some of the estate's own Chardonnay goes through full-barrel fermentation and maturation. The fruit is both hand- and machine-picked–the latter at night when the ambient temperatures are lower– gently pressed in modern tank presses and fermented in new Allier barrels. After fermentation, the wine

Brand new stainless steel shows the commitment to thoroughly modern winemaking.

is left in contact with the lees for a number of months, with monthly "battonage" to integrate the flavors. The result is a "New World" style Chardonnay from Spain.

VIÑA UNDURRAGA SA

Lota # 2305, Providencia, Santiago, Chile
Tel: (56) 2 232 6687 Fax: (56) 2 234 1676
*Visitors: Santa Ana winery tours Monday–Friday
9:30AM–1:00PM and 2:00PM–4:30PM*

Viña Undurraga was founded by Don Francisco Undurraga Vicuña in 1885. A well-traveled man, Don Francisco had visited Europe on a number of occasions, including studying there. He brought back cuttings of Riesling vines from Germany and Pinot Noir, Cabernet Sauvignon, and Sauvignon Blanc from France to plant in his new vineyard. These cuttings were taken before phylloxera devastated the European vineyards, and, since Chile is phylloxera-free, they represent some of the few remaining pre-phylloxera vine clones anywhere in the world. A French enologist called Pressac supervised the planting while cooperage was supervised by a Monsieur Perranau,

FACT BOX

WINEMAKER: Hernán Amenabar Correa

SIZE OF VINEYARD: 2,000 acres. In addition 30% of grapes for red wine and 20% for white are bought in

PRODUCTION: 12 million cases total

GRAPE VARIETIES: Cabernet Sauvignon, Merlot, Pinot Noir, Sauvignon Blanc, Chardonnay, Riesling Sémillon, Gewürztraminer

RECOMMENDED VINTAGES: Gewürztraminer 1997, Chardonnay Reserva 1996

The winery and visitors center at Undurraga.

who worked with Kentucky and Bosnian oak.

Undurraga claims to be the first company to export bottled wine from Chile. The order went to the United States in 1903.

Undurraga, still a family concern, now own some 2,000 acres of vineyard. The first estate, Santa Ana, has 350 acres of vines; the Codigua Estate comprises some 620 acres; both are situated in the heart of the Maipo region. The climate here is Mediterranean, with mild winters and warm summers, but cool nights which help retain freshness in the grapes. The Codigua Estate is close to the Pacific Ocean and the cooling effect of the Humboldt current makes it ideal for the white varieties, Chardonnay and Sauvignon Blanc.

Most grapes are picked by hand, despite most of the vineyards being fairly flat. Undurraga has two wineries. The larger of the two is at Talagante, where the Chardonnay is vinified. Chardonnay is whole-bunch pressed in pneumatic presses. This means the must is cleaner to start with, with less solid matter in it, making clarification easier. Fermentation for the reserva featured here is in French oak barriques of 60 gallons at 61–64°F. Subsequent aging lasts some four months in the same barrels. After bottling the wines are given a short resting period before shipment.

TASTING NOTES

1995 RESERVA SANTA ANA CHARDONNAY– VALE DEL MAIPO

Medium-lemon gold in color with some green hints. Vanilla and nuts initially on the nose from the French oak, along with cream and butter and some citrus fruit, and lemon peel. Dry with medium acidity and medium weight. Quite youthful still after three years. Alcohol nicely balanced and there's a clean finish.
Rating ★★★

SUGGESTED FOOD PAIRING
Not a blockbuster, so foods should not be too assertive. Try smoked salmon and other moderately flavored fish dishes, and broiled or fried chicken, but not with too strong a sauce. The moderate acid of this wine makes it good on its own as an apéritif.

WEINGUT DR LOOSEN

St Johanneshof, D-54470 Berkastler-Kues, Mosel, Germany
Tel: (49) 6531 3426 Fax: (49) 6531 4248
Visitors: By appointment only

*T*op wine producers throughout the world often seem almost eccentric when talking about their wines. So passionate are they about their product, they become animated in the fashion of the comedy professor. Others are calm and collected, giving an air of total control. One such is Ernie Loosen, proprietor of Weingut Dr Loosen in the Mosel, yet his methods could easily be classed as eccentric.

Ernie Loosen seems to break every rule in the business textbooks in his desire to make fine wine. Tiny and almost inaccessible vineyards, ungrafted vines and organic viticulture, low yields and small volumes. The results, though, are among the finest Rieslings, and therefore finest wines in the world.

The Dr Loosen estate is made up of a series of small vineyards in the middle of Mosel, all within about 12 miles of Bernkastel. Some of the vineyards were Ernie's father's, formerly sold under the St Johannishof label.

FACT BOX

WINEMAKER: Bernard Schug
SIZE OF VINEYARD: 28 acres
PRODUCTION: 6,400 cases total
GRAPE VARIETY: Riesling
RECOMMENDED VINTAGES:
1996, 1995, 1994, 1993, 1990
LOCAL RESTAURANT/HOTEL:
Hotelmoselchild, Urzig

Others belonged to his mother, sold under the Bergweiler-Prum name. The Dr Loosen label started in the late 1980s when

Ernie inherited the estates.

They had been making a loss for Ernie's father, who worked them on a part-time basis. When Ernie took over the advice he was given was that he would have to spend a fortune replanting the vineyard if he was ever going to get decent yields.

Dr Loosen's tasting room.

The vineyard had been neglected: vines were up to a 100 years old and all on their own roots, a recipe for poor profits by any normal measure. Ernie had other ideas. Low yields would give better wine, and the customer would be prepared to pay premium prices once the quality of the wine became known.

Initially Ernie Loosen ran into problems with his staff. Used to the old ways, they were unwilling to change to the new philosophy. Grapes had been harvested all at once—now they were to make a number of differ-ent selections for different wines. Wines had been

Erdener Treppchen vineyards in the Mosel.

fined regularly and filtered three times before bottling, but that was to end, so the wines get only the lightest treatment before bottling. Many of the staff walked out in the early days, to be replaced by people without their preconceived notions. The cellarmaster, Bernhard Schug, for example, came from an agricultural background that had specialized in livestock rather than grapes.

The five Mosel vineyards are Ürziger Würzgarten (the spice garden), Graacher Himmelreich (the heaven vineyard), Wehlener

Sonnenuhr (the vineyard with the town sundial in it), Erdener Treppchen, and Erdener Prälat. Most top Mosel vineyards, like Himmelreich and Sonnenuhr, have slate soil which collects the heat, reflecting it back onto the vines. Prälat and Würzgarten have some weathered sandstone which gives the wines an

extra layer of minerally, earthy flavor.

Ernie Loosen has reintroduced the concept of vineyard classification, which fell out of use with the 1971 wine law. Graacher Himmelreich had always been considered a Premier Cru vineyard, while all of the other Loosen vineyards are on Grand Cru sites. Not surprising, then, that all but a handful of vines are Riesling.

The training used is unusual. Instead of long canes being left, tied to wires or posts, the Loosen vineyards use vertical "cordons," where the main trunk carries a series of short spurs which bear the fruit. This means the grapes grow from the basal buds, which are not as productive as those further along a cane, but labor costs are kept down since no trellis work is needed.

The more basic qualities of wine are fermented in stainless steel but the higher Prädikat grades are fermented in old wooded "Füder" casks, 30 years old and with a capacity of around 260 gallons, so they do not add oak flavors to the wine.

TASTING NOTES

1996 ÜRZIGER WÜRZGARTEN RIESLING AUSLESE

Very pale gold, a typical cool climate color. Attractive, if extremely youthful nose. Mineral and floral notes with a hint of honey, and a very slight earthy quality that could almost be spice—but perhaps that is just power of association; Würzgarten means spice garden. Medium sweet with a firm backbone of acid giving a very finely structured palate and enormous length. This wine is delicious now, but will yield so much more if given a few years of bottle age.

Rating ★★★★★

SUGGESTED FOOD PAIRING

The best accompaniment for wines of this sort is good conversation—they are the perfect vinous drink. The structure, though, means it will complement not too sweet desserts: fresh fruit salad, without too much citrus, would be ideal.

WEINGUT EMMERICH KNOLL

A-3601, Unterloiben 10, Austria
Tel: (43) 2732 79355 Fax: (43) 2732 79355
Visitors: By appointment only

*T*he Wachau valley is narrow and steep-sided, formed over centuries by the Danube. Terraced vineyards overlook the river, benefiting from its reflected sunlight like the finest estates in the Mosel valley in Germany. Like that of the Mosel, the climate here is cool, but with longer and generally more reliable falls. The low temperatures do, however, require long ripening seasons, and grapes here are harvested as late as November.

At the eastern end of the region, on the north bank of the river just as it takes a dramatic turn, lies the small but very scenic village of Unterloiben, home to the Knoll family for over 200 years. Emmerich Knoll is an unassuming man who finds the praise heaped on him by wine critics almost unbelievable, yet his Rieslings and Grüner Veltliners are among the finest in the world.

The Knoll estate, a mere 28 acres, is mostly given over to these two varieties, with about

FACT BOX

WINEMAKER: Emmerich Knoll
SIZE OF VINEYARD: 28 acres
PRODUCTION: 5,000 cases
GRAPE VARIETIES: Grüner Veltliner, Riesling, Feinburgunder, Muskateller
RECOMMENDED VINTAGE: 1995
LOCAL RESTAURANT: Loibnerhof in Unterloiben (the owner is Emmerich Knoll's cousin)

WEINGUT KNOLL
A-3601 UNTER-LOIBEN · WACHAU

one-tenth devoted to Feinburgunder (Chardonnay), Muskateller, and Traminer between them. Four principal vineyards make up the estate: Loibenberg, Schütt, Pfaffenberg, and Kellerberg. Each wine carries the vineyard designation. The soils here are basically gneiss and sandy loess, offering good drainage which keeps the surface dry, and therefore warmer than it might have been. In cooler areas these details make the difference between making good wine and making none at all.

The grapes are not all harvested together. Emmerich Knoll is a great believer in fully ripe grapes and in this climate the whole vineyard will not be ripe at once. Moreover, not all the bunches on one vine will ripen totally evenly, so the harvest is done selectively, with the pickers passing through the vines on a number of occasions choosing the ripest bunches. This is standard practice with sweet wines throughout the world, but is an unusually perfectionist method for dry wines.

Fermentation is carried out in either stainless-steel or large (265–1,190-gallon) old wood barrels. Temperatures are controlled but are not taken to less than 68°F, relatively high. After racking into clean barrels the young wine is allowed to mature in barrel for a considerable time before bottling. Old and large wood is used, adding maturity, not oak flavor. They will be bottled only when Emmerich Knoll feels they are ready—the exact time depends on the wine and the vintage.

TASTING NOTES

LOIBNER GRÜNER VELTLINER 1990

Deepish golden hue with a mature nose of fruit with some honeyed richness to it and a hint of sweet flowers. No oak but the maturity gives the impression that there might be, a smell reminiscent of the very finest mature white Burgundies. Dry, but again the ripeness disguises this, with firm acidity and a full, silky palate feel. Great length.
Rating ★★★★★

SUGGESTED FOOD PAIRING
A wine like this is a fantastic experience on its own, but if matched with food it must be haute cuisine—fine flavors deserve not to be abused. Salmon in a butter sauce and scallops are perfect partners.

WEINGUT FRIEDRICH WILHELM GYMNASIUM

Weberbach 75, 54290 Trier, Mosel, Germany
Tel: (49) 651 97 83 00 Fax: (49) 651 4 54 80
Visitors: Monday–Friday 9:00AM–12:30PM and 1:00PM–5:45PM;
Saturday (April–December) 9:00AM–1:30PM;
tours by appointment only

*T*he Weingut Friedrich Wilhelm Gymnasium has been operating since 1561 when it was founded to supply a source of income for a Jesuit school in Trier. "Gymnasium" here means school or college, a place where students' *minds* are enlightened, so it's not just somewhere to exercise their bodies. Over the centuries the Gymnasium has educated many famous poets, politicians, and philosophers, as well as leaders of industry, their courses partly funded by the vineyards.

Vines have been donated over many years by patrons of the church, parents of students, and grateful graduates. Most are on the gray slate for which the Mosel is famed–hard dark rock that collects the heat of the sun, reflecting it back onto the vines, helping the ripening. This far north every little bit of heat helps.

Friedrich Wilhelm Gymnasium owns parts of some of the most spectacular vineyards in the

FACT BOX

WINEMAKER: Günter Welter
SIZE OF VINEYARD: 70 acres
PRODUCTION: approx. 20,000 cases
GRAPE VARIETIES: Riesling 80%;
Rivaner (Müller-Thurgau), Kerner
RECOMMENDED VINTAGES:
1996, 1995, 1993, 1990, 1989, 1983

Mosel. The wine featured here comes from an almost vertical west–southwest-facing vineyard just opposite Trittenheim, so steep that on a map the contour lines almost merge with each other. It is not surprising, therefore, to find that four out of five vines are Riesling. The rest is Müller-Thurgau–vinified here to dryness and sold under its alternative name of Rivaner–and Kerner. The Rieslings come in all styles from bone-dry to fully sweet, depending on the vintage conditions.

German winemakers put a premium on grape ripeness, a result of being so far north and having such a cool climate. In an average year Friedrich Wilhelm Gymnasium, like all German growers, will have grapes ripe enough to make QbA wines. If the weather is kind, the grapes will be riper, or can be left on the vine to become riper, and QmP wines–Kabinett, Spätlese, Auslese, Beerenauslese, or even Trockenbeerenauslese–will result. Each grade of wine is made from riper grapes than the previous one, the last being made from shriveled, nobly rotten berries.

Most, but not all, of the grapes are grown on steep hills where machine picking is impossible. Fermentation for the better wines is in oak, but, as befits an aromatic variety, this is old wood. Füder barrels up to 50 years old are used. Bottling is early, to preserve the aromatic fruit flavors.

The sign of great German wine is the perfect intensity and balance of the fruit, along with an amazing ability to age gracefully. At 23 years old as I write, the top 1976s are

Trier / Mosel

Mosel - Saar - Ruwer
1995
Graacher Himmelreich
Riesling Kabinett

Produce of Germany · Qualitätswein mit Prädikat · A.P.Nr. 35610241496 · alc.8% vol.
GUTSABFÜLLUNG FRIEDRICH-WILHELM-GYMNASIUM · D-54290 TRIER   750 ml

drinking beautifully now. Generally, the basic QbAs are ready when they are still young; the higher grades benefit from more time. The wines from Friedrich Wilhelm Gymnasium are set apart from many by the fact that even the lesser wines survive some bottle age. Their simple and remarkably inexpensive Graacher Himmelreich Riesling QbA 1990 still, in 1998, tasted youthful, without any hint of the seven years' bottle age it has had.

The Trocken (dry) and Halbtrocken (literally medium-dry but really off-dry) are perhaps the least successful wines from this company. The austere acidity of Riesling from as cool an area as the Mosel needs the hint of sweetness that the sweeter styles have. If you are looking to buy Trocken wines, seek out Pfalz or Baden examples.

TASTING NOTES

TRITTENHEIMER APOTHEKE RIESLING SPÄTLESE 1995

Very pale gold in color with a very youthful, pronounced, fine floral nose. Quite closed at first, taking some time to fully release into the glass and come to the fore. Medium-sweet but seemingly drier than it really is because of the racy Riesling acidity that forms a strong backbone to the wine. This is only 8% alcohol but the intense flavor on the palate and perfect balance mean that the lack of alcohol is hardly noticeable. Keep for another five to ten years to allow the best of the flavors to develop.

Rating ★★★★★

SUGGESTED FOOD PAIRING
Delicately spiced dishes, such as Vietnamese cuisine, work well with a wine of this style.

WEINGUT GEORG BREUER

Geisenheimerstrasse 9, 65385 Rüdesheim, Germany
Tel: (49) 6722 1027 Fax: (49) 6722 4531
Visitors: Daily April–November; by appointment at other times

*T*he Breuer estate in Rüdesheim, one of the best parts of the south-facing hillside which is the Rheingau, has suffered amazing peaks and troughs in its fortunes over the years since its founding in 1880. Now performing at its near-perfect best, it was not long ago that the wines were supermarket fodder.

In Victorian times the wines of the Rheingau were very highly prized. Auction prices and surviving merchant lists put the prices on a par with, or above, the first growths of the Médoc. Even in the mid-sixties the top estates were getting sensible prices for their wines, but by the 1970s, the market turned away from fine German wines toward inexpensive, mass-produced, medium-sweet wines like Liebfraumilch

FACT BOX

WINEMAKER: Bernhart Breuer ("cellarmaster")

SIZE OF VINEYARD: 57 acres total–15 acres in Rauenthal, 42 acres in Rüdesheim

PRODUCTION: 6,000–10,000 cases total approx.–2,500 bottles of featured wine

GRAPE VARIETIES: Riesling (for this wine–90% of total vineyard), Pinot Noir, Pinot Gris

RECOMMENDED VINTAGES: 1996, 1994, 1993

LOCAL RESTAURANT: Bistro Berg Schossberg, on the estate

and Piesporter Michelsberg, selling as much on price as quality.

Despite the outstanding location, and high proportion of Riesling in the vineyard, the Breuer estate was, until 1975, selling to supermarket groups, ever more keen on lower prices at the expense of quality. At this point the company was being mismanaged and wine was being sold too cheaply. Bernhart Breuer, on his return from

extensive travels in Europe, presented his father Georg with an ultimatum. He went to his father and said, "Either we change or I go." Remarkably Georg resigned, leaving his son to get on with the task of re-forming the company.

By 1984 the firm's reputation was improving to the extent that Bernhart was elected first president of the Charta Association, a group of Rheingau growers dedicated to restoring the quality and image of the region's wines to their former glory. Moving away from the easy-drinking medium-sweet styles, the Charta

Large old oak barrels maintain the fruit flavors
of the grapes.

Association believes that wines should not be sweetened, and that classic German Riesling should be dry or off-dry, with marked acidity and greater concentration than had been the case.

Like all Charta group members, Bernhart Breuer is concentrating more on the vineyard than the winery. Low yields, unusual in most of Germany, and careful selection are the keys, he believes, to fine-wine production. While not organic, the Breuer vineyards are using smaller quantities of chemical sprays each year. Not, says Bernhart, to be organic as such but because experience has shown that better wines result–chemicals increase yields to the detriment of quality.

In the cellar, too, there is a noninterventionist policy. Breuer likes to recount the story of a trainee New World winemaker who joined the firm for a couple of years. Keen to get on he wanted to do all sorts of treatments to the wine, but was told to just watch the wine, and keep everything clean. Good Riesling makes itself–not for nothing do the top German estates use the term "cellarmaster" rather than winemaker.

TASTING NOTES

1994 RÜDESHEIM BERG SCHLOSSBERG

Very pale lemon in color with some green hints. Intense, steely and minerally character with sharp green fruits, limes and greengages. Dry to the taste with a full flavored yet light-bodied palate. Racy acidity and great concentration of mineral flavors. Still very young, this is a wine to put away for a few years yet.

Rating ★★★★★

SUGGESTED FOOD PAIRING

A wine like this deserves to be tasted properly so simply cooked fine ingredients are required. The intensity of flavor would make this a good match for most fine food. The clean flavors of nouvelle cuisine, and of Vietnamese food would work well, if the latter is not too spicy.

WEINGUT H & R LINGENFELDER

Hauftstrasse 27, D 67229, Grosskarlbach, Pfalz, Germany
Tel: (49) 6238 754 Fax: (49) 6238 1096
*Visitors: Cellar-door sales; tastings and informal tours,
time permitting*

*T*o produce truly fine wine from a good, rather than a great, vineyard means that the winemaker needs to know the vineyards and the vines more intimately. He or she will have to consider every detailed aspect. Rainer Lingenfelder of Grosskarlbach has such devotion.

Grosskarlbach is a small village in the north of Bad Dürkheim. The terrain here is fairly gentle, but just behind the vineyards are the Haart mountains, protecting the region from rain, just as the Vosges, the French continuation of the Haart, do further south. The soils are variable–some calcareous, some sand, and some loess. Although the slopes are gentle, some of the Lingenfelder vineyards have to be terraced to retain the soil. Rainer is very fond of pointing out to visitors the difference between his Freinsheimer Goldberg

FACT BOX

WINEMAKER: Rainer Lingenfelder
SIZE OF VINEYARD: 37 acres
PRODUCTION: approx. 13,000 cases
GRAPE VARIETIES: Riesling, Scheurebe, Pinot Noir, Spätburgunder
RECOMMENDED VINTAGES: 1997, 1996, 1992, 1990, 1989
LOCAL RESTAURANT/HOTEL: Hotel Winzergarten, Restaurant Luther

vineyard, just over the parish boundary, and his neighbor's. His terraces have retained the soil, maintaining a water supply to the vine roots. On the next plot the soil has washed down the hill, and the vines at the top of the hill are under severe stress. It is such attention to detail that sets Lingenfelder apart from the rest.

Rainer Lingenfelder, who, with his father Karl, and uncle, Hermann, is in charge of the company, is the 13th generation of the family to be involved in vine growing. Initially Rainer resisted joining the family business but after a long tour of the world, which included time in wineries in Australia, Bordeaux, New Zealand, and Egypt, he returned to Germany to take a position as top winemaker of Blue Nun, the highly successful Sichel brand.

Weingut Lingenfelder has developed a reputation for its full-bodied dry wines, in contrast to the normal view of German wines on the export market. Many are made at Spätlese level–riper grapes fermented to dryness giving remarkably high alcohol levels, but always in balance with thoroughly ripe flavors.

The three main grapes grown are Riesling, Scheurebe, and Spätburgunder (Pinot Noir). Spätburgunder is normally used for a barrique-aged red wine, but in poorer vintages rosé is made. Scheurebe is an interesting grape, providing wines that are pungently aromatic and grapefruit-like when young, a flavor that is tamed when the wines are a few years old. Rainer Lingenfelder produces probably the best Scheurebe in the world, and he is a firm believer that in the right sites its quality can equal Riesling. Opinions are, however, divided on this and, however good, Scheurebe rarely matches the elegance of Riesling.

TASTING NOTES

1996 RIESLING

Pale golden color, really shining in the glass. Intense, but still very, very youthful nose of limes and pineapples and very floral. A slight hint of honey as well, but as yet totally undeveloped. Dry, with the classic Riesling streak of acidity but in no way austere, these grapes were very ripe so there is a full-flavored, aromatic quality about the palate. The alcohol is quite high for a German Riesling at 13% but it is totally in balance and holds the wine together. Many Trockens can be rather hard but this has the richness to be appealing even in youth, although it will improve for many years yet.

Rating ★★★★

SUGGESTED FOOD PAIRING

A wine of this intensity can stand up to many quite full-flavored foods like wurst.

WEINGUT HANS WIRSCHING

Ludwigstrasse 16, 97346 Iphofen, Germany
Tel: (49) 9323 87330 Fax: (49) 9323 873390
*Visitors: Monday–Saturday 8:00AM–6:00PM;
Sunday 10:00AM–12:30PM*

*F*ranconia, on the banks of the Main, towards the eastern boundary of the major wine regions in Germany, has always been highly sought after in its native Bavaria, despite being more expensive than wines from the other regions in the country. For this reason the wines are rarely exported. When they are, they are not well understood. The traditional Bocksbeutel reminds many customers of the medium-dry Portuguese rosé, so the wine stays on

FACT BOX

WINEMAKER: Werner Probst
SIZE OF VINEYARD: 170 acres
PRODUCTION: 37,500 cases
GRAPE VARIETIES: Silvaner, Riesling, Müller Thurgau, Weisser Burgunder, Scheurebe, Portugieser, Blauer Spätburgunder
RECOMMENDED VINTAGES: 1996, 1993
LOCAL RESTAURANT: Iphöfer Kammer, in the market square

the shelf. The bottle shape is unpopular with many sommeliers who cannot fit it into the racks, and the drier style of the wine is quite different from most consumers' expectations. Yet the effort of getting to know Franken wines is well worth it.

The river Main, like the Mosel, forms steep hillsides as it takes its gigantic W-shaped path from between Frankfurt and Bamberg. As in the Mosel area, vines are planted on the steepest slopes, safe from frost and with good exposure to the sun. There is a saying in German viticulture: "where the plow can go, no vine should grow."

Weingut Hans Wirsching is now run by the 15th generation of one family. The main vineyard lies on the southern slopes of the Schwanberg, encompassing the vineyards of Julius Echterberg, Kronsberg, Kalb, and Burweg. Principally planted on steep slopes, these vineyards are protected by the woods to the north and east. Here the dark Keuper soil collects the heat of the sun in summer, and the falls are generally long and the climate fairly mild. This gives the vines a long ripening season so that, while collecting sugar in the grapes, they also have enough time to collect flavors.

Dr Heinrich Wirsching continues the philosophy his father, Hans, employed. He was a firm believer that if a vine is forced to produce too much fruit the life

TASTING NOTES

1990 IPHÖFER JULIUS-ECHTER-BERG RIESLING SPÄTLESE TROCKEN

Very pale lemon yellow with green hints from relative youth and cool climate. The nose is aromatic and pronounced, just beginning to develop the sealing-wax hints of maturity, but still with some of the floral, perfumed characters of the young Riesling. Dry, with a streak of fine fruit acidity. Full flavor but only medium weight, showing the concentration and finesse of a truly fine Riesling. Long, clean finish.
Rating ★★★★

SUGGESTED FOOD PAIRING
Quite full-flavored wine, so this will go well with German sausages and charcuterie, as well as smoked fish.

Hillside vineyards of Franconia contribute to the firm
flavors in the wine.

of the vine will be diminished, quite apart from the reduction in
wine quality, so they are extremely careful not to overstress the
vines. Low yields are the order of the day here. Vines are pruned
accordingly and unusually for Germany a green harvest is carried
out, cutting off a proportion of the bunches halfway through the
summer. This allows the vine to concentrate its efforts on bringing
the most out of the remaining bunches.

Press-yields, too, are strictly controlled, only the gentle first
pressings being used to ensure only the finest must is fermented.
Modern cellars with outstanding hygiene ensure the fruit flavors
are uncorrupted. Purity of grape flavors is typically the aim
of Franken producers.

Silvaner, that most Frankish of
Franconian grape varieties, is
the most widely planted on
the Wirsching estate, with
over a third of the total
area. A few sweeter wines
are made but most wines
here–indeed, most Franken
wines–are made dry, to go
with food.

WEINGUT JULIUSSPITAL

Klinikstrasse 5, 97070 Würzburg, Franconia, Germany
Tel: (49) 930 393 1400 Fax: (49) 931 393 1414
*Visitors: Monday–Thursday 8:00AM–4:30PM; Friday 8:00AM–
12 NOON; store open Monday–Friday 9:00AM–6:00PM;
Saturday 9:00AM–3:00PM*

*T*he Weingut Juliusspital belongs not to a family or a company, but to a charitable foundation, established in 1576. Today the charitable work continues, but also the wine estate has become one of the most famous in Franken, and one of the finest in Germany.

With the excellent vineyard holdings owned by Juliusspital this is hardly surprising. These include parcels in five of the finest

FACT BOX

WINEMAKER: Horst Kolesch

SIZE OF VINEYARDS: 314 acres

PRODUCTION: 83,000 cases

GRAPE VARIETIES: Silvaner, Müller-Thurgau, Riesling, Kerner, Scheurebe–used unblended in varietal wines

RECOMMENDED VINTAGES: 1994, 1993

LOCAL RESTAURANT: own restaurant, Weinstube, on the corner of Klinikstrasse and Barbarossa Platz

The Juliusspital foundation in Würzburg.

vineyards in Franconia. At Würzburg, Juliusspital own part of the famous Stein vineyard that so often gives its name to the whole of the Franken production, sometimes called Stein wine, just as Rhine wines are called Hock.

These vineyards have a diverse selection of soil types, suiting different grape varieties. Riesling accounts for nearly one in five vines grown but almost twice as much vineyard is given over to Silvaner. Elsewhere this variety is considered something of a workhorse grape, good but not outstanding. In Germany Silvaner has always been considered one of the country's two top grapes.

Still it is the Rieslings that really shine. Hand-worked steep vineyards, cultivated entirely in environmentally sound ways, rise up above the Main, collecting the sunshine so vital this far north. Vinification is very traditional. Other grapes might go into stainless steel but the truly noble grapes, Riesling and here Silvaner, will be vinified in old wooden barrels. No new wood, no hint of vanilla or smoke here. It's big old barrels, many over a century old, that add complexity and maturity without giving wood flavors. All the wines are bottled in the traditional dark-green Franken Bocksbeutel embossed with the seal of the foundations and its year of establishment.

TASTING NOTES

1994 WÜRZBURGER STEIN RIESLING SPÄTLESE TROCKEN

Very pale lemon-yellow with a touch of residual carbon dioxide showing careful bottling and storage. Initially a weak nose which develops in the glass to reveal floral hints of youngish Riesling and a minerally, earthy character typical of Franken, and in particular, Stein wines. Dry with a steely acid backbone and intense yet austere fruit, echoing the mineral characters of the nose. Great length.
Rating ★★★★

SUGGESTED FOOD PAIRING
White meats in general, and asparagus, but this wine also has the flavor and structure to work with the German white sausage.

WEINGUT MAYER AM PFARRPLATZ

Pfarrplatz 2, A 1190, Vienna, Austria
Tel: (43) 1 37 33 61 Fax: (43) 1 37 47 14
Visitors: Heurigen open daily until midnight

*M*ayer am Pfarrplatz is unusual in this book in that it is the only wine estate that sells most of its wine through its own tavern. Vienna is famous for its waltzes, its cafés and their chocolate cake, but it has also been an important wine producing city for centuries. In the third century the Roman emperor Probus promoted grape growing in the area, a tradition which has continued ever since.

There is also another tradition that all wine lovers who go to the city should know about; the Heurigen. Heurige has two meanings. It can mean the new wine of the vintage, still fizzy from the fermentation, but it also refers to the hospitable and very traditional taverns, most in Vienna, where producers can sell their own wine, usually served with food. One of the best known of all Viennese Heurigen is the Mayer house. The Mayer family has been involved with

FACT BOX

WINEMAKER: Mario Galler
SIZE OF VINEYARD: 61 acres
PRODUCTION: 20,000 cases
GRAPE VARIETIES: Riesling, Grüner Veltliner, Chardonnay
RECOMMENDED VINTAGES: 1996, 1995
LOCAL RESTAURANT: Heurigen Mayer am Pfarrplatz

TASTING NOTES

1996 GRÜNER VELTLINER

Pale lemon color with quite considerable viscosity in the glass. Very attractive nose, delicate and very fine, with floral hints and some white pepper character. Dry with crisp acid backbone and medium weight and alcohol. The general feel on the palate is one of great harmony and balance.

Rating ★★★

SUGGESTED FOOD PAIRING

Local sausage and charcuterie.

vine growing in Vienna since 1683. Their vineyards and winery are operated on organic lines to protect the environment. The lack of protective chemicals puts extra strain on the requirements for near perfect cellar hygiene. Cellar work and bottling have to be carried out with painstaking attention to detail.

The house itself, an unprepossessing twin gabled building in the parish square in Heiligenstadt was, in the nineteenth century, occupied by the composer Ludwig van Beethoven. Beethoven is believed to have written the Ninth Symphony, probably his most famous work, while he was living here. The family have tried to preserve the original character of the house as much as possible.

As is fitting for a Heurige, the wines are made to preserve the initial fruit. The grapes are grown on chalky soil in a mild to cool climate, thus preserving their characters. They are hand picked and destalked to avoid unnecessary astringency. Gentle pressing using the latest in press technology follows, and the fermentation is carried out in cool conditions. When appropriate, the wines see a little wood, normally old wood for the whites with a small per-

centage of new wood being used for their red wines. The Grüner Veltliner is made to be drunk young and sees very little oak, being bottled soon after fermentation is finished.

WEINGUT PRAGER

A-3610 Weissenkirchen, Wachau NR 48, Austria
Tel: (43) 02715 2248 Fax: (43) 02715 2532
Visitors: Monday–Saturday 7:00AM–6:00PM

*A*t Wachau the great Danube has carved a narrow, steep-sided valley, reminiscent of the port district in northern Portugal. The Danube brings with it warm air currents from the Pannonian plain, which, along with the cooler air entering from the side valleys, gives a long ripening season. Often the grapes are still on the vines in November.

Weingut Prager is based in the middle of the Wachau region, near the small and very picturesque town of Weissenkirchen. The estate, like so many in Austria, is small, only 30 acres under vines. About a quarter of this is Grüner Veltliner, Austria's native grape, while the remainder is split between Riesling and Chardonnay, here called Feinburgunder.

Franz Prager, the owner of the estate, was one of the founder members and first chairman of the Vinea Wachau Nobilis Districtus. This is an association of vine growers and

FACT BOX

WINEMAKER: Toni Bodenstein
SIZE OF VINEYARD: 30 acres
PRODUCTION: 6,000 cases total
GRAPE VARIETIES: Grüner Veltliner, Riesling, Chardonnay (Feinburgunder), used as varietals
RECOMMENDED VINTAGES: 1995, 1993, 1990
LOCAL RESTAURANT: Landhaus, Bacher in Mautern

WEINGUT
P R A G E R
A · 3610 WEISSENKIRCHEN

RIESLING
SMARAGD 1995
WEISSENKIRCHNER KLAUS

BRODUCT OF AUSTRIA · WACHAU
WHITE TABLE WINE
QUALITÄTSWEIN MIT STAATL. PRÜFNR. L. F. 03496
ALC. CONT. 13,0% BY VOL. · net cont 750 ml

winemakers whose aims, despite the rather pretentious name, are very laudable. It is one of the strictest wine-quality classification systems in the world. Each wine must not only come from certain designated sites but must also achieve a level of quality judged by the most exacting standards. The top classification is "Smaragd," or Emerald. These wines are made from grapes grown on the steepest rocky slopes. They are only made in good vintages and the rules require a higher level of ripeness in the grapes than for the lower categories, although they are usually vinified to dryness.

The Prager estate is currently run by Franz Prager's daughter, Ilse, and her husband, Toni Bodenstein. Running a small estate like this may not be a full-time job, but few can have quite the range of outside interests that Toni has. A published historian, he is also on the boards of two banks. His passion is, however, wine. The Rieslings from this estate are elegant and delicate, fine fruity flavors, without the oily gas character of the German equivalents. Toni's view of Grüner Veltliner has changed over the years. Once he considered it "a weed" but has now come to appreciate the grape. The answer, he says, is in rapid and gentle pressing. Too slow, or too hard, and the wine becomes clumsy. Prager Grüner Veltliners are typically fruity, with tropical fruit characters rather like a very muted Gewürztraminer in youth, developing a spicy, earthy character with a little age.

For the Smaragd Grüner Veltliner the must is fermented in large 530-gallon wooden vats, the lesser wines are fermented in stainless steel.

TASTING NOTES

GRÜNER VELTLINER SMARAGD 1990 RIED ACHLEITEN

Pale-straw-colored with now fully mature nose, spicy and a little earthy but still with sweet tropical fruit notes as well. Dry with marked acidity, but the maturity has rounded off the edge so this does not seem to have the austere character that some Austrian wines can have in youth.

Rating ★★★★

SUGGESTED FOOD PAIRING

Plainly cooked white fish or scallops work well with this quite subtle-flavored wine.

WEINGUT REICHSRAT VON BUHL GMBH

Weinstrasse 16, D-67146 Deidesheim, Pfalz, Germany
Tel: (49) 6326 965010 Fax: (49) 6326 965024
*Visitors: Monday–Friday 8:00AM–6:00PM; Saturday–Sunday
10:00AM–5:00PM–Historic cellars, garden, and free tastings.
Function rooms available for large parties by appointment*

*T*he Pfalz, sometimes called the Palatinate, is one of the two largest regions in Germany. It is, in effect, the continuation of the Alsace vineyards, west of the Rhein, stretching northward from the French border. Its gentle rolling plains are covered by vineyards enjoying a climate protected by the densely wooded Haart mountains, the range that, across the border in France, becomes the Vosges.

The best part of the Pfalz is the central Mittelhaart district, around the towns of Forst, Deidesheim, and Ruppertsberg. Here Riesling accounts for nine out of ten vines planted, a measure of the inherent quality of the site, Riesling being a fussy vine. Reichsrat von Buhl owns a significant share of these premium sites.

FACT BOX

WINEMAKER: Frank John

SIZE OF VINEYARD: 125 acres

PRODUCTION: 39,000 cases

GRAPE VARIETIES: Riesling 88%; Grau- and Spät-burgunder (Pinot Noir & Pinot Gris) 10%, Gewürztraminer 1%, Scheurebe 1%

RECOMMENDED VINTAGES:
1996, 1993, 1989

LOCAL RESTAURANTS/HOTELS:
Hotel Restaurant Hatterer, Weinstraße 12, Deidesheim and Hotel Deidesheim Hof, Trorkplatz, Deidesheim

The tasting room at Reichsrat von Buhl.

Established in 1849, the estate rapidly achieved a distinguished reputation in the export markets, gaining high awards at exhibitions in Paris, Brussels, and Chicago. At the time the finest wines of Germany regularly commanded higher prices than the great wines of Bordeaux and Burgundy, and the von Buhl wines were, by 1896, among the highest of any. No surprise then that von Buhl Riesling was chosen to toast the official opening of the Suez Canal that year. Unfortunately, Armand Buhl, then head of the firm and very much responsible for developing its reputation, died in Luxor, Egypt, shortly afterwards.

In 1989 the company entered a leasing arrangement with a Japanese wine company which has allowed for the investment needed to maintain the historic quality

1996er Forster Kirchenstück Riesling Spätlese Trocken

of the wines. Huge investments in both vineyards and cellars have enabled von Buhl to again gain distinctions on the international wine exhibition circuit.

All of the wines come from their own vineyards, a total of about 125 acres spread over the three main Mittelhaart towns, including nearly a quarter of the small, but exquisite, Forster Kirkenstück Vineyard, just behind the church in the picturesque village of Forst. Here the volcanic loam soil is ideal for Riesling. Kirkenstück is classified as among the best vineyards in the Pfalz. Yields are kept low to concentrate the flavors in the grapes, which are vinified in modern cellars in as reductive a manner as possible to preserve the fruit flavors. Gentle pressing using the latest in pneumatic presses is followed by natural settling and cool fermentation in stainless-steel vats. No oak is used here. After fermentation the wines are allowed a period of maturation on the yeast lees to help the flavors and the structure of the wine integrate and add a certain body to the wine.

TASTING NOTES

1996 FORSTER KIRCHENSTÜCK RIESLING SPÄTLESE

Pale lemon-yellow with fragrant notes of apricots and very ripe white peaches, still very young and fruity. Medium-sweet with fine, racy Riesling acidity and intense flavor and body and an almost interminable length. Picked very late, but without rot, the grapes must have been very ripe for a Spätlese as the flavor concentration is verging on Auslese levels. Delicious now but this is a wine that will develop and improve for at least a decade.
Rating ★★★★★

SUGGESTED FOOD PAIRING
Smoked fish dishes and Asian cooking where the sweet/sour character works well with the sweetness and acid of the wine.

Harvesting in Forster Kirkenstück.

WELTEVREDE WINE ESTATE

PO Box 6, Bonnievale 6730, South Africa
Tel: (27) 2346 2141 Fax: (27) 2346 2460
*Visitors: Monday–Friday 8:30AM–5:00PM;
Saturday 9:00AM–3:30PM*

*W*eltevrede is in the picturesque Robertson area, inland from Stellenbosch and Franschoek. Driving from Stellenbosch or Cape Town one travels through the garden-like areas by the coast before beginning to climb, high over the hills and into Robertson and Worcester. At the top of the hill the landscape changes, and suddenly you feel you really are in Africa, and not just a very warm part of Kent. The soil is drier and the vegetation browner. The climate is hotter and drier here, less affected by the cooling influence of the oceans.

The estate was first started by Klaas Jonker, who bought 720 acres of what was then uncultivated scrubland at the base of the Riviersonderend Mountains. He was the first to plant vines in the area.

FACT BOX

WINEMAKER: Simon Smith
SIZE OF VINEYARD: 370 acres
PRODUCTION: 158,500 cases
GRAPE VARIETIES: Colombard, Sauvignon Blanc, Chardonnay, Gewürztraminer
RECOMMENDED VINTAGES: 1998, 1994, 1992, 1991
RESTAURANT/HOTEL: on the estate, serving lunch; also guest house (sleeps two) available

The next generation, Japie Jonker, took over in 1933 and Lourens, a former air force pilot, after him in 1969. Lourens has extended the estate during his tenureship by purchasing two adjoining farms, consolidating them into one property.

Over the years Weltevrede has produced a number of firsts. It was the first estate in the area to bottle its own wines, the first to have a red Muskadel accepted as "certified" by the authorities, and the first to use new French oak in the maturation of white wine–now virtually standard practice for some varieties. A full range of wines is made, from the sweet fortified "muskadels" to elegant Chardonnays, including Privé du Bois, the first oaked white, now made using Chardonnay and Sauvignon. In 1996 Weltevrede released its first Cap Classique sparkling wine, made in the same manner as champagne.

Gewürztraminer was another first for Weltevrede. Planted in 1980, it was, at the time, the only example of the variety in the Robertson area. Grapes are harvested early in the morning, when they are still cool from the night, to help avoid high fermentation temperatures. After crushing, the skins are left in contact with the must for about eight hours to pick up aromas and flavors. A long, cold fermentation is arrested just before it is complete by centrifuging the must to remove the yeast. This results in an off-dry wine without any chemical additions such as sulfur dioxide, which would dull the flavor.

TASTING NOTES

GEWÜRZTRAMINER 1997

Very pale in color, surprisingly so for this variety, but with quite significant legs showing. Light on the nose too, very young and fresh with light pineapple and slightly spicy notes. Faintly rather than pungently aromatic. Off-dry on the palate, with medium, balanced acidity, light body, and fairly light alcohol. Good overall balance, however. A well-made wine for current drinking.

Rating ★

SUGGESTED FOOD PAIRING

This is the sort of wine which is excellent on its own or as a thirst-quenching beverage on a hot day. It is, therefore, very good with light, summer foods–salads and cold meats.

GLOSSARY

ALCOHOL: potable alcohol as contained in alcoholic drinks is ethanol; sometimes called ethyl alcohol.

ALCOHOL, ACTUAL: the amount of ethanol present in a wine, measured as a percentage of the total volume and shown on the label.

ALCOHOL, POTENTIAL: is the amount of alcohol which would be produced by a complete fermentation of any sugar remaining in the wine. This is occasionally shown on the label after the actual alcohol.

ANAEROBIC: able to operate without oxygen. The yeast which cause fermentation are anaerobic.

BARRIQUE: cask with a capacity of approximately 60 gallons. This is the traditional size in Bordeaux, but it is now used extensively throughout the world. While wines fermented in barriques take on a distinctive oaky flavor, new wood gives more flavor than old.

BOTRYTIS CINEREA: fungus which attacks the grape berry. It usually forms unwanted gray rot, but in certain cases can result in the desirable noble rot.

BOTTE traditional large barrels, used in Italy, of various sizes up to approximately 4,240 gallons. These add very little flavor to the wine.

BUSH TRAINING: training of vines as free-standing plants. Low-cost option used in warm, dry areas. Can result in great concentration of flavors.

CASK: any wooden barrel, usually made of oak, used for fermentation and maturation of wines. Numerous sizes are made, but most are between 60 and 132 gallons. Generally a horizontal wooden vessel is called a cask, and the larger vertical ones are referred to as vats.

CLONAL SELECTION: selection of plants from a particular variety for specific, desirable features (which may include early ripening, low (or high) yield, or disease resistance). This is a scientific approach to something grape growers have been doing in a random fashion since the beginning of viticulture. The vines are propagated by taking cuttings so each clone will retain the features of the parent plant.

CORKINESS: an all too common, but random fault in wine caused by a faulty cork tainting the wine. Detectable by a musty, dirty smell and flat taste. Corky wines should be returned to the supplier for a replacement or refund. Note that one corky wine in a case does not necessarily mean the rest will be.

CROSSING: breeding of new vine varieties by sexual

propagation between two different varieties of grape vine.

DENSITY OF PLANTING: the number of vine plants per area of land, usually expressed as vines per hectare in Europe. Varies from 3,000 vines to 10,000 or more per hectare (a metric unit equal to approximately 2.5 acres). Low plant density has the advantage of lower establishment costs but higher density is generally considered to give higher wine quality.

FERMENTATION: the conversion of sugar to alcohol by the action of yeast enzymes.

FINING: removal of suspended matter in a wine by the addition of a fining agent such as bentonite or egg white, which acts as a coagulant.

FIXED ACIDITY: the acidity in wine detectable only on the palate, composed of tartaric, malic, and lactic acids. An important part of a wine's structure.

HYBRID: a vine variety resulting from the cross-pollination of two vines of different species.

LEES: the sediment of dead yeast cells which collects at the bottom of any fermentation vessel once fermentation is over. For many white wines the lees will be stirred during maturation to add yeast flavor and palate structure.

MALOLACTIC FERMENTATION: conversion of harsh malic acid into softer lactic acid by the action of a naturally occurring bacteria.

MUST: unfermented grape juice before it becomes wine.

NOBLE ROT: benevolent form of *Botrytis cinerea* which concentrates the sugars of ripe grapes, essential for most of the finest sweet wines.

PHYLLOXERA VASTATRIX: the most important insect pest of the vine. It devastated European vineyards in the nineteenth century until it was discovered that its effect can be stopped by grafting the *V. vinifera* on to American rootstock.

RACKING: drawing off clear wine from a cask or vat and moving it to another, leaving any sediment behind.

RESIDUAL SUGAR: unfermented sugar remaining in the wine after bottling. It is what makes medium and sweet wines sweet.

SULFUR DIOXIDE (SO_2): highly reactive and pungent gas which is used in winemaking as an anti-oxidant and antiseptic. Used in almost all wines. Wines sold in the American market must be labeled as containing sulfites.

TARTARIC ACID: the acid responsible for most of a wine's acidity.

VINIFICATION: winemaking.

VITICULTURE: grape growing.

VOLATILE ACIDITY: acetic acid in a wine. A small amount exists in all wines, but excessive amounts indicate a fault.

AUTHOR'S
ACKNOWLEDGMENTS

A book may only have one name on the cover, but many other people are involved, particularly in the case of non-fiction, where research and administration are more important than inspiration and imagination. This book could never have been published without the help of all the producers. I thank them and where appropriate, their UK agents, for all the samples, pictures, and information supplied.

Contacting them, organizing the photography and delivery of wines to me, and somehow managing to keep cheerful throughout it all was Clare. Thanks for all the hard work and the patience.

Wine tasting should not be a lonely business, but it can be when deadlines are involved. For all their help with the tastings, occasionally unwittingly, Michael and Gareth deserve a mention.

For putting up with even more disturbed weekends, delayed outings, and general absences, thanks and apologies to the three girls in my life, Catherine, Rosalind, and Isobel.

PICTURE CREDITS

pg 10 e. t. archive; pg 11 Roger Viollet; pgs 12, 17 Klein Constantia; pg 14 *top* Agricola Flli. Tedeschi S.R.L.; pgs 14 *bottom*, 21, 28, 30, 91, 243 Janet Price; pgs 15, 16 Rosemount Estates Limited; pgs 18, 20, 22, 24 *top*, 25 *top*, 63 *top*, 64 *bottom*, 172, 173 179 *top*, 223Godfrey Spence; pg 24 *bottom* Inniskillin Wines Inc.; pg 33 House of Nobilo; pgs 35, 37 Berry Bros & Rudd Ltd.

INDEX